ALBION'S PEOPLE

Social and Economic History of England

Edited by Asa Briggs

ALBION'S PEOPLE
English Society, 1714 – 1815

John Rule

Professor of History, University of Southampton

Longman
London and New York

Longman Group UK Ltd
Longman House, Burnt Mill, Harlow,
Essex CM20 2JE, England
and Associated Companies throughout the world.

*Published in the United States of America
by Longman Publishing., New York*

First published 1992

British Library Cataloguing in Publication Data
Rule, John
  Albion's people: English society, 1714–1815.
  – (Social and economic history of England)
  I. Title II. Series
  941.07

    ISBN 0–582–08916–6

Library of Congress Cataloging-in-Publication Data
Rule, John, 1944–
    Albion's people : English society, 1714–1815 / John Rule
      p. cm. – (Social and economic history of England)
    Includes bibliographical references and index.
    ISBN 0–582–08917–4 (cased). – ISBN 0–582–08916–6 (pbk.)
      1. England–Social conditions–18th century. 2. England–Economic
    conditions–18th century. 3. Social classes–England–History–18th
    century. I. Title II. Series.
    HN398.E5R79 1992
    306'.0942'09033–dc20   91–21964
                                                                CIP
                                                                AC

Set in baskerville

Produced by Longman Singapore Publishers (Pte) Ltd.
Printed in Singapore

Contents

List of Abbreviations

Econ. H.R. Economic History Review. All references are to the Second Series

Jn. Econ. Hist. Journal of Economic History

Smith, Wealth of Nations All references are to the edition of E. Cannan first published in 1904 and reprinted in two volumes by Methuen in 1961

List of Figures

List of Tables

Introductory Note

This is the latest volume in an established series which sets out to relate economic history to social history. Interest in economic history has grown enormously in recent years. In part, the interest is a by-product of twentieth-century preoccupation with economic issues and problems. In part, it is a facet of the revolution in the study of history. The scope of the subject has been immensely enlarged, and with the enlargement has come increasing specialization. There has also been a change in the approach to it as a result of the collection of a wider range of data and the development of new quantitative techniques. New research is being completed each year both in history and economics departments, and there are now enough varieties of approach to make for frequent controversy, enough excitement in the controversy to stimulate new writing. Interest in social history has boomed even more than interest in economic history since the first volume in this series was published, and debates continue both about its scope and its methods. It remains the purpose of this series, however, to bracket together the two adjectives economic and social. There is no need for two different sets of historians to carry out their work in separate workshops. Most of the problems with which they are concerned demand cooperative effort. However refined the analysis of the problems may be or may become, however precise the statistics, something more than accuracy and discipline is needed in the study of social and economic history. Many of the most lively economic historians of this century have been singularly undisciplined, and their hunches and insights have often proved invaluable. Behind the abstractions of economist or sociologist is the experience of real people, who demand sympathetic understanding as well as searching analysis. One of the dangers of economic history is that it can be written far too easily in impersonal terms: real people seem to play little part in it. One of the dangers of social history is that it concentrates on categories rather than on flesh and blood human beings. This series is designed to avoid both dangers, at least as far as they can be avoided in the light of available evidence. Quantitative evidence is used where it is available, but it is not the only kind of evidence which is taken into the reckoning.

Within this framework each author has complete freedom to describe the period covered by his volume along lines of his own choice. No attempt has been made to secure general uniformity of style or treatment. The volumes will necessarily overlap. Social and economic history seldom moves within generally accepted periods, and each author has had the freedom to decide where the limits of his chosen period are set. It has been for him to decide of what the 'unity' of his period consists.

It has also been his task to decide how far it is necessary in his volume to take into account the experience of other countries as well as England in order to understand English economic and social history. The term 'England' itself has been employed generally in relation to the series as a whole, not because Scotland, Wales or Ireland are thought to be less import or less interesting than England, but because their historical experience at various times was separate from or diverged from that of England: where problems and endeavours were common or where issues arose when the different societies confronted each other, these problems, endeavours and issues find a place in this series. In certain periods Europe, America, Asia, Africa and Australia must find a place also. One of the last volumes in the series will be called 'Britain and the World Economy'.

The variety of approaches to the different periods will be determined, of course, not only by the values, background or special interests of the authors but by the nature of the surviving sources and the extent to which economic and social factors can be separated out from other factors in the past. For many of the periods described in this series it is extremely difficult to disentangle law or religion from economic and social structure and change. Facts about 'economic and social aspects' of life must be supplemented by accounts of how successive generations thought about 'economy and society'. The very terms themselves must be dated. Above all, there must be an attempt to relate society to culture, visual and verbal, separating out elements of continuity and discontinuity.

Where the facts are missing or the thoughts impossible to recover, it is the duty of the historian to say so. Many of the crucial problems in English social and economic history remain mysterious or only partially explored. This series must point, therefore, to what is not known as well as what is known, to what is a matter of argument as well as what is agreed upon. At the same time, it is one of the particular excitements of the economic and social historian to be able, as G.M. Trevelyan has written, 'to know more in some respects than the dweller in the past himself knew about the conditions that enveloped and controlled his life.'

ASA BRIGGS

Preface

The last decade and a half has been an active time with respect to eighteenth-century history. After a longish period of relative neglect compared with the centuries on either side, the 1700s have returned to the foreground of historical scholarship. In social history, interest in social protest and crime not only opened up those specialist areas but posed bigger questions about social relations and the exercise of power. Re-estimating rates of change in output in both manufacturing and agriculture led to a strong challenge to traditional views of economic 'revolutions' but has not, in my view, invalidated the old concepts as completely as some would claim. Especially significant was work using new methods and new data in population history. This confirmed the perception of those scholars who had stressed the key role of fertility in driving the demographic revolution. A new urban history has emerged as something to set against the over-rustication of the 'proto-industrialists'. Trade-union history has escaped the constraints of the Webbs' definitional rigidity and the bicentenary in 1989 focused attention on 'Britain's avoidance of revolution'.

All these challenges met with responses. That is why this book has been six years in the writing. The thud of the latest *Past and Present, Economic History Review* or *Social History* dropping through the letterbox brought anticipation and a slight sinking of the heart at the near-certainty that yet another article on the social and/or economic history of the long eighteenth century would have to be read. Gone are the days when 'keeping up with the literature' was easier for eighteenth-century historians than for most of their colleagues. By the time this book appears, yet more important arguments and findings will have been printed. There has to be a moment to stop. All textbooks are interim, those on the eighteenth century, at this time, especially so. Findings have, however, to be assessed and presented to students and to the less specialised world of readers; tentatively I offer a synthesis in this and its companion volume, *The Vital Century: England's Developing Economy 1714–1815*.

The world of eighteenth-century history is still a smaller one than that of the nineteenth. My debt to around twenty historians on whose work I rely and from whom great inspiration is gained from occasional meetings at seminars or shared examination duties will be obvious from citations in the text and in the footnotes. Walter Minchinton was supportive and prompt in helping me on several matters, especially on the slave trade. Roger Wells and I have been brought together for various academic purposes in recent years and have been able to find time to discuss many matters of common interest. It has been especially warming to have been once more in contact with Edward Thompson on his welcome return to eight-eenth-century history.

Throughout I have offered approximate conversions of pre-deci-mal prices. Yet converting sums which do not amount to even the smallest coin now in use vividly indicates a problem of comprehen-sion for the post-1970 generation. (Next year we shall be admitting to the universities, polytechnics and colleges many students during whose lifetime no one has walked on the Moon!) I will repeat a paragraph from a previous book:

> Not only decimalisation separates today's students from the wage and price data of 1750–1850: even more of a problem is the exceptional inflation of recent times. I was once offered in 1962 employment as a clerk at £3.00 for a five- and-a-half-day week. Between me and the skilled wages of, perhaps, £1.50 a week of a craftsman in the early nineteenth century yawns no gap of comprehension equal to that of the modern student on an inadequate grant of perhaps £30 a week . . . in the middle of our period (1795) . . . a farm labourer could expect to earn no more than 8s (40p) in the south of England . . . . Another 20p to 30p a *week* would have very substantially relieved him; a further 80p would have placed him among the well-paid.

An apology:

> Thus I set pen to paper with delight,
> And quickly had my thoughts in black and white.
> For having now my method by the end,
> Still as I pulled it came, and so I penned
> It down, until it came at last to be
> For length and breadth the bigness which you see

And John Bunyan did it all without the word-multiplying technology of the Amstrad PCW8256. For the first time I don't have a typist to thank, and only myself to blame! Instead I will thank my patient family, Ann, Geoffrey and Helen, and Towan and Ky, two mongrels of determination, whose 'prioritisation' of walks in a nearby wood from time to time got me away from the green screen.

J.G.R.
Hampshire, 31 March 1991

FORENOTE

The divisions between economic and social history are fluid. *Albion's People* and *The Vital Century* are intended to be able to stand on their own, but several topics which could have been covered in either have been more fully treated in *The Vital Century*. Among them are the organisation of labour and its conditions of work, the consequences of enclosure and the so-called 'consumer revolution'.

Acknowledgements

The publishers are grateful to the following for permission to reproduce copyright material:

Oxford University Press for figs. 1.1 and 1.2.

Whilst every effort has been made to trace the owners of copyright material, in a few cases this has proved impossible, and we take this opportunity to offer our apologies to any copyright holders whose rights we may have unwittingly infringed.

CHAPTER ONE

The Background

POPULATION GROWTH

Around the middle of the eighteenth century, after two decades of
stagnation, the population of England entered a new phase of
growth. Steady at first, the annual rate of increase from 1741 to
1771 was around 0.5 per cent. Growth then accelerated so that from
1771 to 1811 the annual average was over 1 per cent. The meaning
of these percentages is revealed in the outcome. The Hanoverian
dynasty began its rule in 1714 over 5.25 million English subjects. By
the time of Waterloo, a century later, George III had 10.5 million.
Growth had continued, unchecked, through the forebodings of
Malthus and the hyper food crises of the 1790s and 1800/1. The
economy was discovering new supportive powers and although
around the turn of the century the Malthusian trap threatened to
snap, its jaws did not close. The escape was in part due to the
agrarian sector very nearly managing to feed an expanding population, despite the fact that most of the working population no
longer farmed; but more significant in the long term was the
emerging ability of the economy to export manufactured goods to
pay for imported cereals. In short, the industrial revolution broke
through age-old constraints which had until then imposed a population ceiling of around 5 million.[1]

Economic historians have tended to regard the rate of population growth in eighteenth-century England as 'optimal' for economic progress. There is much truth in this. A slower rate would not
have expanded the market to the necessary extent, nor supplied the
labour for a significant increase in total employment. A more quickly growing population, anywhere near the rates of much of the

1. For a fuller discussion of population growth, see J.G. Rule, *Vital Century*,
pp. 5–28.

underdeveloped world of our time, would have pressed too hard on the resources of the economy. Increasing output would have been unable to keep even marginally ahead of demographic increase and income per head would have fallen, bringing widespread poverty and, for much of the population, destitution.[2] All this may seem clear to the hind-sighted historian, but how does a society *experience* changes of this kind?

Some of the effects were certainly felt. Higher food prices and a greater degree of shortage in the markets brought widespread food rioting in years of bad harvest such as 1757, 1766, 1773/4, 1795/6 and 1800/1. Increasing competition in the labour market prevented money wages, *in general*, from matching the growth of the economy and accordingly real wages after the 1760s hardly improved for most workers. The population growth rate was optimal rather for employers than for them, and the 'reserve army of labour' across the Irish Sea confirmed their disadvantage. There were regions of significant exception. In the expanding industrial areas of the North and Midlands the labour market was much more favourable to the workers. However, the most important point is that the developing English economy managed to absorb so much of the augmented labour force. There was not full employment. Seasonal underemployment was endemic in many trades. Under the putting-out system of manufacture the organising merchant capitalists tended to keep the number of home-based out-workers at the need level of brisk times rather than of slack. As the century progressed the agricultural labourers of the South increasingly experienced what can best be described as chronic structural underemployment, with large numbers unable to get work for a full year and many able to get hired only a daily basis. There was deep and widespread poverty, but no slide into mass destitution. It was, however, to be the second decade of the nineteenth century before any clear upward trend in real wages for most workers set in.[3]

The mechanics of population growth have been largely confirmed by a major study. *The Population History of England 1541–1871* by E.A. Wrigley and R.S. Schofield has brought new techniques and the aid of the computer to fresh data to demonstrate that a rising birth rate was more important than a falling death rate. That is not to say the latter was unimportant. Greater fertility can increase population only to the extent that mortality permits. The death rate

2. For a clear statement on the 'optimal' nature of population growth, see H.J. Perkin, *Origins of Modern English Society*, pp. 101–6.
3. For the standard of living, see Chapter 7 below.

has to be at least permissive. In fact over the eighteenth century mortality stabilised. The soaring peaks associated with famine and epidemics were lowered. The plateau remained high – expectation of life at birth was still only thirty-five years in 1780 and forty in 1826 – but ironically Thomas Malthus at the turn of the century was drawing attention to the fearsome effects of population crises at the very moment when, so far as England was concerned, soaring mortality peaks were ceasing to be part of the demographic pattern. Nor did the Plague trouble Britain after the seventeenth century. Smallpox, which had threatened to assume its deadly mantle, was brought under control by inoculation and vaccination. Even cities and large towns began to prove capable of natural increase. Studies of Leeds, Exeter, Norwich and Nottingham all show an excess of births over deaths in the second half of the eighteenth century, although *rapid* growth was still possible only through immigration. In Nottingham it still provided 60 per cent of an increase of 11,000 inhabitants between 1779 and 1801.[4]

All this mattered. Against constant fertility, mortality changes could still have produced a population increase of around 0.5 per cent a year and may indeed have been particularly responsible for the growth over the middle decades. According to Wrigley and Schofield, however, against a constant mortality, increasing fertility would have produced a rate three times as high. Once married, women had children at very much the same rate from the time of Elizabeth to that of Victoria. What began to happen in the eighteenth century was that fewer of them stayed unmarried and, more important, the average age of women at first marriage fell significantly. A reconstitution of the parish register data from a sample of twelve parishes shows a fall from 26.5 years in the second half of the seventeenth century to 23.4 by the first half of the nineteenth. From such a change, if it is sufficiently general, can come substantial population growth. Not only do extra births come from the backward extension of marriage over the most fertile years, but the interval between generations also shortens.[5]

Was the fall in marriage age widespread? Although so far only a small number of parish reconstitutions have been completed, general tendencies which can be clearly discerned in the period

---

4. A convenient summary of the main argument of Wrigley and Schofield, *Population History*, is provided in E.A. Wrigley, 'Population growth: England, 1680–1820', 1985, reprinted in Digby and Feinstein, *New Directions*, pp. 105–116 See also P. Corfield, *Impact of English Towns*, pp. 99–123; P. Borsay (ed.), *Eighteenth-century Town*, Introduction, p. 7.

5. Wrigley and Schofield, *Population History*, p. 255.

strongly suggest so. The decline in living-in service and in apprenticeship released some young people from institutional constraints on early marriage. But more generally a fall in the age at marriage was related to a change from a 'peasant' to a 'proletarian' marriage pattern. Peasant societies, that is societies of small land occupiers, tend to marry late. There is a need to inherit or otherwise obtain a farm, perhaps through saving on the part of both the intending man and woman. For the minority who did not farm, there was the equivalent need to acquire a craft practice. In contrast, a waged proletarian when he reaches adult earnings is as capable of supporting a family as he will ever be and is not under the same economic pressure to delay marriage. Expecting to acquire neither land nor the means to follow life as an independent craftsman, he has no expectations to justify caution.[6]

'Proletarianisation' here is not used in the special sense of Marx and Engels to describe the process by which the factory labour force was formed, but generally as a shorthand for the protracted process by which the working classes became overwhelmingly *waged*, dependent on selling their labour power and no longer owning the means of production, nor directly selling their product. Mixed occupations, where very small-scale farming supplemented a living from a waged employment such as weaving or mining, remained widespread through the eighteenth century, but what matters is the main means of living. It has been suggested that in the mid sixteenth century around a quarter of the English population depended on wages; by the mid nineteenth century 80 per cent did. There are sound reasons for believing that the eighteenth century saw especially rapid change in this respect.[7]

In the first place, there was the considerable spread of manufacturing into the countryside and, as Professor Wrigley has indicated, the rural non-farming population grew more quickly over the eighteenth century than did the farming population. Labelling it 'proto-industrialisation', historians have recently stressed the significance of this development, which was not confined to England.[8] Textiles, hosiery, cutlery, nails and hardware were produced in cottages to which merchant capitalists 'put out' materials and from which they collected and marketed the product. Thus the system became wide-

6. For a general argument on these lines, see D. Levine, 'Industrialisation and the proletarian family', *Past and Present*, **107**, 1985 pp. 168–203.

7. See Rule, *Labouring Classes*, pp. 18–20.

8. Wrigley, 'Urban growth and agricultural change: England and the Continent in the early modern period' in Borsay (ed.), *Eighteenth-century Town*, pp. 54–5. For proto-industrialisation generally, see L.A. Clarkson, *Proto-industrialisation.*

spread in the woollen cloth districts of the West Country, in the cotton districts of south Lancashire and in the hosiery knitting east Midlands, and in worsted production in the West Riding, although Yorkshire woollen cloth continued to be made by small independent clothiers until the coming of the factory. It was also to be found in the Black Country where especially nails, but also other hardware items, were made up in countless small forges attached to cottages. Around Sheffield cutlery was made up in villages, although it was usually inferior to that made in the town itself. Similarly in the Warwickshire villages around Coventry, cheaper silk ribbons were woven than those produced by the skilled artisans of the towns.[9] In effect rural manufacturing was based on piece rates paid to out-workers. Some capitalists employed very large numbers – larger than those concentrated in the early factories. The system had developed as merchant capitalists began to draw upon the spare labour provided, especially in pastoral districts, by a rising rural population. As it grew it began to impart a demographic momentum of its own. This process has been well described by Hans Medick and David Levine in the context of textile regions. The unit of labour in cottage-based manufacture was the *family*. Once children had passed through infancy, their contribution in performing the subsidiary tasks needed around the weaving loom, or the knitting-frame, increased the family's earning potential. Thus, it is argued, not only was early marriage permitted by the fact that maximum earning potential came sooner in the life-cycle, but there was a positive advantage from larger family size.[10]

Levine found that in the Leicestershire knitting village of Shepshed the mean age of women at first marriage was 28.1 in 1600–99, but fell with the introduction of the hosiery manufacture through 27.4 in 1700–49 to 24.1 in 1750–1824. Of course, early-marrying need not necessarily have produced larger families, but Levine found that fifty-five marriages when the bride was between twenty and twenty-four produced a mean completed family size of 5.6, whereas fifty-one marriages where the age range was twenty-five to twenty-nine, produced one of 4.5. Although the switch to a manufacturing-based economy did make for a slight increase in child mortality, the effect on the reproduction rate was formidable. At

9. For the organisation of manufacturing generally, see Rule, *Vital Century*, Chapters 4–6.
10. See H. Medick, 'The proto-industrial family economy: the structural function of household and family during the transition from peasant to industrial capitalism', *Social History*, I, 3, 1976, pp. 291–315; Levine, *Family Formation.*, pp. 58–87.

the rate of 1600–99 population would have taken 250 years to double; at that of 1750–1824, only forty years.[11] The interest in proto-industrialisation has certainly produced valuable insights, but its demographic impact should be kept in perspective. It was hardly the only force operating in the direction of population increase. In part at least the high initial growth of manufacturing villages was due to in-migration of young adults, who not only added their own immediate numbers but very soon contributed their high fertility.

This was also the case with a second form of wage-dependent rural community: the mining village. The majority of miners were coal miners employed on the coalfields in the North-East, York-shire, Lancashire, the Midlands and on smaller fields in Cumbria and Somerset. They numbered between 12,000 and 15,000 by 1700 and exceeded 50,000 by 1800. Metal mining was also of growing importance. Cornish mines, tin and copper, probably exceeded 10,000 by 1800, and when iron miners and the lead miners of the Peaks and north Pennines are added, metal miners altogether must have numbered more than 13,000. Miners also married early and mining villages had during their expanding years a high rate of in-migration of young adults. A study of the Somerset/Wiltshire bor-der area has shown that mining parishes there had significantly higher birth rates than non-mining parishes.[12]

Urban birth rates were also influenced by the in-migration of young adults but in towns, too, the proportion of the labour force which could be described as 'proletarian' was increasing. This was not only due to the overall increase in the size of the labour force in an era of urban growth, but also to a shift in the employment structure of several large trades. In London especially, but also in large provincial towns, the eighteenth century saw the growth of a class of *permanent journeymen*, that is skilled artisans, who had very little prospect of becoming self-employed master craftsmen because of the increasing costs of setting up in business. In 1745 a writer supporting the London tailors in a wage dispute defined a journey-man as:

> one, who has by apprenticeship or other contract, served such a portion of his time to that particular business which he professes to occupy, as renders him capable to execute every branch or part of the trade, whereby he is at full liberty, if his ability and condition of life will

11. Levine, *Family Formation*, pp. 61, 74.
12. For estimates of the mining population, see Rule, *Experience of Labour*, pp. 28–9; S. Jackson, 'Population change in the Somerset–Wiltshire border area, 1701–1800', *Southern History*, **7**, 1985, pp. 128–9.

permit, to set up in the world as a master of his profession; and is only called a Journeyman while he continues to serve under the direction of others at certain wages.[13]

Increasingly, work was carried out in the workshops of employers. By this time, few of London's several thousand tailors, 'as common as locusts' and 'as poor as rats',[14] were independent masters. In hat manufacture by 1777 only fifty masters still worked up their own materials and the ratio was even larger in the case of Clerkenwell's 8,000 watchmakers, where in 1795 one master alone employed more than 100 out-workers and put his name on the product 'though he has not made in his shop the smallest wheel belonging to it'. Small self-employed shoe makers decreased in numbers. A man could buy for two shillings enough leather to keep a family for a week. A special trade, leather cutting, had emerged to cut hides into pieces a small shoe maker could afford. By 1738 the larger shoe makers were trying to increase their hold over the trade by seeking a prohibition on the sale of less than whole hides, which cost around £10: 'the master shoemakers do not care that journeymen should work for themselves'. The print workers used the near-impossibility of becoming masters in their trade as a justification for a wage increase in a pamphlet of 1809. A quantification based on rate data for 1800 suggests that in London only around 5 to 6 per cent of the working-class population were self-employed.[15] The same situation prevailed in many provincial trades like paper making and calico printing, although in centres of hardware manufacture such as Sheffield and Birmingham, the line between independence and waged employment was less firmly drawn and frequently crossed in both directions.[16]

The growth of mining and manufacturing in rural and urban forms is not, however, the whole picture. England was unique in its pattern of agriculture in that the most substantial labour input came from a landless proletariat. It formed soonest in areas where commercial farming developed. Levine has shown how in the Essex village of Terling, only 35 miles from the huge market offered by London, by the seventeenth century a few farmers already employed most of the village's land workers. The age at marriage became relatively low, as with little prospect of owning land,

13. Rule, *Experience of Labour*, pp. 32–3.
14. *Ibid.*, p. 33.
15. *Ibid.*, pp. 33–4; L.D. Schwarz, 'Income distribution and social structure in London in the late eighteenth century', *Econ. Hist. Rev.* XXXII, 2, 1979, pp. 256–7.
16. Rule, *Experience of Labour*, p. 36.

postponement had little point. It became lower still after 1780 when a shift to a more labour intensive form of agriculture led to a less strict application of the settlement laws (below, pp. 135–7). In the Leicestershire village of Bottesford, where framework knitting was kept out by the control of the Duke of Rutland, women's age at marriage was still at a mean of 26.5 in 1800 and fell thereafter only when a more labour-intensive form of agrarian agriculture was adopted.[17] The growth of commercial agriculture was stimulated by the higher food prices after mid century. A reinforcing process was at work. The demand in the food market was increasing both because population was growing and because a larger fraction of it, in country as well as in town, no longer produced much of its own food. For a generation, the practice of employing young people from their teens to their early twenties as living-in farm servants diminished the demographic impact. Farm service, according to one writer, was a 'covenanted state of celibacy', but in the South and the East it was in rapid decline by the late eighteenth century. In those regions the populations of agricultural villages began to grow. The direct demographic impact of poor relief systems related to family size seems to have been slight, but since it also encouraged the employment of married rather than young single men, the Poor Law clearly imposed no constraint on early marriage. It is hardly a coincidence that the great population pessimist Thomas Malthus was the rector of a southern agricultural parish.[18]

It would seem that the argument for linking population growth in a general sense to the takeover of a 'proletarian demographic regime' is a very strong one, resting as it does on several clearly observable changes in the structure of employment both urban and rural. But more specifically the timing of changes in nuptiality may have been linked in some way to changes in living standards. In what way precisely, it is hard to establish. Wrigley and Schofield suggest a pattern of 'dilatory homeostasis'. By this they mean that the statistical correlation they have discovered between changes in nuptiality and turning points in the standard of living indices works with a time lag, with the turning points in the age at marriage following those in the real wage level after a delay of around twenty years. Accordingly the relatively prosperous years of the early eighteenth century, with low food prices and slow population growth, could have generated an optimism over taking the plunge, which

17. Levine, *Family Formation*, pp. 94–6, 119–26.
18. A. Kussmaul, *Servants in Husbandry in Early Modern England*, Cambridge UP, 1981, pp. 4–9, 112.

set in train a tendency towards earlier marriage that worsening times took a while to dispel.[19]

URBANISATION AND LABOUR

In 1815 most English people still lived in the countryside, but a third by then were living in towns. This was a significant proportional increase over 1714 and in aggregate terms trebled the urban population from 1 to 3 million. This does not overstate the growing urbanisation of eighteenth-century England. It takes a baseline of 5,000 inhabitants for towns and no account of the fact that many of those living in the countryside had at one time or other lived and worked in towns, for the population contained a large youthful mobile element. The England of 1800 was in many ways nearer to that of 1851, when the urban and rural populations were officially measured as equal, than it was to the seventeenth century.

On the continent any increase in aggregate urban populations which did take place was explained largely by the further domination of sprawling capital cities. That was not the case in eighteenth-century England. There, provincial towns set the pace. London's share of the total population remained unchanged from 1700 to 1800 at around 11 per cent. By 1750 the combined population of the provincial towns matched it and by 1801 their population was almost double that of the capital. Not all towns grew; smaller market towns especially suffered. There was a fall of 18 per cent in their numbers between 1690 and 1792. Their decline was more than matched by the growth of others, however: regional centres, manufacturing towns, ports and spas. This decline of small market towns was in itself part of the process of 'urbanisation'. In the mid seventeenth century these towns had been 'adjuncts in physical appearance, function and administrative authority of the age-old agrarian structure'. By 1760 a great number of them were developing into urban centres with very different administrative structures, and with 'a variety and profusion of town amenities unknown to earlier generations and no doubt with a novel degree of impact on their rural neighbourhoods'.[20] English urban growth was, as Dr Corfield

19. Wrigley and Schofield, *Population History*, Chapter 10, but see also the Introduction to the 1989 paperback edition.
20. E.L. Jones and M.E. Falkus, 'Urban improvement and the English economy in the seventeenth and eighteenth centuries' in Borsay (ed.), *Eighteenth-century Town*, p. 119.

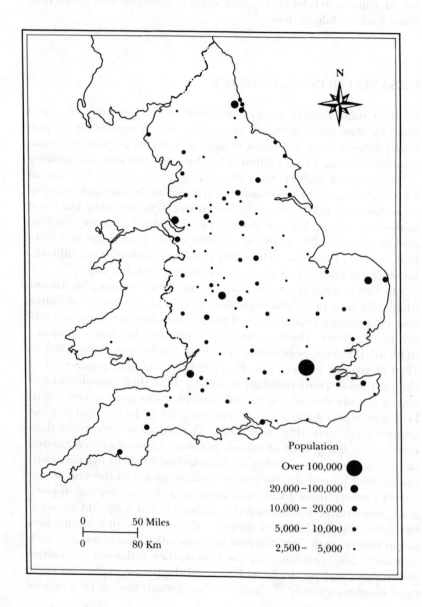

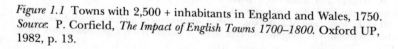

Figure 1.1 Towns with 2,500 + inhabitants in England and Wales, 1750. *Source:* P. Corfield, *The Impact of English Towns 1700–1800.* Oxford UP, 1982, p. 13.

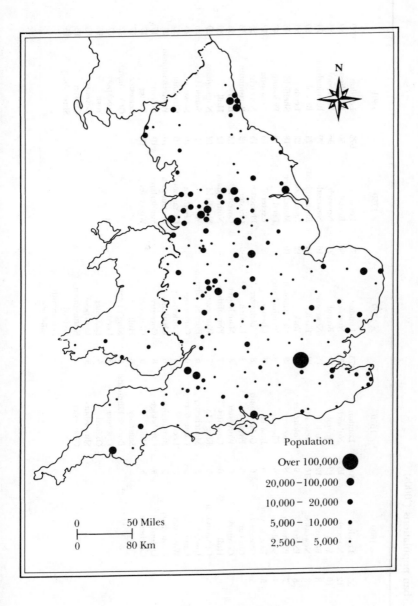

Figure 1.2 Towns with 2,500 + inhabitants in England and Wales, 1801.
Source: P. Corfield, *The Impact of English Towns 1700–1800*. Oxford UP,
1982, p. 14.

Table 1.1 Urban populations ('000s)

c. 1520		c. 1600		c. 1670		c. 1700		c. 1750		1801	
London	55	London	200	London	475	London	575	London	675	London	959
Norwich	12	Norwich	15	Norwich	20	Norwich	30	Bristol	50	Manchester	89 [a]
Bristol	10	York	12	Bristol	20	Bristol	21	Norwich	36	Liverpool	83
York	8	Bristol	12	York	12	Newcastle	16	Newcastle	29	Birmingham	74
Salisbury	8	Newcastle	10	Newcastle	12	Exeter	14	Birmingham	24	Bristol	60
Exeter	8	Exeter	9	Colchester	10	York	12	Liverpool	22	Leeds	53
Colchester	7	Plymouth	8	Exeter	9	Gt Yarmouth	10	Manchester	18	Sheffield	46
Coventry	7	Salisbury	7	Chester	8	Birmingham		Leeds	16	Plymouth	43 [b]
Newcastle	5	King's Lynn	6	Ipswich	8	Chester		Exeter	16	Newcastle	42 [c]
Canterbury	5	Gloucester	6	Gt Yarmouth	8	Colchester	8–9	Plymouth	15	Norwich	36
		Chester	6	Plymouth	8	Ipswich		Chester	13	Portsmouth	33
		Coventry	6	Worcester	8	Manchester		Coventry	13	Bath	33
		Hull	6	Coventry	7	Plymouth		Nottingham	12	Hull	30
		Gt Yarmouth	6	King's Lynn	6	Worcester		Sheffield	11	Nottingham	29
		Ipswich	5	Manchester	6	Bury St. Edmunds		York	10	Sunderland	26
		Cambridge	5	Canterbury	6	Cambridge		Chatham	10	Stoke	23 [d]
		Worcester	5	Leeds	6	Canterbury		Gt Yarmouth	10	Chatham	23 [e]
		Canterbury	5	Birmingham	6	Chatham		Portsmouth	10	Wolverhampton	21 [f]
		Oxford	5	Cambridge	6	Coventry		Sunderland		Bolton	17
		Colchester	5	Hull	6	Gloucester		Worcester		Exeter	17
				Salisbury	5	Hull				Leicester	17
				Bury St Edmunds	5	King's Lynn				Gt Yarmouth	17
				Leicester	5	Leeds	5–7			Stockport	17
				Oxford	5	Leicester				York	16
				Shrewsbury	5	Liverpool				Coventry	16
				Gloucester	5	Nottingham				Chester	16
						Oxford				Shrewsbury	15
						Portsmouth					
						Salisbury					

Shrewsbury
Sunderland
Tiverton

Notes:
a Including Salford.
b Including Devonport.
c Including Gateshead.
d Stoke and Burslem.
e The Medway towns: Chatham, Rochester, and Gillingham.
f Wolverhampton, Willenhall, Bilston, and Wednesfield.

Source: E.A. Wrigley 'Urban growth and agricultural change: England and the Continent in the early modern period' in P. Borsay, The Eighteenth Century Town, Longman, 1990, p. 42.

puts it, 'multi-centred, not focused on a single city'.[21] This wider spread (see Figures 1.1 and 1.2; Table 1.1) reflected the intimate links of the towns with surrounding regional economies, as well as the growing specialisation of some, for even those normally considered manufacturing centres were in reality multi-functional (Table 1.2). The dual economy was not marked in England, where towns were hardly 'islands of modernity'. Far from it, they were 'pace-setters for rural England'; the leading edge of a developing economy. Professor Daunton has rightly contended that in eighteenth-century England, towns were no longer 'parasitic' but had become engines of growth.[22] Following his work and that of Peter Clark and Penelope Corfield, the dynamism of urban England is now effectively contrasted with the paralysis affecting continental towns. According to Professor Clark, 'both older and newer towns gave significant, if sometimes indirect impetus to economic growth: they were a vital lead sector in the wider modernising processes affecting English society'.[23]

It was not only in the quantitative sense that the contours of the urban nation were forming. The idea that there was an 'urban renaissance' beginning at the Restoration and accelerating over the next hundred years has been urged by Dr Borsay. He has pointed to the widening of provincial elites by the inclusion of middling people from the professions, the merchants and prosperous traders. The expansion of the urban sector was consequent upon the growth of the economy and especially of consumption. It was not just the obvious resorts like Bath which participated. Other towns too, especially regional and county capitals like Bristol, Norwich, York, Lichfield, Lancaster and Warwick, were involved, with only the lesser market towns missing out. Physically the renaissance was manifested in public buildings and in the replacement of timber and thatch by brick and tile in front-street buildings. Culturally it was evident in the 'civilisation' of country manners, the commercialisation of upper- and middle-class leisure and the need for even the rusticated squirearchy to spend some time in town. Its class dimension was the expansion of the middle ranks and its occupational one the growing numbers employed in the service and 'luxury' trades.[24] At Shrewsbury between 1750 and 1775 every third new

21. Corfield, *Impact of English Towns*, p. 10.
22. *Ibid.*, p. 186; M.J. Daunton, 'Towns and economic growth in eighteenth-century England' in Abrams and Wrigley (eds), *Towns in Societies*, pp. 245–77.
23. P. Clark (ed.), *Transformation of English Provincial Towns*, p. 14.
24. Borsay, *English Urban Renaissance*.

Table 1.2 Occupations in nine provincial towns in the 1790s from the *Universal British Directory* (percentages)

Occupational group	Bath	Bolton	Bristol	Chester	Colchester	Maidstone	Nottingham	Plymouth (inc. dock)	Wolverhampton
Agriculture	1.2	0.8	0.9	1.2	7.8	0.4	1.1	0.3	1.4
Building	5.3	3.5	5.3	5.2	6.4	6.4	6.3	3.6	4.0
Manufacturing	23.6	49.3	29.7	27.7	30.7	39.1	48.5	25.6	53.2
Transport	1.0	0.4	0.8	2.3	3.6	0.0	0.1	5.1	0.4
Dealing	54.4	30.9	36.1	27.1	28.2	44.4	23.4	40.0	28.8
Professional and public	12.4	10.1	12.2	15.1	13.6	7.7	9.7	14.8	7.0
Domestic service	1.9	0.5	1.6	2.2	2.3	1.2	2.9	2.7	1.2
Proprietors and independents	0.2	4.5	13.0	18.5	7.4	0.8	8.0	6.6	3.6
Miscellaneous	0.0	0.4	0.4	0.7	0.0	0.0	0.0	1.3	0.4
Number	1,197	596	3,134	1,200	528	248	728	1,483	771
Approximate 1801 population	33,000	18,000	61,000	15,000	12,000	8,000	29,000	40,000	13,000

Source. P. Clark, *The Transformation of English Provincial Towns*, Hutchinson, 1984, p. 28.

freeman was connected with the 'world of luxury and leisure', whereas between 1650 and 1675 every third entrant had been a textile or leather worker. To Dr McInnes this signifies an alteration of the 'whole style and ambience of the town', but he is reluctant to make the emergence of Shrewsbury in a new guise as a leisure town representative of a general phenomenon. To him Borsay's renaissance is too sweeping, for the many small towns which were largely bypassed were probably more familiar to the country people than were county capitals. Borsay has responded by insisting that diffusion was indeed wide, if obviously unequal. If the idea of an urban renaissance is a little overstated, it remains true that there was an urban dynamism in eighteenth-century England which contrasts with a seventeenth-century stupor and with contemporary experience in Europe. This fits ill with attempts to characterise eighteenth-century England as an *ancien régime*.[25]

Urban populations were young, but in this they only accentuated a more general feature of a national population which owed its growth to a rising birth rate. Defining the 'dependency ratio' as the number of persons aged below fifteen and over sixty per thousand people between those ages, Wrigley and Schofield have measured it as moving from a low of 624 in 1671 to a peak of 857 in 1826. The increase was particularly steep after 1731. Then at 670, it rose to 750 by 1770 and 800 by 1790.[26] In short, eighteenth-century England was increasingly burdened with children, for the contribution of the over-sixties was slight. Even by the end of the eighteenth century it had become clear that poor relief was needed not only to support those impotent through old age or infirmity, the orphaned and widowed and, occasionally, those unable to find work, but also to supplement those whose 'common' wages were inadequate to support their families. The desirability of children working from an early age was hardly disputed. Most modern historians have assumed accordingly that it was usual for eighteenth-century working-class children to work. That, as Dr Cunningham has shown, tends to confuse desirability with availability. From this perspective the districts whose local economies afforded plentiful opportunities for child employment were looked upon as favoured. Defoe was only the best known of eighteenth-century writers who commended child labour *in the particular instances* he chanced upon. These were all in

25. A. McInnes, 'The emergence of a leisure town: Shrewsbury 1660–1760', *Past and Present*, **120**, 1988, pp. 58, 87; Borsay, 'The emergence of a leisure town: or an urban renaissance?', *ibid.*, **126**, 1990, p. 190.
26. Wrigley and Schofield, *Population History*, pp. 443–4.

the textile areas. Around Norfolk he found 'no hand out unemployed, if they would work; and that the very children after four or five years of age could everyone earn their own bread'. In the West Riding he saw 'hardly anything above a few years old, but its hands are sufficient to itself'. He made similar comments at Taunton and in Essex. Other writers similarly make specific rather than general references to child labour. Arthur Young, for example, remarked of Manchester in 1771: 'large families in this place are no incumbrance; all are set to work'.[27] The implication that in many places they were an 'incumbrance' is one that would have struck a note with many parents and most Poor Law officers. That children's labour was useful within the family economy of many households, and that in some districts they were able to earn independently, is clear. It can help explain some significant regional differences in living standards as well as the spread of poverty over the family cycle, but, especially in the agricultural districts, there was little in the way of *regular* paid employment for children. Such opportunities as there were no doubt were eagerly seized upon, but they were by no means so extensive as to make child labour a general and daily experience.

In the eighteenth century adult work too was often more irregular and less intense than it became with the advent of modern forms of industrial labour. 'A flush and ebb is common to almost all trades' wrote a pamphleteer in 1719, complaining that the improvident poor lacked the foresight to save for rainy days. Frost and snow, too, prevented many trades from working. Calico printers could not wash their fabric. Shoe makers could not sew when their waxed threads were frozen. Building workers lost up to three months in a bad winter, such as that of 1740 when a sad procession of bricklayers and their labourers, with hods in sable, begged through the streets of London. Adam Smith considered that such workers needed wages half as high again as the ordinary level to compensate. House painters lost several weeks in London; when the 'season' was in progress the gentry did not want tradesmen in their houses. Adverse winds could prevent the east coast colliers from plying the coal trade to London, and as a consequence colliers on the north-eastern field had a month-long holiday around Christmas.[28]

27. Examples cited in Rule, *Experience of Labour*, pp. 42–3. The argument is presented in a developed form in H. Cunningham, 'The employment and unemployment of children'.

28. Rule, *Experience of Labour*, p. 51 and *Vital Century*, pp. 189–197 for these and other examples.

Summer brought brisk employment and longer daylight hours to many trades but for some, like paper making which needed a constant and steady flow of stream water, it brought slack times. So too did it to other trades, such as silk throwing, where the mills were water powered. As the so-called 'consumer revolution' reached only tentatively down through the social order, the 'fashion' trades also had their seasonal aspect. Hatters, dress makers, West End tailors and shoe makers were short of work when the 'quality' left town. Tailors knew this period as 'cucumber time', when poor journeymen could afford little else to eat. According to one source in 1747, they lost up to four months in a year. Some compensation was afforded by court weddings or, especially, deaths. The demand for mourning clothes always brought a welcome rush of work and a higher wage for the time being.[29]

But not all rest was enforced by seasonal or fashionable vagaries. Employers complained throughout the century of the 'leisure preference' indulged by an idle workforce. The only way to make the poor 'sober, industrious and obedient', William Temple remarked in 1739, was to remove the means of 'idleness and intemperance, such as high wages'. The best goods were made when subsistence was expensive and workers were 'obliged to work more and debauch less'. William Hutton, himself a former framework knitter, was less censorious in tone but even he remarked in 1781 that a man who could support his family from five days would not work six. Arthur Young, the great agricultural propagandist, shared his view that 'great earnings' caused all those the 'least inclined to idleness or other ill courses' to work only four or five days. Some complained that the earnings forgone were substantial. Wool combers were accused in 1794 of working only 'half their time' and taking home 10 shillings (50p) when 28 shillings (£1.40) could have been earned. Such a differential seems hardly creditable, but then the complainer was the inventor of a machine designed to replace them! Coming from such sources, as Professor Mathias has pointed out, the question is whether the evidence should be viewed as objective observation or as employer opinion. Probably it comes between the two. As normative reporting it justified the 'utility of poverty' theory of low wages associated with early mercantilism and its emphasis on low export prices. But the attitude can also be found in the writings of those like Defoe who generally supported high wages in the interests of greater consumption. It is also pres-

29. Rule, *Experience of Labour*, pp. 51–2.

ent in unpublished writings devoid of polemical intent. A West-Country clothier bemoaned in his diary that high wages had made his workforce 'scarce, saucy and bad', while a Cornish mine agent explained to his employer in a letter of 1793:

> The common tinners continue to be very refractory and insolent: many of them refuse to work, and have not gone underground for three weeks past – They have no just cause for it; for their wages have been rather too high lately than otherwise; the consequence has been too much brandy drinking, and other bad practices.[30]

As the eighteenth century progressed these labour attitudes may have been in decline but they were still extensive enough at its end. In a seminal article Edward Thompson wrote of the 'characteristic irregularity of labour patterns before the coming of large-scale machine powered industry'. The pattern was one of 'alternate bouts of intense labour and of idleness wherever men were in control of their own working lives'.[31] That a man could control his own pace when working in his own cottage is evident, but the pattern was also characteristic of the small workshops, where men paid by the piece came and went with an irregularity which did not pose too many problems for employers with little investment in fixed capital. Birmingham's 'matrix of small workshops' formed, according to Dr Reid, 'a conducive environment for the survival of immemorial work rhythms'.[32] Sheffield was similarly characterised and a song from there, 'The Jovial Cutlers', neatly captures the pace of a cutler's working week. It describes the cutler sitting by his fire On 'Saint Monday' talking over the enjoyments of the Sunday rather than starting his week's work. His wife enters and berates him for his laziness, her tongue moving faster than his 'boring stick at a Friday's pace'. As every student knows, there is more than one way of putting the necessary number of hours of work together in a week.[33]

In addition, the year was punctuated with holidays. Even such a firm disciplinarian as Josiah Wedgwood could not keep his potters from absenting themselves for the annual wakes. Cornish miners had a monthly holiday when their wages were paid and several days

---

30. *Ibid.*, pp. 53–4; P. Mathias, 'Leisure and wages in theory and practice' in *Transformation of England*, p. 149.
31. E.P. Thompson, 'Time, work-discipline and industrial capitalism', pp. 49–50.
32. D.A. Reid, 'The Decline of Saint Monday, 1776–1876', *Past and Present*, **71**, 1976, p. 77.
33. For the full folk song, see Rule, 'Labour in a changing economy 1750–1850', *ReFRESH*, **12**, 1991 pp. 5–8.

a year peculiar to themselves. Most trades kept an annual patron saint's day as well as Saint Monday.[34] Adam Smith considered that such 'lost days' were the *result* of overworking. Francis Place expressed a similar view.[35] Perhaps sometimes they were, but that was an occasional happening. A strong leisure preference seems to have been more generally characteristic. So prevalent was 'Saint Monday' that it has recently been suggested that its keeping was part of a 'regular' working pattern which had become widespread in urban England well before the factory imposed its special demands on labour. From a study of the local press for Bristol between 1790 and 1850, Dr Harrison has been bold enough to write: 'It is safe to stress that between 1750 and 1850 almost all employed people, particularly in towns, were to be found at work between the hours of 6 a.m. and 6 p.m., Tuesday to Saturday.'

That seems reasonable – although much depends on what numerical meaning is attached to 'almost all' – but the question is over Monday. Harrison reached his conclusion from the fact that 'crowd occurrences', that is meetings or incidents involving large attendance on the part of working people, tended to take place on Mondays. Indeed, he suggests that the observance of Saint Monday was sufficiently widespread to be viewed as an indicator of a *regular* rather than an irregular working week.[36] I doubt it was that clear; there are too many qualifications. Widespread as was the journeyman's proclivity to holiday on Mondays, the suggestion that from 1750 a five-day week was normal is unsound. The employers' view was more biblical, allowing only the seventh day for rest. To them Monday absenteeism remained a problem, not an accepted institution. Further, Saturday in many trades was pay day and an early-finishing one. Nor was employment between 6.00 a.m. and 6.00 p.m. necessarily constant, for hardly any workers were paid by the hour and their masters did not always have work on hand. In the major trade of tailoring, employment was on a half-day basis and journeymen constantly complained that employers took them for only part of the day. *If* a five-day week had been normal in urban England by 1750, then the time-discipline effect of the factory would have been even more significant, for its six-day week would have been a novel imposition.

34. N. McKendrick, 'Josiah Wedgwood and factory discipline', *Historical Journal*, IV, 1961, p. 46; Rule, *Experience of Labour*, pp. 56–7.

35. Adam Smith, *Wealth of Nations*, I, p. 92; M. Thale (ed.), *The Autobiography of Francis Place*, p. 123 footnote.

36. M. Harrison, *Crowds and History*, pp. 108, 121–5.

To a small extent a persistent leisure preference may have limited the share of any increase in consumption from the growth of the economy which went to the lower orders. But the main explanation of the slow overall improvement in real incomes before 1820 is that the economy, although growing, was doing so only slowly and, as Professor Crafts has indicated, real wage growth was similar in the long run to per capita income growth with little evidence of a marked shift in income distribution towards or away from the working classes. He has calculated increases per capita in national output as only 0.31 per cent between 1700 and 1760. Growth in national output continued at very much the same rate between 1760 and 1780, but faster population growth led to stagnation in the level of income per head, which Crafts calculated rose at only 0.01 per cent per annum. From 1780 to 1801 a faster rate of economic growth kept ahead of population increase to restore a per capita growth rate of 0.35 per cent. But increasing shares going to investment and government expenditure between 1780 and 1801 might well have meant that consumption per head in those years fell behind income per head in its rate of increase. From 1801 to 1831 income per capita increased by 0.32 per cent per annum.[37] Crafts' figures are generally more pessimistic than those of earlier estimates. Deane and Cole, for example, in their pioneering book of 1962, while they were slightly more pessimistic for 1760–80 when they calculated a decline of 0.04 per cent, calculated per capita growth to have been 1.08 per cent from 1780 to 1801 and 1.61 per cent from 1801 to 1831. These figures are respectively twice and three times the Crafts estimates.[38] However, even if Crafts' figures are to a degree pessimistic, there is no room for any strong improvement in the level of consumption of goods and services by the lower orders.[39]

THE 'CONSUMER REVOLUTION'

Who, then, did consume the increased volume and range of consumer goods and services which undoubtedly were produced in eighteenth-century England and which have led some historians to

37. N.F.R. Crafts, *British Economic Growth*, Chapter 2.
38. P. Deane and W.A. Cole, *British Economic Growth 1688–1959*, Cambridge UP, 1969. For a fuller discussion of their findings, see Rule, *Vital Century*, pp. 28–38.
39. This is the conclusion reached by Crafts, *British Economic Growth*, p. 112.

insist on a 'consumer revolution'? In effect this is to ask who benefited from the fact that, however narrowly, output *did* outpace population growth. The great landowners mostly did, through the inheritance practice of primogeniture and through legal devices like strict settlement to keep their estates intact and to hold on to their share of the land. Indeed, there was a gradual shift in the pattern of land-holding towards those having 3,000 acres or more, who, on Professor Thompson's estimate, held between a fifth and a quarter of English land by 1790. Their gain, a gradual one of around 5 per cent a century, was at the expense of small rather than of middling owners. The former group, that is those holding less than 300 acres, had held between a quarter and a third of English land. By 1790 they held less than a seventh.[40] During the agricultural depression from 1730 to 1750 which was most pronounced in the lighter-soil regions, rent arrears piled up and many farms simply could not be let. Once the cereal price trend turned up from mid century, however, the incomes of the large land-holders moved steadily with it.[41] As Dr O'Brien has pointed out, few of them were the committed, innovating, improving landlords so beloved in the traditional 'heroic' presentation of the agricultural revolution. They did not have to be. In some districts, such as Cumbria, entrenched forms of customary tenure might have restricted landlords' opportunities to raise rents, but in general they were able to consolidate and re-let their farms on old enclosed areas, and where they did enclose their not inconsiderable investment brought them the opportunity to re-form and re-let their farms at increased rents. Thereafter the farmers tended to take on a large share of the burden of investment in agricultural improvement. The great power of the Hanoverian aristocracy rested on substantial economic foundations. Some were especially fortunate in that portions of their estates were taken up in urban development with huge enhancement of their rent income, or in the existence beneath their fields of coal or metals.[42] Landlords began to spend more time in town and their consumption habits developed accordingly. They did not consume

40. F.M.L. Thompson, 'The social distribution of landed property in England since the sixteenth century', *Econ. H.R.*, XIX, 1966, p. 512. For a fuller discussion of land-holding and inheritance, see Rule, *Vital Century*, pp. 40–47 and the sources cited therein.

41. For the general movement of prices, etc., see E.L. Jones, 'Agriculture 1700–80' in Floud and McCloskey, *Economic History of Britain*, pp. 66–86.

42. P.K. O'Brien, 'Quelle est exactement la contribution de l'aristocratie britannique au progrès de l'agriculture entre 1688 et 1798?', *Annales ESC*, Nov–Dec 1987, No. 6, pp. 1391–409.

only luxuries; they had armies of servants to dress and huge house-holds to equip and maintain. Nevertheless the English aristocracy was a tight elite and very much smaller than was the case on the continent. It might have led, but it could not on its own have sustained, a 'consumer revolution'.[43]

Farmers did well – so well that their over-furnished parlours and their wives' pianos had become objects of clichéd derision by the end of the eighteenth century. As for the urban middle class, they derived status from material possessions and assumed life-styles perhaps more than did any other social group. In fact it was the large proportionate size of the middle-income groups which distinguished English society. Increasing numbers with a margin to spend after 'necessities' make it possible for some historians to see 'rising expectations' and 'social emulation' driving an expansion in domestic consumption which was a key condition for the industrial revolution.[44] But how far down the social scale did the consumer revolution reach? Professor Eversley has suggested that 'what seems necessary for growth is that very exceptional expenditures should become a little less so'. He stresses the importance of 'decencies', items like soap, some household utensils and a few cotton garments which came between absolute necessities and luxuries, as well as to an increasing consumption of imported 'groceries' like tea and sugar. Taking an income of around £50 a year as the threshold, he suggests that around 3 million of the population were to be found above it by 1800.[45] In terms of adult male earnings a number of the better-paid artisans from the 'honourable trades' were included, while even rural manufacturing groups like hand-loom weavers and framework knitters enjoyed periods of full employment and high earnings which took them in from time to time. Dr McKendrick has pointed out that where opportunities for the employment of women and children existed, family earnings could bring a significant number of households into the group. The problem is that the language used to describe the so-called 'consumer revolution' tends to be rather stronger than the statistics which support it. Eversley considered that the necessary home market expansion needed only around 15 per cent of the population in 1750 and 20 to 25 per cent

43. For the idea of a 'consumer revolution', see especially McKendrick, Brewer and Plumb, *Birth of a Consumer Society*, and the discussion in Rule, *Vital Century*, pp. 256–60.

44. For example Perkin, *Origins of Modern English Society*, pp. 91–7.

45. D.E.C. Eversley, 'The home market and economic growth in England 1750–80' in Jones and Mingay (eds), *Land, Labour and Population in the Industrial Revolution*, Arnold, 1967, pp. 211–14.

by 1780 to be within the income range £50–£200. A very small section of the labouring classes was part of this.[46]

The rise of Britain as a world power over the eighteenth century was facilitated by an ability to raise her tax yield to a level significantly higher in per capita terms than her main rival, France. Direct taxation on land and immovable property was responsible for only a fifth of government income by 1793. Financial success derived from indirect taxation. Dr Porter has suggested that the ability to tax 'commodities purchased by the populace at large' reflected the 'burgeoning prosperity of the trading and labouring classes'. Taxation fell on bricks, starch, glass, salt, printed fabrics, paper, soap, candles, leather and, especially, alcohol. Home-produced goods were taxed through the efficient Excise and were hardly subject to the loss through smuggling which so reduced the yield of import duties. Certainly, relative to the population of France, Britain's income distribution favoured the imposition of an effective but increasingly regressive form of taxation which placed only a light and diminishing burden on the landed classes. It is, however, as unsafe on this as on any other basis to write generally of the 'prosperity' of the labouring classes, especially after cereal prices began to rise from around 1760. Indirect taxation must have lowered the ability to purchase non-essentials for a sizeable number of marginal households. And it was not only tax yield per head which rose over the later eighteenth century; so, too, did expenditure on poor relief. National expenditure in 1748–9 was £689,971. It passed through £1.5 million by the time of the American Revolution to reach £4,077,891 in 1803.[47]

Large numbers of England's labouring poor were consumers in a very different sense. The waged proletariat entered the market from necessity and overwhelmingly for food. In some years of high food prices for groups like the southern farm labourers, even the wages of full employment could hardly buy enough. As Dr Berg has pointed out, 'the home market grew in the eighteenth century, but its expansion was based on changing social relations and not on a national trend of rising living standards'.[48] Rioting over food prices

46. N. McKendrick, 'Home demand and economic growth: a new view of the role of women and children in the industrial revolution' in McKendrick (ed.) *Historical Perspectives: Studies in English Thought and Society*, Europa, 1974, pp. 184–90.

47. R. Porter, 'English society in the eighteenth century revisited', in J. Black (ed.), *British Politics and Society from Walpole to Pitt*, pp. 33–4; J.G. Rule, 'Land of lost content? The eighteenth-century Poor Law', *Revue française de civilisation britannique*, VI, No. 2, 1991, p. 19.

48. M. Berg, *Age of Manufactures*, p. 99.

and industrial disputes are both proletarian forms of protest, and both were common in later eighteenth-century England. Bare necessities, and hardly enough of those, were what entered the rural hovels and the urban cellars and attics inhabited by the poor. To write of *mass* consumption of non-essentials in the eighteenth century is therefore inexact; for the masses life remained a struggle.[49]

Among journeymen tailors there was a high level of 'consumption'. Hundreds died of it every year – so many that they became the 'wretched emblems of death'. It was widely accepted that hard as was the lot of the country labourer, manufacturing workers fought a special struggle against ill health. Adam Smith wrote of the 'peculiar infirmity' of each trade, and 'grinder's rot', 'weaver's bottom' and 'hod-carrier's shoulder' are but a sample of the litany which confirms his observation. Potters, painters and plumbers suffered from lead poisoning along with gilders and glaziers, while those who actually produced the lead in the notorious Whitechapel works seldom lived more than a dozen years after taking up the business. Arsenic similarly served those who refined copper, and mercury poisoning drove the hatter mad. In a range of trades from coal mining through cutlery grinding to sugar baking, a deadly dust had an equally pernicious effect.[50] There was ample justification for the remark of a pamphleteer in 1782:

> Scarcely are we fed, lodged, clothed, warmed, without sending multitudes to their grave. The collier, the clothier, the painter, the gilder, the miner, the makers of glass, the workers in iron, tin, lead, copper, while they administer to our necessities, or please our taste and fancies, are impairing their health and shortening their days.[51]

Such people made the goods for the 'consumer revolution'; that is, they did so until it consumed them.

POWER AND THE LAW

Some people inverted the consumer revolution. Their struggle was with the law and the extremes to which it went in protecting

49. For the frequency of food rioting and of industrial disputes, see Chapter 8 below. They are clearly 'proletarian' protest forms; a member of a subsistence economy does not riot in a market, while industrial disputes involve wage-earners.
50. Rule, *Experience of Labour*, pp. 74–92 for these and other illustrations.
51. *Gentleman's Magazine*, LII, 1782, p. 526.

property. Some stole as a way of life; many more did so from time to time as a means of survival. The thousands of women and girls who sold themselves on the streets were part of their world too, as were beggars, tricksters and vagrants of all kinds. Watches, jewellery, silk handkerchiefs and other consumer goods passed through their hands – out of the pockets of 'superior' folk and into the receiving grasp of fences. Wigs were stolen too. There was a canting term for this speciality: 'wool pulling'. Those who stole wigs did not wear them; there was a market for second-hand wigs and they supplied it. Since wigs were usually valued above the level which made theft a capital offence, it was a dangerous trade – one in which you risked your life.[52]

The struggle to exist was fought in a manner of ways. At all times large numbers of the population were engaged in it. In years of bad harvest or trade depression their numbers significantly increased, as they did at the end of wars when the discharged and the laid-off further swelled normally high levels of unemployment and under-employment. It was the other side of an eighteenth-century world of style and social emulation for which its existence *and* its subordination were necessary conditions. Adam Smith recognised this very clearly.

> In a Society of a hundred thousand families, there will be perhaps a hundred who don't labour at all, and yet, either by violence, or by the orderly oppression of the law, employ a greater part of the labour of the Society than any other ten thousand in it. The division of what remains after this enormous defalcation, is by no means made in proportion to the labour of each individual. On the contrary those who labour most get least.[53]

That was why, in 'civil society', laws were necessary.

> Laws and governments may be considered . . . as a combination of the rich to oppress the poor and preserve to themselves the inequality of the goods which would otherwise be soon destroyed by the attacks of the poor, who if not hindered by the government would soon reduce the others to an equality by open violence.[54]

This was not simply a matter of physical force. With no standing

52. See P. Linebaugh, *The London Hanged*, for the most persuasive linking of crime to the development of the capitalist mode of production over the eighteenth century.

53. From an early draft of the *Wealth of Nations* cited in D. Winch, *Adam Smith's Politics*, Cambridge UP, 1978, pp. 88–9.

54. Adam Smith, *Lectures on Jurisprudence*, R.L. Meek, D.D. Raphael and P.G. Stein (eds), Oxford UP, 1978, p. 208.

army and a police system that was literally medieval, the British state appeared weak in comparison with some continental powers. That was an illusion. It was no weak state which provided the force to put together one of the greatest commercial empires in history. But it does serve to indicate the complexities of state power and of class hegemony. From the settlement of 1688 through to the revolutionary era of the 1790s, the political system was stable. Edward Thompson has described the period as 'a hundred years of comparative social stasis so far as overt class conflict or the maturation of class consciousness was concerned'.[55] Indeed, until the defeat of the second Jacobite rising in 1745 the only serious challenge to the Hanoverian dynasty and the aristocratic Whig elite had been presented by the Tory supporters of an alternative monarchy. As William Blake knew, there was more than physical force to securing that subordination.

> The twenty-eight cities of Albion stretch their hands to thee
> Because of the oppression of Albion in every city and village.
> They mock at the Labourer's limbs: they mock at his starv'd
>   children:
> They buy his daughters that they may have power to sell his sons:
> They compell the Poor to live upon a crust of bread by soft mild
>   arts:
> They reduce the Man to want, then give with pomp and ceremony:
> The praise of Jehovah is chaunted from lips of hunger and thirst.[56]

Ideology in various forms legitimated power. Established religion was especially important in associating 'Church and State'. As Dr Jonathan Clark has detailed, there is an important sense in which every Anglican priest was an agent of the state and played a part in ensuring that the claims of the elite to govern were hardly disputed.[57] After the outbreak of the French Revolution in 1789 a much more considerable effort was required from the ruling class. Events across the Channel inevitably stimulated intense political debate in Britain and brought a deep polarisation of opinion. In the early 1790s the campaign for parliamentary reform was stimulated by the example of France and secured greater public support than ever before, but its very success allied to the fear of a French inva-

---

55. E.P. Thompson, 'The peculiarities of the English' in *The Poverty of Theory*, Merlin, 1978, p. 322.

56. William Blake, *Jerusalem*, 1804–20, Chapter 2.

57. J.C.D. Clark, *English Society*, is a major, but controversial work which asserts that until 1828–32 when it was destroyed by Catholic emancipation and by the great Reform Act, Hanoverian England was an *'ancien régime'* society and polity in which the aristocratic/Anglican hegemony was not significantly threatened.

sion after 1793 brought a conservative reaction. The ruling class proved itself as adept at the 'mild arts' of persuasion and propaganda as in the role of repression. From Edmund Burke down it exploited the threat to the constitution, to the established Church and to 'property' so effectively that it split the Whig party, drew the middle ranks of society to its side and even, playing upon traditional anti-French feeling, nurtured into being a genuine popular loyalism. Although the Younger William Pitt tended to think of himself as an 'independent Whig', the label 'Tory' was increasingly applied to a ministry which defended the royal prerogative, supported the privileges of the Church of England, cultivated patriotic sentiment in the nation at large, encouraged militant loyalists and suppressed the freedom to dissent. What the 1790s saw was on the one side the emergence for the first time of a genuine popular radicalism, republican and even insurrectionary at its edges, and on the other controlled rather than wholesale repression legitimated in the dissemination of a conservative ideology of considerable force and appeal. As Professor Dickinson has expressed it, the latter was sufficient in the outcome 'to swamp the radical cause and to drive the reformers underground'.[58] It was not to be a permanent victory. Conservatism and loyalism were widely supported only so long as radicalism could be associated with the revolutionary excesses of the French and the military threat of Napoleon. Very soon after these ended in 1815, and in the economically depressed post-war years, the cause of radical reform speedily and effectively revived.

The conservative propaganda offensive urged the people not just to appreciate their 'constitution' and stand by their Church, but also to value their freedom under the law. As Douglas Hay and others have pointed out, it was a special contribution of the eighteenth century to place alongside religion and a widely accepted conservative political ideology a third element: the rule of law.[59] Through it, protecting the property rights of the possessing classes could be generalised into the protection of all property. Rhetoric about the security of the few poor goods in the cottage home could

58. For the extent of 'popular conservatism', see H.T. Dickinson, 'Popular conservatism and militant loyalism' in Dickinson (ed.), *Britain and the French Revolution 1789–1815*, Macmillan, 1989, pp. 103–26. For popular radicalism, see J. Stevenson, 'Popular radicalism and popular protest 1789–1815', *ibid.*, pp. 61–82. For insurrectionary intent, see R.A.E. Wells, *Insurrection: The British Experience, 1795–1803*, Alan Sutton, 1983. The enforcement of the repressive legislation is subtly analysed in Clive Emsley, 'An aspect of Pitt's terror: prosecutions for sedition during the 1790s', *Social History*, VI, 2, 1981, pp. 155–84. The indispensable classic account is that in E.P. Thompson, *The Making of the English Working Class*.

59. See below, pp. 244–9.

hide the way in which the more valuable 'properties' of the poor, their 'rights' through apprenticeship, wage regulation and under the Poor Law, were disregarded and ultimately removed. Eighteenth-century law underpinned the market economy while it undermined the moral one.

Political stability gave emerging capitalism one of its preconditions: relative tranquillity in the social order. Equally significantly, it enabled the *economic* subordination of labour to capital to be substantially accomplished by 1815. This did not reflect weakness on the part of the elite. It was the outcome of a 'positive permissiveness'. In the first place, through its role in the enclosure process and in estate consolidation generally, the landed elite was actively playing a part in the subordination of agricultural labour. Christopher Hill has perceptively brought together revealing phrases from enclosure's propagandists: 'open war against cottages'; forcing labourers to 'work every day in the year'; 'their children will be put to labour early'. Enclosing the commons, especially by depriving the lower orders of any chance of economic independence, would secure the 'subordination of the lower ranks of society'.[60]

Of course, capitalism and the market economy with their associated relations of production were not created by the eighteenth-century state, but capitalism as a system triumphs only when it becomes identified with the state. As Corrigan and Sayer have pointed out, what was happening in the eighteenth century was 'the construction of the typical state/economy relation of bourgeois societies, whereby the former secures the conditions in which the latter can "freely" operate *through* the inflection of older forms'. The state's agency in this respect can be overlooked, for it moved through permitting rather than enacting and by making new relationships appear natural even though 'what was permitted for some was experienced as imposition for most'.[61] But what it did enact should not be overlooked. Its statutes, for example, banned trade unionism in specific trades before the general prohibition of 1800. A series of laws criminalised the appropriation of raw materials by out-workers as putting-out manufacture spread. Even though statutory apprenticeship was not removed until 1814, it had been long

---

60. C. Hill, *Reformation to Industrial Revolution*, Penguin, 1969, pp. 269–7.
61. P. Corrigan and D. Sayer, *The Great Arch: English State Formation as Cultural Revolution*, Blackwell, 1985, pp. 91–2. This very suggestive book has been undeservedly neglected by historians – one suspects because the authors have been placed further beyond the pale by the fact that they are sociologists rather than by the fact that they are Marxists.

disregarded and its extension to new trades refused.[62] In an age when labour was being freed, 'employment', a form of contract made in a labour market, was replacing 'service'; many wanted the best of both worlds and still spoke partly within the old discourse of 'master and servant'. Indeed, the last act governing the relations of employment and hire which was so entitled was not passed until 1823.[63] In a time of industrial conflict in the west of England woollen industry in 1756, the clothiers expected to be freed from legislation regulating wages because 'we think it absolutely absurd and repugnant to the Liberties of a free people, and to the Interest of Trade that any Law should supersede a private contract honourably made between a master and his Workmen'. But they also argued that laws enforcing certain wages on employers tended to 'invert the Laws of Society, and to destroy that due subordination which ought to be religiously preserved in all Communities. The Weavers by this Act will be rendered more our Masters than we are now theirs.'[64] The economy demanded a more mobile labour force, but the vagrancy accompanying its creation was still viewed by many within an older paradigm of 'masterless men'.

---

62. See Rule, *Experience of Labour*, pp. 107–14.

63. 4 George IV c. 4; it was used regularly in the 1850s and 1860s and not repealed until 1875.

64. Reprinted in W.E. Minchinton, 'The petitions of the weavers and clothiers of Gloucestershire in 1756', *Trans. Bristol and Gloucs Arch. Soc.*, **73**, 1954, pp. 222–3.

CHAPTER TWO

The Upper Class

INHERITANCE AND OFFICE-HOLDING

'Class' as a means of describing social divisions came into some use before the end of the eighteenth century, as Dr Corfield has recently shown.[1] It had to appear, because existing terms were too static for those who sensed a growing fluidity. The old language not only denied mobility, it hid opposing interests. Talk of 'rank conflict' would indeed be a contradiction in terms. Even if the sense of a society in flux was increasing, it was far from general and many of those attempting social description continued to do so in the older terms of a 'Great Chain of Being', a well-ordered sequence of ranks and degrees. This was divinely ordained; part of a natural order of things which both implied that social position was a matter of birth and sanctioned an authority structure which should not be challenged. Even though the class structure which was to be characteristic of nineteenth-century industrial society was emerging, it would be anachronistic to talk even of a developing class consciousness until the last decades of the eighteenth century. Clearly there is little sign till then of the ideologies which both develop from and form that consciousness. But however the social order is described, there is no doubt who both headed it and were uniquely cohesive as a social group.

'Nobody', according to Henry Fielding in 1752, described 'All the people in Great Britain, except about 1200'.[2] Probably he was making a wry comment on 'society', but it is a fair indication of the size of the elite within the governing classes. It has become a commonplace to counter ideas of a bourgeois revolution happening in seventeenth-century England by stressing that over the eighteenth

1. P. Corfield, 'Class by name and number'.
2. *Covent Garden Journal*, 4, 14 January 1752.

century the aristocracy not only retained their social and political power but actually increased it. Further, it is stressed that this power was held and exercised without significant challenge, there being, as Professor Cannon has put it, 'a massive consensus, based upon the widespread acceptance of aristocratic values and aristocratic leadership'.[3] Because only first sons inherited, the hereditary titled classes were exceptionally small in eighteenth-century Britain. Only 1,003 persons held peerages during the whole of the eighteenth century. Few new peerages were created before its closing decades and existing peers discovered a talent for long living – a hundred of them held their titles for fifty years or more (Lord Fitzwilliam headed the list with 77 years!). Professor Cannon has tabulated the number of peers on 1 January at several points.

Table 2.1 Number of peers on 1 January 1720–1800

1720	1740	1760	1780	1800
190	183	181	189	267

Source: J. Cannon, *Aristocratic Century: The Peerage of Eighteenth Century England.* Cambridge UP, 1984, p. 15.

The peerage need not be considered coterminous with the aristocracy. Not only would younger sons and perhaps daughters consider themselves as part of the latter, but so too would the hereditary knights, the baronets. The newly created Lord De Dunstanville may have been proud to take his seat in the upper house in 1796, but the seat he had been occupying in the Commons as Sir Francis Basset, Bart had been one of the five he owned in west Cornwall. That was two more than his nearest peer neighbour Lord Falmouth and three more than the county's premier nobleman Earl Mount Edgecumbe. Basset's peerage merely confirmed his position as the most powerful man in his copper-rich locality and, indeed, the only other person to approach his position was his kinsman Sir John St Aubyn who remained a baronet. It is clearly difficult to draw a line between men like this and the peerage or even between it and for the time being untitled landowners such as the Cokes of Norfolk. Yet, as Cannon has pointed out, even if we add English peers, baronets and knights together to comprise a titled social elite, the numbers still remain small, and given the rapid population growth after

3. J. Cannon, *Aristocratic Century*, pp. viii, 10.

mid century show a pronounced relative decline as well as a slight actual one from 1,323 in 1700 through 908 in 1750 to 1,126 in 1800. The judgement of Professor Mingay that 'between the main body of the peerage and the great majority of the gentry there yawned always a measurable social gulf' seems sound given that it excepts a small, but significant, minority of that class.[4]

The peerage, slightly augmented, did not make up a complete ruling class. Some others shared in the ownership of power in particular spheres, for example local communities or corporate towns. But the aristocrats were paramount. They dominated high politics and the major offices of state. Peers were differentiated by their sitting in the House of Lords, alongside the spiritual lords, the archbishops and bishops. Yet even accepting the general view that the power of the upper chamber was declining relative to that of the lower, the hold of the aristocracy on the reins hardly slackened. Cannon suggests that peerage patronage over seats in the Commons increased around fourfold between 1715 and 1785. In the former year sixty-eight borough MPs were controlled by the peerage; in 1786, 210 were. As for their actual membership, fifty sons of peers sat in the House in 1734, seventy-two in 1780 and eighty-two in 1796. If we add the Irish peers who also sat, the 'peerage element' rose from 8 per cent in 1713 to 21 per cent in 1796. In the House of Commons in 1784, in addition to 107 sons of peers and Irish peers, there also sat forty-six blood relatives of peers and twenty-two sons and brothers-in-law. Representation of the landed interest did not end there. Eighty-four baronets sat, sixteen of their sons and eleven of their sons-in-law. This cohesiveness of the House of Commons in the eighteenth century, from which sprang common values and great confidence, was the real basis of what was 'one of the most exclusive ruling elites in human history'.[5]

Their hold over the great offices of state was even more emphatic. When Henry Pelham added the Duke of Bedford to his cabinet in 1744, ducal representation rose to seven. Between 1782 and 1820 cabinet office was held by sixty-five men of whom forty-three were peers and fourteen sons of peers. Alongside the domination of civil office was a parallel one in the Army and Navy. In the former the system of army purchase was the essential enabling factor. By 1800 a colonelcy in the cavalry cost £5,000 and of 102 colonels of regiments in 1769, fifty-four were peers or their sons,

4. *Ibid.*, pp. 31–2; G.E. Mingay, *The Gentry: The Rise and Fall of a Ruling Class*, Longman, 1976, p. 4.
5. Cannon, *Aristocratic Century*, pp. 104–15.

grandsons or sons-in-law, as were more than 40 per cent of the generals and 70 per cent of the field-marshals. There was scant chance of the Army not sharing the values of the rulers. Domination of the Navy was less marked. Long periods on a man-of-war tended to appeal only to the dedicated and afforded only a distinctly cramped life-style. Nevertheless, aristocratic influence at the top was prevalent enough.[6]

Holders of major office could hardly avoid performing service in return for the advantages, some would say spoils, that it brought, but there were many offices which were sinecures, while some, like that of Paymaster General, needed some input but were mainly sought for the opportunities of profit they afforded. The Earl of Ranelagh, the Duke of Chandos, Walpole and Henry Fox all founded fortunes from brief tenures of this office. Unlike landed estates political office could not be inherited, but tenure was usually for life. It was secured through political influence and connections – a channel to lucrative position which, in comparison with the slower accumulation of direct profits from the land, has led one historian to remark cynically, 'Political influence could do more to maximise profits than could four-course rotations.'[7] Of course, land and the income and influence derived from it remained the foundation of aristocratic wealth and power. But being commonly inherited under terms of strict settlement it lacked mobility as an asset and only through mortgage could it release liquidity. That is why other forms of income were important, and it was in the expectation of profit that the patriciate expended so much in pursuit of parliamentary influence. E.P. Thompson has been an exceptionally stern critic of 'Old Corruption', as later reformers and historians summarised the political system of pre-1832 Britain. He has written of 'a patrician banditti' who 'contested' for the 'spoils of power' to the extent that 'the State was itself among the prime objects of prey' and of a 'parasitism' on the backs of the smaller gentry who paid the land tax. (It was in this sense also a parasitism on the backs of the lower orders who bore the burden of a system of indirect taxation which was increasingly regressive in its effects.) While it is true that the ruling class of eighteenth-century Britain may have been less venal than those of most *ancien régimes*, it still needs to be remembered that 'Old Corruption' was not simply a term of abuse, it was a serious shorthand for a political system ultimately resting on the expectation that advantage should be gained not only from

6. *Ibid.*, pp. 115–20.
7. E.P. Thompson, 'Eighteenth-century English society', p. 139.

office but from the vote of the elector; from a seat in parliament or from the representation of a borough. From the 1780s the proponents of political reform began to uncover it in statistical detail, but well before then writers like Swift, Fielding and Smollett could employ a comparison between high politics and the criminal underworld as a common figure of satire.[8]

According to Thompson the system was based on 'networks of place, pelf and patronage'.[9] The first two we have indicated; the third describes the method through which they were achieved. As Professor Plumb has put it:

> The letter bag of every M.P. with the slightest pretensions to influence was stuffed with pleas and demands from voters for themselves, their relations or their dependants. Places in the Customs and Excise, in the Army and Navy, in the Church, in the East India, Africa and Levant Companies, in all the departments of state from doorkeepers to clerks: jobs at Court for the real gentry or sinecures in Ireland, the diplomatic corps, or anywhere else where duties were light and salaries steady. These were the true coin of politics.[10]

The court and government patronage systems developed to provide a parliamentary majority, and so meticulously described by Sir Lewis Namier and his associates, were, as Professor Perkin suggests, 'the visible topgrowth of a plant whose roots and branches ramified throughout society'. From the lucrative state offices down it amounted to a 'system of personal selection from among one's kinsmen and connections' through which 'property influenced recruitment to those positions in society which were not determined by property alone'.[11]

With the great divisions of the seventeenth century at rest in a general atmosphere of conditioned tolerance, religion in the eighteenth century was a stabilising feature. Indeed, the role of the established Church in propping up the social order was hugely important, with the village parson being the most frequently encountered representative of authority for most people. The aristocracy could place a hold over ecclesiastical office alongside their domination of military and state offices. This hold was twofold, being expressed both through the holding of high positions and by

8. *Ibid.*, pp. 139, 141–2.
9. P. Corrigan and D. Sayer, *The Great Arch. English State Formation as Cultural Revolution*, Blackwell, Oxford, 1985, p. 89.
10. J.H. Plumb, 'Political man' in J.L. Clifford (ed.), *Man versus Society in Eighteenth-Century England*, Cambridge UP, 1968, p. 6.
11. H.J. Perkin, *Origins of Modern English Society*, pp. 44–5.

the lay patronage over church livings. The first was of increasing significance, for while only four of the eighty-five eighteenth-century bishops appointed before 1740 were aristocrats, of the seventy-six appointed after that date twenty were. In 1808 the aristocratic-born held nine of the twenty-six archbishoprics and bishoprics. The right to present to livings was a more widespread advantage, a way of providing for relatives and for those to whom favours were owed. In the 1720s and 1730s forty-nine peerage families had at least eight livings each in their gift, and Cannon has suggested that there was an increase over the later eighteenth and early nineteenth centuries, though with some regional variation.[12]

The extraordinary cohesiveness of the aristocratic faction of the ruling classes was further enhanced by the way in which their sons were educated. In particular they used the great public schools to fit them for public life. There was a marked shift away from private education to the schools. From a sample of 954 peers, Cannon has found that of those born between 1711 and 1740, 58.6 per cent went to one of the four great schools of Eton, Harrow, Westminster or Winchester. Of those born after 1740, 72.2 per cent did. The self-confirming classical curriculum reinforced their perceptions of their position in society, as it further did for those who went to university. At a time of declining enrolments at Oxford and Cambridge, the increasing percentage of peers who attended suggests a growing dominance, especially over the colleges they favoured like, especially, Christ Church at Oxford and Trinity, St John's and King's and Clare at Cambridge. The importance of a handful of schools and colleges to the sons of the peerage was obvious in terms of acquaintanceship networks and in the inculcation of shared values.[13]

THE ARISTOCRACY AND THE GENTRY

At the level of national politics and national institutions, the aristocracy was dominant. The prolonged political stability which followed the settlement of 1688 had provided a situation in which, with the grand issues dormant, the ascendancy of an elite, the so-called 'Whig oligarchy', had been paralleled by the degeneracy of

12. Cannon, *Aristocratic Century*, pp. 61–5.
13. *Ibid.*, pp. 34–49.

institutions and their absorption into a corrupt system. The consequence of elite entrenchment was the opening of a gap between
them and the majority of the middle and lesser gentry, but it is
difficult to see that the latter lost power and influence in the
countryside. In the context of local government and in the exercise
of everyday authority, a wider concept of the ruling class is needed.
In a sense this is paradoxical for the great house was the most manifest mark of the aristocrat, dominating or even creating the local
landscape. Hanoverian England saw what has been described as a
'truly astonishing' building and rebuilding of country houses involving an immense expenditure not only on house building but, because of the arrival of the landscaped park (preferably by Capability
Brown) as the status symbol *par excellence*, on levelling hillocks,
damming and diverting streams to manufacture lakes and on the
planting of thousands of trees. As the century progressed, style
changed from the classical Palladian to the renaissance of the or-
nate Gothic, but spending hardly abated. Thomas Coke was thirty
years (1734–64) building Holkholm Hall. By 1800 the park around
it had been stretched to 3,000 acres. Even so, it was smaller than
the 5,000 acres laid out in Cumberland by the Duke of Norfolk in
his concern to outdo Lord Lonsdale's 4,000-acre Lowther Park.
Capability Brown worked at 188 separate places between the 1750s
and his death in 1783, while his most important successor
Humphrey Repton, who began in the 1780s, had designed 220 gardens by his death in 1818.[14]

Obviously it was not only in their building that the great houses
were important to the local economy. In only three months' stay at
Thoresby in 1736, the Duke of Kingston ran up a bill of £1,477.
Employment of the estate servants was important, although the
£2,300 annual wage bill of Earl FitzWilliam in 1815 was significantly
inflated by the collieries on his south Yorkshire estate.[15] Even those
of its neighbourhood who were neither purveyors to it nor permanent employees of it expected something from the great house.
William Jenkin, a steward for an absentee landowner, wrote to his
employer in the hungry year of 1801:

> My neighbour has just communicated to me the contents of a very
> polite letter from J. Buller Esq. inclosing a draft on his bankers for
> £100 towards a fund for procuring corn for the poor families in this

14. M. Reed, *The Georgian Triumph 1700–1830*, Paladin, 1984, pp. 114–18; J.V.
Beckett, *Aristocracy in England*, pp. 327–35.
15. Beckett, *Aristocracy in England*, p. 338.

populous parish. Sir John St Aubyn who has but a very small estate here gave £5. 5s.[16]

The expectation is not only that the landowner should contribute but that he should do so in proportion to his local standing. Whether it was for corn subscriptions, school provision or winter fuel, or special cases of individual misfortune, the steward rather than the landlord was the person in direct contact with the poor. Historians have much overstated the face-to-face dimension of paternalism. It was the steward who informed his employer where charity was deserved and where it was expected. Jenkin wrote to his employer on behalf of the widow and children when a poor miner was killed in a mine which was partly on his estate: 'a neighbouring gentleman and one of the lords of the mine, was so kind as to send the poor woman a guinea. I took the liberty of doing the like on your behalf.' On another occasion he reminded his employer of 'some little assistance' he had made to poor mining families and continued: 'Please excuse me for mentioning it now . . . the poor creatures are enquiring whether anything of that sort is to be hoped for this year.' When the estates passed into other hands in 1812, he wrote:

> I have taken the liberty of using thy name and money to the amount of £12 or £14 in the course of last year, in relieving some unfortunate families, some of whose husbands or near relations have either been killed or hurted in Tin Croft and other of thy mines. I did not take the liberty of troubling thee with these little matters as they arose, but as I used to do in thy Uncle's time charge it in one sum at the end of the year.[17]

During the food crisis of 1812 he wrote that one of the lords who had not yet subscribed was in fact a liberal, humane man who 'may do something handsome, when his steward shall think fit to write to him'. On the death of the 'venerable' steward of Lady Basset who had served her and her husband for fifty years, an obituarist applauded a man who:

> while besides most zealously carrying into effect the benevolent designs of his noble patrons, he has been careful to bring under their consideration every case in which they might, with advantage to deserving persons, or with benefit to the neighbourhood, gratify the first desire of their hearts – the desire to do good.[18]

16. County Museum Truro, Mss. Letterbooks of William Jenkin, 29 April 1801.
17. *Ibid.*, 27 February 1799; 28 May 1798; 17 January 1800.
18. *Ibid.*, 17 April 1812; *Cornwall Gazette*, 9 July 1841.

Thus, while the recipients of charity might bless the generosity of the lord, it was the mood of his steward they had to observe. Peers and gentry often put aside annual sums for charity but they rarely concerned themselves with the details of its distribution. The Earl of Thaney thus dispensed £100 a year in Westmorland, and Samuel Whitbread distributed around £2,000 in 1800. Usually, however, the sum set aside was less than 10 per cent of annual income. From an estate-derived income of £2,500 in 1806, Sir John Bridger set aside £35 which was 1.4 per cent.[19]

Sometimes the aristocrats sought to provide an improving example for the populace to follow. Lord De Dunstanville had built a chapel of ease on his estate and walked the mile to it every evening from his manor, 'which he makes a point to do as an example to the people'. His neighbour and kinsman Sir John St Aubyn set an example of a different kind with his fifteen illegitimate children by two local women.[20] Along with charity went ceremony. The great must be seen to be such. Family weddings, christenings and funerals provided occasions. The Duke of Rutland's coming of age in 1799 was celebrated over three days of festivities at a cost of £60,000. When the Duke of Newcastle's body was brought back to his Sussex home in 1768, the procession from London was headed by two porters on white horses followed by eight domestics on grey horses, a gentleman carrying the late Duke's coronet, the hearse drawn by six horses, four four-horse coaches of mourners, with the rear being brought up by a gentleman and six mounted servants. It was not an exceptional example in a country in which, according to one lady, there was 'more pomp at their funerals than weddings'. The funeral and mourning expenses for the Duke of Kingston in 1726 came to £1,475.[21] There were other events, too, which could occasion treating. When it won a lawsuit against the Basset family in 1798, the Lanhydrock family provided all the miners on its Cornish estate with a mug of ale which they drank at a nearby inn and 'huzzaed on the occasion'. Three years later when the verdict went the other way, the steward of the Lanhydrock estate wrote:

> I hear nothing on the side of our honourable, noble, generous opponents but huzzaing and shouting, and their grand display of ribbons. As they passed through Redruth they drew the admiration of multitudes of women and children – Horses and asses decorated with the Ensigns of victory.

19. Beckett, *Aristocracy in England*, pp. 354–6.
20. J. Grieg, *The Farrington Diary*, Hutchinson, VI, 1926, pp. 141, 255–6.
21. Beckett, *Aristocracy in England*, pp. 344–5.

Sour grapes, of course. The only reason that this steward on the first occasion had held back from having the church bells rung was for fear it would subject 'the poor ringers to the malice of insolent, revengeful Tyranny', indicating the consequences of displeasing Lord De Dunstanville, as Sir Francis Basset had by then become, in his own kingdom.[22] It was also expected that the family from the great house would take the lead in sponsoring the local celebrations due on national occasions like coronations, naval or land victories, royal weddings, and on the recovery of George III from illness in 1789. On this last occasion the Earl of Gainsborough entertained the whole parish of Exton in Rutlandshire 'in a most bountiful manner; the town was illuminated, a large bonfire made, and a pipe of ale given to the people in the streets'.[23]

Grand as such aristocratic occasions were, they probably differed only in their lavishness from the expectations the community laid on the gentry. The country gentlemen, those 15,000 squires who lived from their lands, were a less elevated but even more essential component of the rural ruling class than were the aristocracy. Some of them also had their part to play on the national stage as back-bench members of the Commons. Professor Perkin has correctly pointed out that the power of the landed classes 'always came back to the social control of the *ordinary squire* over his tenants and villagers' (my italics). For most inhabitants of rural England, the 'great house' was not the near-palace of the super-magnate but the still imposing manor of the squire.[24]

Professor Cannon is perhaps trying too hard in his portrayal of *The Aristocratic Century* when he seems to imply that through filling the office of Lord Lieutenant, the aristocracy ruled at county level. Certainly, 255 of 294 holders of the top county post over the eighteenth century were peers or sons of peers. The key role of the Lord Lieutenant was in advising the Lord Chancellor on the appointment of the justices of the peace, for it was these men who held the everyday reigns of power both judicial and administrative in the countryside, both as individuals dispensing summary justice or crucially determining who should be committed for trial, and collectively as the bench at quarter sessions. The number of justices of the peace increased with the population and the volume of work. There were 2,560 in 1680 and 8,400 by 1761. Their jurisdiction covered matters such as highways, bridges, the licensing of

22. Jenkin Mss. 22 June 1798, 11 February 1801, 11 August 1801, 15 June 1798.
23. Beckett, *Aristocracy in England*, p. 345
24. Perkin, *Origins of Modern English Society*, p. 42.

alehouses, collecting taxes, directing the operation of the Poor Laws and, though with increasing desuetude, the regulation of apprenticeship wages, food prices and poor rates as well as the criminal law when other than capital felonies, which went to the assizes, were concerned.[25]

If it had been the case that justices were selected from a large willing population of qualified gentlemen, that is Anglicans worth above £100 a year from 1732, or that removal and replacement occurred to any extent, then the role of the Lord Lieutenant would indeed have been crucial. In fact the problem was rather the finding of willing bodies of acceptable social position. The large house might dominate the countryside, but increasingly its owner spent his time in London and was but intermittently at hand either to rule or to supervise the ruling of others. As the eighteenth century progressed, the upper gentry began to display the disinclination for everyday governing which already characterised the aristocrats. Indeed, before the century had ended the bench could be filled only by enlisting the clergy. Perhaps it was the burden of the work which increasingly deterred country gentlemen from being active on the bench, though most made sure that their names were entered on the Commission. In late-eighteenth-century Kent only a quarter of the qualified gentry were becoming justices, and the situation was hardly different elsewhere. It was the clergy, who were usually present and who through their vestries had in any case the major responsibility for local administration at parochial level, especially of the Poor Law, who filled the gap, providing 25 per cent of the Commission in Hertfordshire by the 1750s and a third by 1800; 31 per cent in Oxfordshire in 1775 and 20 per cent in Wiltshire in 1786.[26]

Only a small minority of the Anglican clergy ever became justices, even those whose livings were good and connections sound. The number of clergymen in the Commission at any one time never exceeded 10 per cent of the ordained population. Those who were selected came from parsons, vicars and rectors of good background and comfortable incomes from tithes and increasingly prosperous glebe farms. Many of them were pluralists. Most of them had some property, in some cases very considerable property. Vicars of modest family on poor livings as well as the poor curates on scanty stipends were well out of this league. But that does not imply that the non-justice clergy were any more likely to differ in social attitudes from the country gentlemen. A conscientious parson in

25. Cannon, *Aristocratic Century*, pp. 121–3; Beckett, *Aristocracy in England*, pp. 385.
26. Beckett, *Aristocracy in England*, pp. 385–7.

1800 remarked of a neighbouring clergyman: 'Poole . . . seems a Squire Buck Parson rather than a Divine, a man of some fortune but not much religion, yet good tempered.'[27] Professor Porter has described the parson as 'the squire's spiritual half-brother'.[28] In truth he was often his real brother, and not uncommonly the parson *was* the squire. The aristocracy made use of higher church office for their second sons, but it was the middling and lower gentry who were always soliciting for rich livings for their sons. The case of Squire 'Black' John Borlase of Pendeen in the far west of Cornwall is instructive. The Squire had nine living children, five of them sons, and was to live to the age of eighty-nine. Clearly there would have been problems if even his eldest son, who by the time of his father's death had fourteen children of his own, had had to live in style from the estate. Accordingly when his elder son failed to find a suitable position in office, he placed him in the single family living and then had to seek another for his second son. Walter became Vicar of Madron in 1720 and William Rector of Ludgvan in 1722. But a living apiece would not adequately support the two sons as their families increased, and John Borlase used his influence to secure two more. As William later recalled:

> In the year 1732, the Rev. Mr James Millett who had been 55 years vicar of St Just (the parish in which I was born, and wherein my father had the most considerable property) dying, and . . . my elder brother, having then the two considerable vicarages of Madron and Kenwyn, the one from Bishop Weston and the other from his father; the father thought there was reason to apply to the then Lord Chancellor King in favour of me, his second son, then rector of Ludgvan. This application was of little service, but by the recommendation of Sir William Morice of Werington in Devon, bart., the Lord Chancellor consenting to present me to the vacant vicarage, ordered me to go and thank Sir William Morice for the favour.

Fourteen years later William Borlase was again to call on the influence of Morice to secure a post as midshipman for one of his sons. However, the point here is that when Walter Borlase inherited the family estate in 1755, he combined its running with two good livings as well as with the vice-wardenship of the Stannaries, a leading position in the Cornish tin-mining industry. Technically he was a 'clerical' magistrate, but clearly he was rather more than that.[29]

27. J. Ayres, *Paupers and Pig Killers*, p. 35.
28. R. Porter, *English Society*, p. 83.
29. P.A.S. Pool, *William Borlase*, Royal Institution of Cornwall, Truro, 1986, pp. 1–2, 25, 33.

Compared with continental aristocracies, the great landowners of England spent a good deal of time on their country seats, though of course not a few of them were the owners of other sizeable properties which they hardly visited. Nevertheless, these sojourns were becoming shorter over the eighteenth century. The tendency of the patriciate to metamorphose into an urban leisure class was frequently commented upon. A writer in the *Gentleman's Magazine* in 1737 ascribed rural poverty to the fact that the 'chief nobility and gentry' resided largely in London 'in the utmost extravagance, and but rarely go into the country with any other design than to squeeze a supply of money out of their tenants'.[30] It is certainly an exaggerated impression of a tendency which can in any case hardly be quantified. However, there was concern enough for some to justify the Game Laws on the grounds that the opportunity to shoot game or hunt deer was just about the only incentive for the aristocracy to spend any length of time at home: 'the Country Gentlemen should not be constrained in their diversions otherwise they will desert the countryside as a place not fit for a gentleman to live in'. This remark was made in 1804 by a West Country parson with a comfortable living and himself the second son of a Welsh squire. Although in no sense a 'hunting parson' (he remarks, when he lent his son the family horse to go on a fox hunt, that it was the first time the animal had been thus employed), he kept a gun and was not averse to accepting an invitation to use it. Nor did he decline an invitation to a stag hunt in 1803 and in his description of the meet he provides a fascinating glimpse of the 'company' assembled by a peer in his locality.

> Got to the Hounds, a vast concourse of Gentlemen. At last we moved on about three miles to Lord Fortescue's. He joined the Company which was very numerous, there was an Irish Lord, Lord Lisle, a Sir — Northcote, Mr Chichester and several of the First Gentlemen in Devonshire and several of the Clergy, in all about a hundred.

These meetings the parson approved of: 'It brings the Chief Gentry of Devonshire together which is a glorious sight.' Not much to boast about in the number of titles, though. It it is a reminder that the rural domination of the titled aristocracy was qualified not only by their long urban absences, but also by the fact that in many counties they were very thin on the ground – Cornwall or Kent, for example, would hardly have differed from Devon.[31]

30. Beckett, *Aristocracy in England*, p. 338; *ibid.*, pp. 362–6 for the increasing attractions of London.
31. Ayres, *Paupers and Pig Killers*, pp. 100, 90.

That the aristocracy were the 'leisured class' was axiomatic. Although some in the upper reaches of a few select professions, notably the law, the Church and the Army, might be considered 'honorary' holders of that status, it was the ability to live from property without working which was the fundamental mark of the 'gentleman'. In the eighteenth century 'leisure' came to be defined fully as much in terms of conspicuous consumption as in those of idle time. We have already referred to the work of those historians who have seen the aristocracy as the originators and prime movers in a 'consumer revolution' one of the manifestations of which, it is argued, was a general commercialisation of leisure. For many it was a matter of concern that social emulation was leading the middle classes to neglect their businesses and the lower classes into a crime-supported idleness. No one, however, extended this criticism to the aristocracy or upper gentry or, for that matter, so long as it was at a lower level of extravagance which did not ruin their fortunes and mortgage their estates, to the middling and lower gentry. Henry Fielding was typical in seeing the life-style of the upper classes as of no 'political' significance.

> In diversions, as in many other particulars, the upper part of life is distinguished from the lower. Let the great therefore answer for the employment of their time to themselves, or to their spiritual governors. The society will receive some temporal advantage from their luxury. The more toys which children of all ages consume, the brisker will be the circulation of money, and the greater the increase of trade . . . . To the upper part of mankind time is an enemy, and (as they themselves often confess) their chief labour is to kill it.[32]

In fact he was, in 1751, echoing Bernard de Mandeville's infamous 'Fable of the Bees', a work considered the epitome of infamy when it appeared almost thirty years earlier.

> . . . whilst luxury
> Employ'd a Million of the Poor,
> And odious Pride a Million more.

Several aristocrats increased their fortunes very considerably from urban property. The Bedfords were getting £2,000 a year from Bloomsbury in 1700 and four times as much by 1771, while the Grosvenors were drawing £12,000 in rent by 1802 from the development of their lands south of Oxford Street. Despite such examples, there remains truth in the contemporary notion that a wealth

---

32. Henry Fielding, *An Inquiry into the Causes of the Late Increase in Robbers*, 1751 collected works, ed. T. Roscoe, Henry Bohn, 1849, p. 765.

derived largely from the country was being increasingly dissipated in the town. In general the 'quality' seems by the mid eighteenth century to have spent from six to nine months in 'town'. That is the assumption gained from inverting the regularly repeated assertion that metropolitan tailors were 'out of business about three or four months in the year' and comparing it with that for house painters who were idle 'at least four or five months'. Their busy period began in April or May and continued 'till the Return of the Company to Town in Winter'.[33]

For the most part the gentry did not as much stay in London as visit it. Perhaps combining business with pleasure, they might take lodgings for brief residences perhaps once a year, and in most cases not that often. In fact, as the gentry came increasingly to emulate the urban style of the aristocracy, the transformation of a number of provincial towns was the main consequence. By the early eighteenth century they had already followed the elite to Bath and had in their turn been followed to the extent that by the 1770s, Smollett's Squire Bramble could find nothing to admire in a town which had sadly declined over the thirty years he had known it.

> Every upstart of fortune, harnessed in the trappings of the mode, presents himself at Bath, as in the very focus of observation – Clerks and Factors from the East Indies, loaded with the spoil of plundered provinces; planters, negro-drivers, and hucksters from our American plantations, enriched they know not how; agents commissaries, and contractors, who have fattened in two successive wars, on the blood of the nation; usurers, brokers and jobbers of every kind; men of low birth, and no breeding . . . all of them hurry to Bath.[34]

By that time, however, the gentry could avoid the bustle and disturbing crowds of the spas by enjoying a growing range of genteel pleasures closer to home. Along with an urban upper-middle and professional class they were the main market for the theatres, ball and assembly rooms and covered promenades which were central to the 'urban renaissance' discovered by the new generation of urban historians in towns as far apart as Truro and Ludlow.

When the gentry concentrated on rustic pleasure, their sport *par excellence* was fox hunting. Chasing vermin behind slow hounds had little appeal to the aristocracy. Interest did quicken after 1753 when the Quorn hunt with its lustier hounds packing across pastured Leicestershire acquired sufficient cachet to bring in the young bloods

---

33. Porter, *English Society*, p. 72; R. Campbell, *The London Tradesman*, 1747, rept David & Charles, 1969, pp. 104, 193.
34. Tobias Smollett, *Humphry Clinker*, 1771.

and make the sport much more acceptable by the early nineteenth century as well as involving the participation of the farmers over whose fields they chased.[35]

It was, however, the aristocracy who gave the English one of their most revered institutions: horse racing, with its ultimate level of participation as a mass spectator sport reaching down to the betting proletariat. Lord Grosvenor was spending around £7,000 annually by the later eighteenth century by which time the 'sport of kings' was coming to be shared in a different way by the masses. In the 1720s crowds at Newmarket may have represented, according to Defoe, 'a vast concourse of the nobility and gentry' but they hardly exceeded a few hundred souls. No more did they at Ascot, Epsom, Doncaster or Goodwood, but by the end of the century the race meeting was beginning to be watched by a 'crowd' in both senses. As well as the great race courses, smaller meetings across the country were becoming a regular feature of the social calendar.[36]

We have dwelt a little on matters of life-style as well as on the analysis of power, for as Professor and Mrs Stone have pointed out, the nature of a 'ruling' elite is best approached from an examination of 'all those from whose ranks' it might be drawn. They present the 'county elite' as being made up of three overlapping groups (not ranks, for some in the second and third could be both richer and in some senses more powerful than those in the first).

> The first was the local power elite which ran the affairs of the county and was mostly recruited from the much larger ranks of the second, which was the local status elite . . . . The third was the local elite of wealth, which included most members of the other two, and also such newcomers to the landed classes as were both resident in suitable houses and prepared to spend lavishly in order to obtain either status or local power or both.[37]

The Stones see the ownership of great houses as the most effective defining characteristic, as not all aspired to the burden of great estates. This of course included the 'squires' who might range in 'style' from the hard-drinking, wench- and fox-chasing Squire Western to the judicious, conscientious, charitable and cultured Squire Alworthy. Henry Fielding's famous bipolarity is representative enough stereotyping, although it might be noted that Smollett's Matthew Bramble combined the irascible conservatism of

---

35. Beckett, *Aristocracy in England*, pp. 347–9.
36. *Ibid.*, pp. 357–9.
37. L. Stone and J.F. Stone, *Open Elite*, p. 39.

the former with generous impulses, which he preferred to indulge covertly, equal to those of the latter.[38] By the later eighteenth century the 'Westerns' were a shrinking but only slowly dying minority, for there seems little doubt that the elite in general considerably improved in manners over the period.

Inevitably a broad definition of an elite invites problems at the margin. Consider the case of the Reverend William Holland who became Vicar of Over Stowey in Somerset in 1789 and also held the nearby living of Monkton Farley. A second son of a Welsh gentleman who traced his line back two centuries to a duke, he had some claim to birth. His living allowed him good comfort, with two resident servants as well as day help, but his diary clearly shows a man who *worked*, not only at his calling and at his duties connected with parish affairs from poor relief to highway upkeep. He kept no higher servant to intermediate between him and the host of local builders and other tradesmen, nor housekeeper to handle his purchases of supplies. All of this he attended to himself and watched every penny. He not only supervised the work on the glebe farm and garden, he seems to have rolled up his sleeves and participated. Over the twenty years covered by his diaries, he only once visited London. In fact he learned about goings-on there either from the newspapers or from letters from his regular correspondent, the Duke of Somerset. What he shared with the nobleman was an interest in physiognomy. On his trip to London he was invited to dine at the duke's Grosvenor Square residence, 'In stile, on Plate and vast quantities of Plate and China around us'. However, he was so unsure of his standing that he left Mrs Holland in their lodgings, she, though included by the duke, not having received a specific invitation from the duchess. It was the wrong understanding. Poor Holland went alone to find the duchess 'said but little and I fear was displeased'. The duke waited twelve years before writing again. When Holland chose company it was usually that of the neighbouring gentry and clergy. His parish contained a number of tenant farmers – substantial men, but not gentry. If they are given a title in his diaries, it is always 'Farmer'. From time to time he entertained them, but it was invariably an element of business over, for example, tithes or church wardenships. There seems no doubt that he considered himself their social superior and that they hardly challenged his estimation: 'After dinner young Farmer Landsey came in saying, ". . . that wench Carter, I caught her stealing

38. Western and Alworthy were created by Henry Fielding, *Tom Jones*, 1749, and Bramble by Smollett in *Humphry Clinker*.

potatoes . . .. Do ye, if your Honor be so good as to speak to her, She'll mind what you say." ' Holland was not himself a justice, but several of his friends were. When he had a tithe dispute needing resolution in his favour, he brought it before a clerical justice: 'He is an odd tempered man but a tolerable good justice, a poor stick at church, and not a very accommodating Parish Priest.'[39]

It is difficult to place such men socially. The clergy were perhaps a special case. Some of them by blood, connection, wealth and position clearly belonged to the 'county elite' in the wider sense. All the clergy were university educated but many without connections or background remained in curacies or poor livings, permanently excluded from the style as well as the substance of the gentleman. But there were others, like Holland, who seem to have owned no property of note yet nevertheless enjoyed a level of social acceptance above that of commercial people, who might exceed them in wealth. They had in fact a kind of 'honorary' gentleman status, something they shared with lawyers, some doctors and the dons.

Just as patronage provided the arteries of the influence system, so 'paternalism' generally describes the other main manifestation of gentry power. Paternalism is a rather generalised way of defining the relationship between patrician and pleb. It views the relationship from above. The gentry emerge as the 'fathers of their people', generous but firm, expecting gratitude for their charity and deference towards their rule. E.P. Thompson has described paternalism as 'a magical social quantum'[40] which serves historians in allowing them to present an image of a 'one-class society', although blinding them to forms of social conflict which it has no real vocabulary to reveal. Its normative implications are clear and suggest warmth and a natural assent to authority. As myth or as a justifying ideology it is backward-looking, the modes and manners of a previous generation tending to serve as a model against which subsequent degradation and deterioration of social relationships can be pointed out. As such, a romantic nostalgia pervades its presentation. True paternalism, it seems, is always best represented by the 'good old squire', either of blessed memory or surviving as a peculiar anachronism. The ideal and the real are constantly blurred in its discourse. 'The rural patron is beheld no more' concludes Langhorne's poem 'The Country Justice' in 1774, while Richard Polwhele wrote of his fellow Cornishman, the county member of

---

39. Detail from Holland's enormously entertaining diary edited by J. Ayres, *Paupers and Pig Killers*.
40. E.P. Thompson, 'Eighteenth-century English society', p. 134.

parliament Sir William Lemon, 'In him we justly admire the old country gentleman, faithful to his king without servility, attached to the people without democracy.' A short while earlier he had lamented at great versified length the decline of paternalism and the widening of the gulf between the gentry and the people in his poem, 'The Old English Gentleman'.[41]

Of course, the close and mutual knowledge and the reciprocation of beneficent authority with deference on which the relationship depended flourished best in small rural communities where the assumption of social tranquillity could also be reinforced by a parochial religious teaching that property and authority were divinely ordained. It was characteristic, too, of the so-called 'closed village'. Few were so closed as was the parish of Cotesbach in Leicestershire, where in the 1790s Dr Robert Marriot was both parson and lord of the manor.

> The Doctor, if he should chuse to govern, may give laws to all that
> breathe in this place, and indeed the cattle in the field are subject to
> his controul; for not only all the land owns him for its lord, but every
> dwelling also; the patronage of the church, and the living are all his
> own.[42]

At the other end of the scale were the 'open villages', the 'lordless' ones, where land-holding was too fragmented to give any particular proprietor a marked ascendancy. Here smaller property owners could set up nonconformist chapels, vote against nominated candidates and drink in alehouses which did not bear the arms of the great house and remain open only at its pleasure. In the forest areas such as Kingswood near Bristol, or Dean, the independence of the inhabitants and their turbulent resistance to authority were proverbial. Even in the closed villages, the moral authority of the lord could be as much weakened by his own self-interested actions as by broader social changes. Sullen compliance rather than cheerful acquiescence was the reciprocation earned by the squire who was deemed responsible for the enclosure which, John Clare felt, 'trampled on the grave / Of labour's rights and left the poor a slave', or for the landscaping lord whose spreading park engulfed whole villages.

41. *Ibid.* p. 137; R. Polwhele, *The Old English Gentleman*, 1797, p. iv.
42. Quoted in D.R. Mills, *Lord and Peasant in Nineteenth-century Britain*, Croom Helm, 1980, p. 27.

> . . . The man of wealth and pride
> Takes up a space that many poor supplied –
> Space for his lake, his park's extended bounds.
> Space for his horses, equipage and hounds.[43]

SOCIAL MOBILITY

If villages could be 'open' or 'closed', what of the elite itself? Was eighteenth-century England an open society, with a ready mobility characterising it from bottom to top? As the Stones have shown, the contemporary myth that it was has often been repeated by social historians since.[44] Contemporaries reacted to what was perceived as an intrusion of moneyed newcomers into the aristocracy and gentry; those described by Oliver Goldsmith as 'trade's unfeeling train' were often seen as rushing into the countryside and snapping up estates and country seats. So far as the upper crust of peers and baronets was concerned, there is practically no substance to such claims. The eighteenth-century titled aristocracy was one of the most closed in Europe, despite the fact that there was no legal definition of noble blood. There were, as we have noted, few creations before Peel began to serve his political interests in the last years of the century, and the accusation made against him in 1814 that 'society was turned upside down and the muck came uppermost' could hardly have been wider of the mark. As Cannon has pointed out, there was no elevation of 'captains of industry, ship owners, forgemasters, textile manufacturers and the like' but of 'persons who for the most part, owed their peerages to years of tactful service at court, to sound voting in the House of Commons, or to the possession of borough interests'.[45]

When the newly orphaned Fanny Hill decided to seek her fortune in London, she had been told 'as how several maids out of the country had made themselves and all their kin forever . . . some had taken so with their masters that they had married them, and kept them coaches and lived vastly grand and happy and some, mayhap, came to be duchesses'. Some hope! This was an extreme form of a myth about a route to ladyship which hardly ever led to

43. John Clare, cited R.W. Malcolmson, *Life and Labour in England*, p. 127; Oliver Goldsmith, *The Deserted Village*, 1769.
44. Stone and Stone, *Open Elite*.
45. Cannon, *Aristocratic Century*, pp. 19–20.

the desired destination and many times brought the hopeful traveller to ruin. Not even for those born much further up the ladder
than Fanny, the daughter of a country labourer, was marriage a
much-taken route into linkage with noble families. Cannon has
demonstrated that snobbish contemporary assertions of the flood-
ing of 'inferior ladies' into the ranks of the great must be treated
with extreme caution. Not only were such liaisons rare, the most
celebrated examples, like Defoe's Mrs Gerrard who married the
Duke of Hamilton, were seldom as low-born as they were presented
– in fact she was the grand-daughter of an earl. Lord Egremont's
famous depiction in 1745 of a 'lucky season for low people's marrying' has been shown to be either misinformed or to be exhibiting
a distinct inverted hyperbole. Youthful indiscretions or the last-
minute longing of old bones apart, marriage among the eighteenth-
century peerage seems to have been less exogenous than it was in
the centuries before or after. Some ravaged estate fortunes might
be repaired by marrying sons, though hardly heirs, to the daughters
of wealthy tradesmen, but very rarely indeed were peers' daughters
sold to their sons.[47]

The peaks were hardly to be scaled by even the most persistent
of nouveau climbers. But what of the foothills? We have been arguing that the 'ruling class' of eighteenth-century England needs to
embrace a range of country gentlemen down to the ordinary squire.
Here it can be suggested that there were few barriers to the entry of
those wealthy enough to acquire the magic key of a country estate
and patient enough to wait for social acceptance in their locality.
According to Professor Perkin, the English landowners triumphed
'at a price which few oligarchies have been willing to pay . . . by
opening their ranks to all who could acquire the one necessary
qualification, the purchase price of an estate'. He concedes, however, that after the Restoration the aristocracy at the higher levels
was consolidating rather than expanding, but maintains the 'road to
the gentry was now a beaten one'.

> Now there rose, however, a host of substantial squires and minor peers
> from a great variety of occupations: bankers like the Hoares, Childs,
> Smiths, or Thorntons; government contractors and agents like Sir
> Lawrence Dundas, Earl of Zetland, and John Henniker who became an
> Irish peer; nabobs – in addition to Diamond Pitt, ancestor of the earls
> of Londonderry as well as of Chatham – like Henry Vansittart, father of
> Lord Bexley (who rose still further as Chancellor of the Exchequer),

46. John Cleland, *Fanny Hill or Memoirs of a Woman of Pleasure*, 1748–9.
47. Cannon, *Aristocratic Century*, pp. 76–7.

and Robert, Baron Clive; mere attorneys like Sir Joseph Banks's grandfather and his predecessor Thomas Wright of Sheffield, or Walpole's friend Philip Case of King's Lynn, who left large estates in Norfolk and £100,000 in the funds; and mere inland traders like the Wilberforces of Beverley, the London booksellers who established J.H. Round's ancestors at Birch Hall, Essex, or Joseph Hague of Gloucester, the travelling packman who came home to buy Park Hall at Hayfield. Even domestic service could boast its new landed gentry, like Mr Poynter, the Duke of Kingston's master of horse, who purchased an estate of £200 a year and 'seven miles of manor for sporting', Mr Rogers the stable boy who rose to be Lord Monson's steward and 'a very great landholder', or Henry Isherwood, M.P., son of an inn-servant who prospered as a brewer.[48]

This list, Perkin maintains, could be 'indefinitely extended' but still serves to show 'how open by the eighteenth century was the door to the landed oligarchy'.

Setting out to challenge the hypothesis that a distinguishing feature of English society has been 'the easy access of self-made men to power and status', the Stones have concluded at the end of a lengthy study that 'The traditional concept of an open elite – open to large-scale infiltration by merchant wealth – is dead.' They found the degree of upward mobility 'surprisingly small and not of great social significance'. Yet Perkin's examples are real enough. It may indeed have been the case that most entrants to the ranks of the squirearchy came from those who were in fact rising land-holders rather than men of fortunes made in commerce – the Stones concede that 'professionals' had begun to exhibit a distinct upward mobility, but the evidence still seems strong that the ranks of the landed gentlemen were *not* closed to men of new money. We must look for the explanation rather in terms of the disinclination of the *nouveau riche* to undertake the substance rather than the style of the gentleman than in any barriers to their entry.[49]

Although the growth of commercial and financial capitalism in eighteenth-century England is properly regarded as the main dynamic behind the increase and spread of the middle ranks, it is clear that the merchant élite can be more properly considered as a distinct faction of the ruling class. The great plutocrats of London were as active in the world of finance as in that of commerce. As Dr Porter has put it, many were investors of the kind who grew rich in

48. Perkin, *Origins of Modern English Society*, pp. 56–60.
49. Stone and Stone, *Open Elite*, p. 284.

their sleep. Such men no more than the landed gentry worked for their living, but there was a real distinction in that their unearned income was not derived from rents. A foreign visitor in 1727 considered the elite of London's merchants to be wealthier than 'the sovereign princes of Germany and Italy'. Although *some* of them did move into the landed gentry and aspire to the role of squire, Dr Rogers has shown that these were exceptional. It was far from the intention of the majority thus to change their life. The nabobs returning to buy estates with their profits from the Indies were real enough, but they have tended to obscure the fact that most London-based merchants remained attached to the 'City', or at least became only semi-detached from it.[50]

Dr Rogers has studied the eighteenth-century London aldermen, who were the civic leaders of the capital. They were overwhelmingly engaged in trade, mainly overseas, which they increasingly combined with investments or marine insurance activities. They were very rich. Indeed, it was estimated in 1737 that none could bear the costs of being Lord Mayor on an income of less than £15,000. William Beckford left two estates and a residual fortune of £43,000 in money. Even richer was Sir Samuel Fludyer, a cloth merchant who also dealt in government finance. He left £900,000 in 1786. These were very different people from the bottom part of the 2,000 'big merchants' who Gregory King thought exceeded an income of £400 per annum. In mid century it took an estimated £20,000 in capital to set up as a banker. Fortunes of £100,000 or more were not uncommon among a group which contained some of the richest commoners in England.[51]

Rogers has commented on the fact that by the eighteenth century few of their number were newcomers to the City; most were sons of merchants, while marriages produced an interlocking kinship pattern among this urban elite. By 1750 the age of permanent City dynasties was well under way. Although inter-marriages with the gentry increased during the Hanoverian period, this was less a case of outsiders seeking an entrée to the ruling class than of mutually advantageous bargaining between two different factions of it. The merchant and banking elite in fact possessed considerable autonomy. They rarely left, as Rogers has put it, 'the counting house for the country seat'.[52] Even with fortunes made and marriage links to

---

50. Porter, *English Society*, p. 93; N. Rogers, 'Money, land and lineage', pp. 437–54.

51. Rogers, 'Money, land and lineage', pp. 439–41.

52. *Ibid.*, pp. 445, 448–9.

the landed gentry formed, the aldermen retained their links with the City. They tended to favour modest seats, leaving much of their wealth where it was rather than expending it on the purchase of large squire-making estates. They purchased or had built villas or medium-sized mansions within close reach of the City. Even these they regarded as assets which could at the right moment be sold or exchanged, not as the foundation of a 'family seat' entailed in the interests of lineage.

> The rise of merchant status, the emergence of a polite but not necessarily landed ruling class culture, the facility with which merchants married the quality, the increasing security of non-landed investments, all curbed the obsession with broad acres.

As the linking with land for status became less imperative, something of the same kind can be observed among the smaller merchant elites of provincial cities like Leeds, Liverpool, Bristol or Norwich and Rogers has concluded that by the mid eighteenth century no great social gulf separated them from the gentry – something which was not true of those who made their wealth from manufacturing. The affinity of the City elites with the landed gentry was close enough to place both on the side of the resisters when the industrial and professional classes later joined to challenge the political supremacy of the old order. In any case it would be odd to describe the men from whose ranks came the Lord Mayors of London and the directors of the Bank of England and of the great chartered trading companies, whose support could make or break state borrowing as 'middle class'.[53]

53. *Ibid.*, pp. 450–3.

CHAPTER THREE
Middling People

Writing in 1761, William Beckford considered the 'middling people of England' to consist of 'the manufacturer, the yeoman, the merchant, the country gentleman'. The last named would not have considered themselves correctly placed, for the real middle class of the countryside were the farmers.[1]

THE FARMERS

Beckford's 'yeomen' were increasingly tenants rather than owner-occupiers. Around three-quarters of England's farmland was rented by 1800. The tendency, too, was towards larger units. The decline of the smallholder was neither as dramatic nor as complete as used to be assumed, but in most of the major agrarian counties they were declining. A village parson complained of the landlord's steward in 1809: 'He will at this rate soon depopulate the parish for he turns out all the smaller tenants and the houses are going to decay and we shall soon have nothing but labourers and beggars in the parish.'[2]

At the end of the seventeenth century, Gregory King thought there were around 180,000 freeholders worth between £50 and £84 a year and so better off as a group than the 150,000 tenant farmers on an average income of £44. Joseph Massie writing in 1759 thought the number of freeholders had increased by then to 210,000, but the group was now worse off than the 190,000 tenant farmers. At the beginning of the nineteenth century, Patrick Colquhoun considered that 160,000 tenant farmers on an average

1. Quoted in R. Porter, *English Society*, p. 88.
2. J. Ayres (ed.), *Paupers and Pig Killers*, p. 185.

£120 were significantly better off than all but 40,000 of an equal number of freeholders. Freeholders in general were less able to raise funds for investment in larger farms, and the smallholders who made up the vast majority were increasingly considered a group who toiled hard for small reward.[3] At the same time the tenant farmers prospered, some of the larger ones greatly so. It was they for the most part who made 'Farmer' as much a title as an occupational description. In the diary of a Somerset parson from 1799 to 1815, fifteen named individuals appear as 'Farmer'. They covered a wide range. There were the 'Farmers Rich', two bachelor brothers who lived up to their name in all save generosity, and 'Farmer Lindsey', a hard-bargain driver secretly called 'Jew Lindsey' by the parson. He left 240 gold guineas as well as bills and securities worth £1,800. 'Farmer Dibble' rented a good farm for more than twenty years and saved enough to 'retire to a little estate of his own'. 'Farmer Stone' brought up fourteen children on a small farm and managed it 'with great credit and decency'.[4] Once a year, when his tithes were due, the parson entertained them.

> We were all very merry, especially the Farmers when the strong beer began to warm them a little. Farmer Dibble who seems a poor Honey at other times now began to open his mouth and oratise most wonderfully and poor old Charles Selleck, who seems sunk very much since last year, at last began to display his usual keenness and was wonderfully animated. He is now 82 years of age. Farmer Stone was very deaf and heavy and dull, tho when he had his hearing was as shrewd as any of them. William Hill talked a little at last with his scabby nose, but he has been in disgrace for sometime past about a Bastard Child by his girl apprentice so I could not notice him much. Rich of Pepperil has something mild and modest in his character. Mr Rich and Tom Poole stuck to the Brandy and water and they staid tea after the rest were gone.[5]

Doubtless most of the farmers would have seen themselves in the description the parson later gave of one of their number: 'a careful, industrious, open hearted, fair dealing man'. However, he was usually less ready with a compliment. In 1805, getting more promises than actual cash when collecting for the widows and orphans of Trafalgar, he snorted, 'These farmers are sneaking fellows when put to the push.' Yet if we note occasions other than the tithe

---

3. The social tables of King, Massie and Colquhoun are conveniently included in the statistical tables appended to Porter, *English Society*.
4. Ayres (ed.), *Paupers and Pig Killers*. These farmers appear regularly through the diary.
5. *Ibid.* pp. 201–2.

dinners when farmers figure in his diary, their crucial role in the public affairs of the village is revealed. They were the employers, of course, and that alone would have given them power. But it went beyond that. We meet Farmer Dibble collecting the poor rate, Farmer White collecting the new income tax, and Farmers Marle and Dibble calling about the administration of a village charity. Farmer Marle was also churchwarden. Farmer Stone was an overseer of the poor and called about an order for the removal of a vagrant. Farmers Rich, Buller and Poole saw to the parish roads.

Although it covers the high-price years of the French wars, the diary makes no mention of the over-lavish style of living for which the richer farmers were frequently lampooned. Indeed, the parson described wedding guests in 1810 as 'dress'd very respectably for farmers'. There is no mention of that class of rich and enterprising farmers who had profited from rising cereal prices over the later eighteenth century and enriched themselves from the soaring wartime ones after 1793. Their pretensions were captured in James Gillray's wicked cartoon 'Farmer Giles and his Wife showing off their daughter Betty to their Neighbours, on her return from School'. In this a plump and porcine-featured lass struggles with a piano in a carpeted and lavishly, though vulgarly, furnished parlour. The wife and daughter retiring genteelly from the working life of the farm was a source of much critical comment. The piano-in-the-parlour was its symbol. Arthur Young was scathing in 1792 in the *Annals of Agriculture*, the improving farmers' own journal.

> sometimes I see a piano forte in a farmer's parlour, which I always wish was burnt; a livery servant is sometimes found, and a post chaise to carry their daughters to assemblies; these ladies are sometimes educated at expensive boarding schools, and the sons often at the University to be made parsons. But all these things imply a departure from that line which separates these different orders of beings. Let these things, and all the folly, foppery, expense and anxiety, that belong to them, remain among gentlemen: a wise farmer will not envy them.[6]

Sometimes pride influenced a farmer's choice of mount. A horse bred purely for leisure was something only a gentleman should own, not a farmer: 'in the stable a good nag for his own riding, but not good enough for hunting . . . in equipage he goes no further than a one-horse chaise for his wife'.[7]

6. Arthur Young, *Annals of Agriculture*, XVII, 1792, p. 157.
7. *Ibid.*, p. 151.

The presumption of gentry-aping farmers had been portrayed as a source of ruin long before the 1790s. In a revealing passage of Henry Fielding's novel *Amelia*, published in 1751, a young husband narrates how, having been encouraged to rent a small farm from a friend, he had prospered for a while, but:

> I now fell into many errors. The first of these was in enlarging my business, by adding a farm of £100 a year to the parsonage . . . .. The consequence of which was that whereas, at the end of the first year, I was worth upwards of fourscore pounds; at the end of the second I was near half that sum worse (as the phrase is) than nothing . . . my greatest folly [was in] buying an old coach and harness very cheap . . . and as I considered that the same horses which drew my waggons would likewise draw my coach, I resolved on indulging myself in the purchase.
>
> The consequence of setting up this poor old coach is inconceivable. Before this my wife and I had very little distinguished ourselves from the other farmers and their wives, either in our dress or our way of living, they treated us as their equals; but now they began to consider us as elevating ourselves into a state of superiority, and immediately began to envy, hate and declare war against us. The neighbouring little squires too, were uneasy to see a poor renter become their equal in a matter in which they placed so much dignity . . . . My neighbours now began to conspire against me. They nicknamed me in derision the Squire Farmer. Whatever I bought I was sure to buy dearer, and when I sold I was obliged to sell cheaper than any other. In fact, they were all united, and, while they every day committed trespasses on my lands with impunity, if any of my cattle escaped into their fields, I was either forced to enter into a lawsuit or to make amends fourfold for the damage sustained.

In general, however, farmers felt less obliged to consume conspicuously for status reasons than the lesser gentry. 'Comforts', according to Arthur Young in 1792, were 'the natural inheritance of a farmer who has the enjoyment of a considerable business'.

> A large, roomy, clean kitchen, with a rousing wood fire on the hearth, and the ceiling well hung with smoked bacon and hams; a small room for the farmer and his family, opening into this kitchen, with a glass in the door or the wall, to see that things go right. When company is in the house, a fire in the parlour, very well furnished. At table great plenty of plain things.[8]

Another great farming journalist, William Marshall, used the manner in which Norfolk farmers dined to divide them into three

---

8. *Ibid., loc. cit.*

classes. The lowest class were still 'the same plain men which farmers generally are'. They lived and dined in great measure with
their servants and farm workers. A second class lived 'in the kitchen
with their servants' but dined at a separate table. The highest class
had left the kitchen. They had their 'keeping rooms and other com-
modious apartments'.[9]

Clearly there were different ranks of farmers, but in what proportions? High cereal prices would certainly have increased the number of well-to-do farmers, but they would also have allowed many at
the bottom to hang on, at least until the post-war price collapse of
1816. Massie in 1759 divided a population of 150,000 tenants into
four income groups. The top one earned £150 a year but included
only 5,000 individuals, 3.33 per cent of all farmers. The second rank
earning £100 was twice as numerous, but this still means that less
than 10 per cent of farmers earned more than £100. A further 13
per cent earned £70, so the fourth group who earned £40 made up
more than three-quarters of the tenant farmers. Freeholders were
differently proportioned, for 14.28 per cent of them earned £100
and 28.56 per cent £50. The rest, 56 per cent of the total, earned
only £25 – less than many urban artisans and the cottage ale-sellers
of the countryside. The analysis of the 1801 census returns by Colquhoun is not very helpful in placing all tenant farmers in a single
group of 160,000 with an average income of £120. He divides freeholders at the £200 and £90 levels; the first group contained 40,000
families and the second 120,000. Even allowing for the rapid inflation of the later 1790s this suggests a significant increase in the
income of farmers as a whole, but the income structure probably
remained much the same.[10]

Despite some contrary contemporary opinion, the vast majority
of England's farmers even at the end of the 'vital century' aspired
to comfortable rather than luxurious life-styles. From a public relations point of view, the situation of farmers was hardly enviable.
They were the direct employers of labour in the countryside and as
such responsible for the level of wages and of employment. They
were commonly the administrators of the Poor Law. They were the
frequent prosecutors of the poor for crimes such as wood stealing,
and they benefited from high corn prices while the poor hungered.
In 1801 food rioters labelled them 'unfeeling and griping', but they
were not alone in the view that farmers profited from corn scarcity,

9. William Marshall, *The Rural Economy of Norfolk*, I, 1795, pp. 37–8.
10. See note 3 above.

even to the extent of withholding supplies from understocked markets. A Somerset parson feared in 1801 that the farmers were 'too eager to push the price still higher, too avaricious'. A mine manager shared the opinion. He described them as 'unfeeling, inhumane and rapacious' as well as calling them 'callous' and 'overgrown'. In 1800 nine leading Devon landowners placed an advertisement in the local newspaper giving public notice to their tenants that if any of them withheld corn from the markets, their leases would not be renewed. In the same year *The Times* declared, 'A farmer ought not to be a rich man.'[11]

THE PROFESSIONS

In Samuel Foote's comedy of 1772, *The Nabob*, Lady Oldham tells her brother: 'I have always allowed merchants to be a useful body of men, and considered commerce, in this country, as a pretty resource enough for the younger shoots of a family.' That was indeed the case in a country where no formal rule of derogation kept the aristocracy from involvement in trade. This has often been regarded as a prime manifestation of *downward* social mobility which, more than openness of the elite, marked England as a fluid society. As the Stones have put it:

> the question of whether or not the English landed elite can be
> described as open can be answered with an unqualified affirmative. It
> was indeed open in the sense that there was little to prevent most of
> the male children sliding out of it. Generation after generation,
> younger sons were left to trickle downwards through the social system,
> with only some education, some money, and influential patronage to
> give them a head start in life.[12]

This movement they consider 'one of the most important and most obscure aspects' of the social history of England since the sixteenth century. It is clear, however, that the legacy of funding, education and 'friendship' networks received by younger sons was more often put to effective use in the traditional outlets of the Army, the Navy or the Church, and in the emerging professions, than in the commercial world. By the eighteenth century the upper ranks of the

11. Anonymous letter from Stratton in Cornwall, Public Records Office, H.O. 42.61; Ayres (ed.), *Paupers and Pig Killers*, p. 41; A.K. Hamilton Jenkin, *News from Cornwall*, Westaway Books, 1951, p. 81; *Sherbourne Mercury*, 17? September 1800.
12. L. Stone and J.F. Stone, *Open Elite*, p. 5.

professions enabled a man to hold on to the status of gentleman while undergoing the necessary chore of earning a living.

This compared with the huge continental bureaucracies overinflated to provide the employment needed by large nobilities. As Professor Brewer has explained, the English departments of state 'did not have to fund a bevy of *officiers* whose chief contribution to the state was to drain its resources'. 'Old Corruption', while it allowed the adept and the well-connected to rip off the undeserved profits of office-holding, was never remotely broad enough to provide for all those gentry sons who needed a career and were unsuited to the military or the Church. Many central offices employed 'young Esqrs' who were hardly ever present, but the undeserving fee collectors existed alongside hard-working professionals. It was this dichotomous nature of public service which made it in the eighteenth century both a receiving profession for young bloods and a means of advancement for middle-class entrants. In the late-eighteenth-century Stamp Office, a quarter of all tasks were in the hands of deputies paid from the emoluments of the nominal office-holder. Yet historians are able to discern an underlying institutional definition and formality of procedure which, according to Professor Brewer, indicate in the century after 1688 the development of 'a distinctive administrative order as servants of the crown'.[13] The Excise was the branch which came closest to a modern civil service department; its examination-linked promotions were often contrasted with the patronage which still controlled most appointments in the Customs, although even here the non-performing trough feeders were rather a surcharge on the public than an impediment to the performance of what was by the standards of its time an efficient administration. New 'professional' departments were grafted on to existing ones with their sinecures and pluralities. Professor Aylmer has concluded that public service in the eighteenth century was 'an extraordinary patchwork of old and new, useless and efficient, corrupt and honest, mixed in together'.[14] However, the expansion of the profession to around 10,000 public employees in the main departments by the 1780s was a manifest contributor to the swelling of society's middle ranks. Most civil servants earned from £40 to £80 a year. While many advanced to the solid middle-classness of the upper limit, at any given time the service of the state was

---

13. J. Brewer, *Sinews of Power*, pp. 69–70, 85.

14. G. Aylmer, 'From office-holding to Civil Service: the genesis of modern bureaucracy', *Trans. of Royal Hist. Soc.*, XXX, 1980, p. 106.

significantly expanding the ranks of the lower middle class by employing an army of clerks.[15]

The law

In the parable which begins Robert Campbell's career guide of 1747, *The London Tradesman,* the wife of a wealthy woollen draper turned squire sets out to place her three sons – all of whom she has already made 'serve an apprenticeship to the dead languages'. Now, with the eldest finishing at university and the others leaving Winchester School, they had to be 'brought up to a business suitable to the dignity of the Squire's sons'. The eldest, having been to university and the family having a cousin who was a bishop, went into the Church. The second entered the Navy as a midshipman, while the third 'was destined for the Law and bound a clerk for seven years to a noted attorney'. The purpose of the parable was to expose the folly of putting young men into callings for which they were personally unsuited, but Campbell fully accepted that the law was a profession suitable for the son of a squire.[16]

Recent research has tended to confirm this against the contemporary view of a profession for poor entrants whose penury drove them to pettifogging and cheating. Lawyers will never enjoy the best press: for every victor in a court of law there is a loser. But it seems that a significant majority of entrants to the profession over the eighteenth century came from sound backgrounds. Dr Miles has studied more then 5,000 clerks articled to attorneys between 1709 and 1792. Apprenticeship to an attorney provided the bulk of the practising lawyers in the eighteenth century. 'Solicitor' was not then a generally used term but confined to the few who practised in the Court of Chancery, while the route through the Inns of Court to the Bar was one taken by only a handful; there were only around 400 barristers practising in the mid eighteenth century. Sixty-one per cent of Miles's population of articled clerks came from the lesser gentry, many more than the 34 per cent who came from the 'middle sort' of merchants and 'professionals', and vastly more than the mere one in twenty who entered from the artisanry.[17]

Pushed from the land by a structure of inheritance based on primogeniture and strict settlement, and with the money and

---

15. Brewer, *Sinews of Power,* pp. 64–9 for estimates of the size of the Civil Service.

16. R. Campbell, *The London Tradesman,* 1747, rept David & Charles, Newton Abbot, 1969, pp. 4–9.

17. M. Miles, 'A haven for the privileged', pp. 197–210.

connections needed to place a son effectively in Church or Army hardly ever sufficient to suit a large male progeny, many younger sons seem to have found a haven in the law. Young men born into the lesser gentry or upper middle class were placed into a profession which allowed them to retain that status. Premium levels were high enough to deter the vulgar while being low enough for pockets perhaps already depleted by placing older sons and by the need to maintain the viability of the family estate. Placement was especially sought with successful London attorneys. The national average premium between 1710 and 1750 was £100, but most country attorneys asked only £50 and some still asked as little between 1799 and 1803 when the national average had reached £180. Why, then, was there so prevalent an impression that, according to Campbell, those completing their articles were 'so numerous that there is not bread enough for half of them'? In fact, as Miles suggests, the testing time for the newly qualified attorney came when, with few ready-made vacancies, he had to set up his practice. Those 'gentry' entrants with a sufficient patrimony of money and connections, as well as the increasing numbers with a family practice to enter, could hope to pass through it. The less fortunate might have to leave the profession, scrape a living from it in not too scrupulous a manner or simply continue as journeyman clerks, paid, in 1747, only 10s 6d (52.5p) a week. In short, it was the marginal entrants seeking a move up the social ladder who were more likely to become casualties than those seeking, in Dr Miles's words, 'a haven for the privileged'.[18]

For those who became established, rewards were real enough. There was no scale or typical income. Only a few made their living from a criminal law practice – the modern system of representation by counsel for defendants was still in the future – and most of the remainder made money from side activities as much as from direct fees or commissions. Their special position placed them well for dealing in property and they figure prominently among purchasers in the land market. Many also functioned as money lenders, arranging and, when they had resources enough, making loans and mortgages. Few could hope to be as successful as the Sheffield attorney Joseph Banks who put around £40,000 into land between 1705 and 1727, but as their numbers grew in the provinces (Bristol and Liverpool both had more than seventy attorneys by 1800) they became

18. *Ibid.*, p. 203; Campbell, *London Tradesman*, p. 69.

an increasingly important segment of local society, essential for the operation of the economy and generally prosperous enough.[19]

Medicine

Generally speaking, although entrants to the medical profession did not as noticeably come from the gentry, its upper reaches were well enough esteemed and rewarded.[20] It was still common enough for country physicians to have come to their practices without a period of higher education. Some had simply completed apprenticeships or spent a period learning on the job at a London hospital. As the eighteenth century progressed, however, a period of study at university was increasingly expected to provide an MD – the hallmark of the real doctor. Not obtainable at either of the ancient English universities, it had to be acquired either, very fashionably, at Paris, perhaps at Leiden, or, notably, at the Scottish universities. Edinburgh had 660 medical students by 1800 and they made up over a third of Glasgow's student population. Only doctors licensed by the Royal College of Physicians could practise in London, and that institution had only forty-five fellows in 1745.[21] According to Campbell's guide to the trades of 1747, a good physician had 'the honour to practise a profession the most useful to society, and, in England, the most profitable to himself of any that is effected by human learning'. This was an elite, commanding large fees from well-heeled patients. The practitioner who called on or who was called upon by most of the doctor-using sections of society for most of the eighteenth century was unlikely to have received his training in the same way. Most boils were lanced and most leech-bleeding ordered and carried out by men who had learnt on the job through apprenticeship to an apothecary or surgeon.[22]

Even in London, according to Campbell, of the two ways of becoming a surgeon, attending a university or what would now be termed a 'teaching hospital' was less common and less satisfactory than that after learning Latin and Greek a boy be 'bound to a surgeon of good practice for seven years'. Surgeons formally separated from their traditional joint incorporation with the barbers only in

19. Miles, 'A haven for the privileged', p. 209; Porter, *English Society*, pp. 90–1. See B.L. Anderson, 'The attorney and the early capital market in Lancashire' in F. Crouzet, *Capital Formation in the Industrial Revolution*. Methuen, 1972, pp. 223–55.
20. Miles, 'A haven for the privileged', p. 202.
21. Porter, *English Society*, pp. 90–1.
22. Campbell, *London Tradesman*, p. 41.

1745, when by act of parliament they achieved a London monopoly for Surgeons' Hall with the right to examine all surgeons entering the Navy. Separating from the barbers, the surgeons increasingly associated with the apothecaries to the extent that some degree of proficiency in both fields became the usual mark of the country doctor. Few practitioners were either simple surgeons or simple apothecaries mixing only what doctors prescribed: 'he must only know that Rhubarb is not Jesuits Bark, that Oil is not Salt . . . that requires very little brains', as Campbell put it. The route into general medical practice through apprenticeship to either, or, as was common in the country, to someone practising both was respectable enough. Campbell might scorn the conversation of those who had not been college taught, but he preferred their skills. Although not so highly esteemed as the law, medicine was better regarded than most professions, especially for parents with second or third sons to commence in life.[23] A third of 915 apothecary apprentices entered by their company between 1710 and 1750 have been described as of 'lower gentry status', against 55 per cent of 'lower middle sort'.[24]

A hard-working practitioner, especially one able to inherit the well-cultivated practice of a doctor father, could make a good enough living. They would, however, need to follow their occupation as much as a business as a vocation and charge fees which might lessen the gratitude returned for the healing services they performed. A shopkeeper made a note in his diary in 1760 which was neither the first nor the last of its kind: 'Dr Poole paid my wife a visit and charged me 10s 6d. Really a fine thing it is to be a physician who can charge just as they please and not be culpable according to any human law.'[25] More informative is a long letter from an old family friend written in 1808 to a young man intent on becoming a doctor in his native county.

> Thy object I presume to be the profession of a surgeon and
> apothecary, perhaps in Cornwall. It is doubtless an honourable calling,
> but point out more than a solitary instance, if thou canst, in which
> honour and profit have gone hand in hand. Look at home and see
> how your own medical men have fared. It is much to be doubted
> whether after many years of practice that any one of the Redruth
> apothecaries have provided against what is termed a rainy day. If
> premature old age and sickness of long continuance should seize any

---

23. *Ibid.*, pp. 47, 57.
24. Miles, 'A haven for the privileged', pp. 202–3.
25. D. Vaisey (ed.), *The Diary of Thomas Turner*, p. 214.

one of these, who is to provide for their families, and what is to become of their business, which can only be done by the principals themselves. An assistant might possibly stop the gap for a week, but a surgeon or apothecary is employed for his individual skill, and when he can no longer use this, his business must fail of course. Dr Pryce who has perhaps the best practice in Redruth or its neighbourhood, has seriously complained even to me, and surely he would not have so done unless the shoe pinched somewhere. This pinching is not always obvious, and for this unhappy reason, that a medical man must always look and appear to live genteelly or he is a *nobody*, and if the practice of Dr P. were to be considerably extended what would be the consequence – one pony would not carry him through the day, he must have two or three, and then find me the post boy or butcher that must ride harder and feel more personal fatigue.[26]

Allowing that this was an epistle designed to deter, it remains a sympathetic depiction of what must have been the lot of many country doctors: respect but no easy coming-by of wealth.

There were in Hanoverian England many who sought a living from 'cures' who can hardly be placed within an 'honourable calling'. Quacks and the sellers of patent medicines abounded, as did itinerant drawers of teeth by 'painless' methods. What Dr Porter has termed 'marketplace medicine' was in the forefront of the expansion of advertising and growth of salesmanship which characterised the so-called 'commercial revolution' and afforded many opportunities for women as well as men to exploit. Purchasers presumably came largely from the 'middling ranks', but many also came from those higher echelons, who could after all be easily enough persuaded of the all-embracing curative properties of mineral waters and as readily dispensed advice on purging. For the poorer classes there was little enough money to allow for either doctors' fees or patent medicines.[27] Some saw a doctor from time to time. At Cornish mines, for example, a small sum was deducted from wages to form a fund out of which a surgeon was paid to attend the all too numerous victims of accidents.[28] In extreme circumstances Poor Law overseers might fee a doctor to attend a seriously ill or injured person; more often they might afford something in the way of medicine. In general, however, village resort was likely to have been to persons of their own rank, adept at prescribing or carrying out 'folk' remedies or skilled at activities like midwifery, herb healing or

26. Hamilton Jenkin, *News from Cornwall*, p. 141.
27. Porter, 'Female quacks in the consumer society', *The Clark Newsletter*, **16**, 1989, pp. 1–4.
28. William Pryce, *Mineralogia Cornubiensis*, 1778, pp. 175–6.

wound dressing, or even, at the most rusticated level, supplying charms and the like not far removed from witchcraft. Such 'cunning' persons perhaps expected small fees or 'presents'. They, like the doctors and the quacks, earned something from seeking to cure the sick and broken. There was indeed a medical 'profession' growing in numbers and esteem over the eighteenth century, but the service it offered was still beyond the reach of much of the population.

Teaching

This was not unlike medicine in that although many people could be described as 'professional teachers', many more with no formal training provided an educational service as a means of scraping a living. It was unlike medicine in that not even the upper echelons of pedagogy could confirm their special property of the art of teaching through membership of a 'college' or 'company'. Very few people prospered through pursuing school teaching as a full-time career. It became more difficult to do so as the eighteenth century progressed and schoolmastering became an increasingly crowded occupation. The most rapidly growing area – indeed, with the old endowed grammar schools in decline and state education as yet unforeseen, the only really dynamic area in the eighteenth century – was the private school set up by an individual and depending on the attraction of fee-paying pupils. Advertisements placed in local newspapers to this end are the main source of information on the supply and character of these establishments. We may take as typical an example cited by Professor Plumb of a Leeds schoolmaster who, given the fees he advertised and the capacity of his school, probably made around £40 a year – less than the £1 a week Dr Johnson considered a skilled compositor could earn in the printing trade. Not surprisingly many private schoolmasters, even in sizeable towns, advertised their proficiency at other trades. The Newcastle schoolmaster who in the 1740s sold ink was perhaps a vendor of a product with a closer relation to his main profession than that of his Darlington contemporary who sold hats.[29]

In the eighteenth century the demand for education from a middle-class clientele was drawing out school provision which offered a range of subjects that had not been included in the learning of clergymen, but for most of the century the majority of private

29. J.H. Plumb, 'The new world of children' in McKendrick, Brewer and Plumb (eds), *Birth of a Consumer Society*, pp. 296–7.

schools were still provided by clergymen to support a life-style beyond that afforded by their livings. They taught traditional subjects, preparing perhaps better-off scholars for entry to public schools or university. However, not all, perhaps hardly any, were as successful as the Vicar of Highclere in Hampshire who began a school to teach his own sons and because some neighbouring gentlemen asked him to prepare their sons for university. He proved so good that even his patron, the Earl of Pembroke, sent his sons, and by 1794 he was building a special boarding house alongside his crowded vicarage.[30]

Masters at the great public schools to which the large majority of the sons of the ruling class were sent presumably did well enough, but there were only nine such establishments. Near the top of their profession, too, were the masters at those larger endowed grammar schools, mainly in the bigger towns, which were still flourishing against the general decline of the grammar school. The master of King Edward's School in Birmingham was paid £88 15s (£88.75p) at the beginning of the eighteenth century: comfort enough, but hardly riches. The situation of masters in smaller grammar schools, despite a tendency to reduce free places in favour of fee-paying boarders, was hardly to be envied. Rolls fell with the declining interest in the classical curriculum, and fixed endowments produced declining income in real terms, especially after mid century. Dr O'Day has noted that the £16 per annum paid in 1688 to the master of one such school in the diocese of Lichfield was still unchanged in 1820, by which time, of course, it could not by itself have allowed any kind of living.[31]

Village schoolmasters fared poorly. They neither expected nor could have been expected to live from teaching. The enlightened Marquis of Rockingham paid the schoolmasters' salaries on behalf of seven villages on his estates in the 1760s; the highest was £6. We have no knowledge of what income was enjoyed in that same county of Yorkshire at Barnborough in 1743 to 'an useful person to teach such children as they send to him, to read English and some of them to write, they paying for those they send to him'.[32] It has been noted that over the eighteenth century village schoolmasters increasingly took on the additional employ of parish clerk. A recommendation on behalf of a candidate for a Staffordshire school in 1773 informed that he was not only well qualified for the position,

30. R. O'Day, *Education and Society*, p. 207.
31. *Ibid.*, pp. 171–2.
32. Plumb, 'New world of children', p. 292.

'but also for that of parish clerk, if he should be called to, and chosen to undertake that office'. A Somersetshire man combined in 1779 the offices of village schoolmaster and clerk with the trade of tailoring. Perhaps even that was insufficient to keep him from hunger, for it was at his trial for sheep-stealing that this occupational information was revealed.[33] What is perhaps the most celebrated description of a village schoolmaster was penned by Oliver Goldsmith in 1769. We know nothing of his income, but he at least enjoyed status and respect within his small community.

> The village all declared how much he knew
> 'Twas certain he could write, and cipher too;
> Lands he could measure, terms and tides presage,
> And e'en the story ran that he could gauge.
>
> While words of learned length, and thund'ring sound,
> Amazed the gazing rustics ranged around
> And still they gazed, and still the wonder grew
> That one small head could carry all he knew.[34]

Who would deny such a man his place? Certainly not the parson whom he regularly out-argued. But far more common was another kind of village school. Twenty-five years earlier another versifier had drawn attention to the fact that 'in every village':

> There dwells in lowly shed and mean attire
> A Matron, whom we school mistress name
> Who boasts unruly brats with birch to tame[35]

Here we leave any pretension to a place in the middling ranks as village women, typically widows, provided a minimum of learning to the children of the poor in return for a penny or two. Typically the Dame School was a matter of private initiative, but even when parish authorities had the management of a school for the children of the poor, they often seem to have provided a teacher as if it were a matter of out-relief. The School of Industry set up in Redruth in 1791 was entrusted to the churchwardens and was 'left chiefly to the care of a poor old man (a pauper) to learn the children as best he can'. Injured miners might resort to school teaching. A west Cornwall vestry-book entry for 1807 contains an agreement to pay one such man £12 p.a. 'to take the school'.[36]

33. O'Day, *Education and Society*, pp. 176–7; *Sherbourne Mercury*, 18 Feb. 1799.
34. Oliver Goldsmith, *The Deserted Village*, 1769.
35. Cited in R.H. Hartwell, *Industrial Revolution and Economic Growth*, p. 239.
36. Hamilton Jenkin, *News from Cornwall*, pp. 13–14; Cornwall Records Office, Breage Vestry Minute Book, DDP 18/8/1.

Teaching in the eighteenth century was not a following to which many respectable parents would have entered their sons. It was already an occupation, however, which was showing early signs of becoming one of the few acceptable ones open to girls. It was not only a matter of countless governesses living in genteel and subservient poverty, but as the practice of sending daughters to school increased among the gentry and middle classes, there emerged a sizeable number of private establishments to receive and polish them. Of ninety-one schools advertised in the *Ipswich Journal* between 1783 and 1787, seventeen were run by women.[37] Unlike medicine or the law, there was no formal means of entry. Nevertheless, as the role of clergymen among its practitioners declined relatively, teachers were emerging as an increasingly important fraction of the 'middling classes', earning more respect if never full purses.

Estate management

Embracing land stewardship and spawning associated specialisms like land surveying, estate management was one profession which owed its emergence over the period to the growth and commercialisation of the agricultural sector and it was well established before a recognisable management profession appeared other than exceptionally in the manufacturing and service sectors. At the top of the profession the stewards of large, consolidated estates were responsible for property which could exceed a million pounds in capital value and they could have perhaps £30–40,000 annually in rents and other income pass through their hands. Such men on the bigger estates by the mid eighteenth century earned as much as £400 a year. As early as 1732 the chief steward of the huge estate of the Duke of Bedford had his salary raised to £700 and by 1800 his equivalent on the Duke of Devonshire's estates was receiving an astonishing £1,000 a year. There were few such openings, of course, but the level of application and the complex range of knowledge required to carry out a job which needed skill in rent assessing and in the setting of leases, linked with the need to employ men of probity, integrity and weight, made the general run of salaries high. It took the Duke of Bridgewater six years in the 1720s to persuade a yeoman farmer to act as his steward, eventually getting him for £100, a house and a horse at the duke's cost. Most probably the

37. Plumb, 'New world of children', pp. 294–5; O'Day, *Education and Society*, p. 191 and Chapter 9.

new steward continued to farm his holding, for that was normal practice.[38]

The extent of absentee landlordship meant that owners of even quite modest properties might need to employ an agent of some kind. These commissions were sometimes undertaken by middling farmers, but increasingly by lawyers and also by men who specialised in such work, secured a reputation for honesty and efficiency and who made a sound living by combining several agencies and, perhaps, some venture of their own. One such person whose letterbooks survive to give a fascinating picture of his professional life was William Jenkin of Redruth in Cornwall, whose special skill lay in his knowledge of the copper mining industry of the region, in which activity the estates of his employers were inevitably involved. His activities are listed in a letter of 1808. His first employment was as steward to the Lanhydrock estates which held twenty-four manors throughout the county, with many of those in the west being rich in mineral ores; he was agent to a copper company valuing and dealing in ores on their behalf; he looked after the mining interests of the Marquis of Buckingham (indeed, he had earlier turned down an offer to leave Cornwall to take over the stewardship of the marquis's main estate); he played a small professional role in the management of several mines; he ventured capital in mining in his own right; he had a profitable business in hiring out the mules used to transport ores and another in supplying the mines with leather and the rough canvas they used for sacks; finally, he financed in part a farm worked by his brother.[39]

At this time he was seventy years of age and yet in 1814 he took on another activity as copper buyer in Cornwall for a Swansea smelter. How much did all this bring in? His main agency for the Lanhydrock estate in all probability would have brought a comfortable enough living. For he noted in 1792 that his secondary business as a mine agent earned him around £170 a year. When this is combined with his private capitalist activities as merchant and mine venturer as well as with his estate stewardship it seems unlikely that he earned less than £500 a year. For all this, Jenkin had no formal professional training. He seems to have stepped into shoes already filled by his father and then taken much bigger strides, and it is clear that would-be employers sought him out. In a small town,

38. G.E. Mingay, 'The eighteenth-century land steward' in E.L. Jones and G.E. Mingay (eds), *Land, Labour and Population in the Industrial Revolution*, Arnold, 1967, pp. 3, 9–11.

39. Hamilton Jenkin, *News from Cornwall*, pp. 137–8.

such opportunities would not be sufficiently widespread for a man's son to make as comfortable a living alongside him. In the case of Redruth the only other large estate was owned by Lord De Dunstanville, a hated adversary in a score of court cases over land and mineral rights.[40] What happened to Alfred, the favoured son of William's later middle age, is interesting. The young man was dissuaded from becoming a doctor, advised not to article himself for seven years to his father, and neatly apprenticed to a land surveyor. This gave him both an independent profession for the time being and relevant experience against the time his father was to retire. By 1819 when, at the age of eighty-one, William Jenkin finally relinquished the stewardship he had held for nearly fifty years, he had already been employing his son's assistance and was able to recommend him successfully to the stewardship of Lanhydrock.[41] Although Jenkin called himself a merchant in respect of his part-time wholesale business to the mines, he was primarily a representative of the emerging professional sector of the middle classes. Full-time men of commerce much outnumbered his sort in a 'nation of shopkeepers'.

THE COMMERCIAL MIDDLE CLASS

Adam Smith's description of England as 'a nation of shopkeepers',[42] if it has become trite from over-use, still indicates the most distinguishing facet of her eighteenth-century economy. By 'shopkeepers' is understood the whole population of all kinds of sellers of all kinds of goods. At the apex of the commercial world were the merchants proper: those who engaged in overseas trade. According to Defoe in 1726, 'these only are called merchants by way of honourable distinction'.[43] Campbell in 1747 shared this estimation, claiming that only the merchant selling goods at a profit overseas added 'so much to the national riches and capital stock of the kingdom'. In status and in wealth their range was considerable. A select few, mostly of London, we have already noted, were sufficiently powerful and important to be considered part of the ruling classes. For the most part, however, the merchants are to be considered as the top rank of the middle classes. Nowhere were they more esteemed than in eighteenth-century England.

40. *Ibid.*, pp. 4, 15, 180.
41. *Ibid.*, pp. 145–6, 200–1.
42. Smith, *Wealth of Nations*, II, p. 129.
43. Daniel Defoe, *The Complete English Tradesman*, 1726, rept Alan Sutton, 1987, p. 8.

> [The merchant] sets the whole society at work, supplies them with materials to fabricate their goods and vends their manufactures in the most distant corners of the globe. . . . Wherever he comes, wherever he lives, wealth and plenty follow him. The poor is set to work, manufactures flourish, poverty is banished, and public credit increases.[44]

Robert Campbell was echoing the sentiments of Defoe twenty years earlier that Britain's 'rising greatness' was 'all owing to trade'.[45] There were always self-made exceptions, but for the most part the greater merchants exhibited some of the characteristics of a caste. For every one who bought out into land and sought that route for the social advancement of his progeny, there were many who made sure their sons followed in their footsteps. For every one who sought a marriage alliance with 'the quality', there were many who used matrimony to foster commercial alliances. In *Roxana*, Defoe's last novel written in 1724, the heroine intends to use some of her somewhat irregularly earned fortune to 'place' her rediscovered son. The uncle who is to see to the matter asks:

> . . . what he should go to school to learn? and what Trade she would please put him out to?
>
> Amy said, he should put him to learn a little Latin, and then Merchant-Accounts; and to write a good hand, for she would have him be put to a Turkey-Merchant.
>
> Madam, says he, I am glad for his sake, to hear you say so; but do you know that a Turkey-Merchant will not take him under 4 or 500 pounds?
>
> Yes Sir, says Amy, I know it very well.
>
> And, says he, that it will require as many thousands to set him up?[46]

Here is indicated not only the high cost of entry into an established overseas trading establishment and the capital cost of moving to one's own account once apprenticeship had been completed, but also the realisation that a special kind of education was best suited for a merchant career which was not identical with that provided for the landed classes. There was a tendency for established merchants to apprentice their sons to other merchants to learn the business. But most of those apprenticed to merchant houses were hardly expecting to become traders themselves, or at least not for some time.

44. Campbell, *The London Tradesman*, p. 284.
45. Defoe, *Complete English Tradesman*, p. 219.
46. Defoe, *Roxana: The Fortunate Mistress*, 1724.

A youth educated in this manner, is fit for the Compting house of any Merchant; and when he has served his time to any eminent trader, may earn his bread in a genteel manner in any part of the world. He may serve as clerk in any compting-house at home, may turn out supercargo to any port, and may settle as factor in any of our plantations, or other trading cities in Europe, if he understands the practical part of commerce, writes a good hand, understands accompts, and the trading languages, and has the character of integrity and application; whether he has money or not he may live, not only in the employ of others, but may in time deal for himself to any extent.[47]

Even this distant prospect was for only the more ambitious of those who for the most part, along with their equivalents in lawyers' offices and government departments, entered sums and copied documents as members of that growing fraction of the labour force rescued from the neglect of historians by Professor Brewer: 'In an era which saw a remarkable proliferation of accounts, memoranda and correspondence, the scribe, clerk and copyist contributed both to the growth of commerce and the development of government.'[48]

The most opulent and powerful of the merchants were those of the capital, but as the eighteenth century wore on, the leading overseas traders of the main provincial ports like Bristol, Liverpool and Hull began to narrow the gap. In 1742 the leading traders of the first named were described as 'very rich [but] not like the Merchants of London. . . . I would advise the rich ones among them, if they would be a little more polite and generous, than they usually are, to travel to London, and they will see examples worth their imitation, as well for princely spirit, as upright and generous dealings.' By 1778 the example seems to have been followed, for the port's 'gentry, merchants and capital traders' were described then as 'as polite, and superb in their town and country houses, equipages, servants and amusements, as any in the kingdom'.[49]

But many of Bristol's merchants enjoyed less than spectacular success. Graffin Prankard, unlike most of the richer sort, was not involved in the slave trade. The son of a maltster, he specialised in iron but handled a range of other goods and traded with the American colonies, the West Indies and Newfoundland, as well as with many places in western and northern Europe. He employed agents overseas in several places, including Charleston, Carolina,

47. Campbell, *London Tradesman*, pp. 293–4.
48. Brewer, *Sinews of Power*, p. 68.
49. P.T. Marcy, *Eighteenth Century Views of Bristol and Bristolians*, Bristol UP, 1966, pp. 15–16, 20. For merchants generally, see W.E. Minchinton, 'Merchants in England', pp. 60–71.

from where he took return cargoes in rice, destined ultimately for Hamburg. He began his trading career on a share basis but in 1724 had his first ship built – of 100 tonnes and carrying a crew of eight. Eight years later he built a second, twice as large, at a cost of £2,744, whose first voyage returned a profit of £575. He still joint-ventured from time to time and in 1738 built a third vessel for the north European trade. In the same year he was admitted to the Society of Merchant Venturers of Bristol and began to invest in land. In 1739 things began to go wrong. There was a steep fall in the price of rice. He incurred bad debts and spoiled cargoes and in 1740 badly damaged one of his ships. A second was taken off Scilly by a Spanish privateer. At this point his business seems to have been largely taken over for two years by his brother-in-law and son-in-law, who were both experienced and successful merchants. In 1743 he built a 20-ton sloop, but his affairs never really recovered and he spent most of his time on his farm. By the time of his death in 1756 he had disposed of his commercial interests. There is no reason to suppose that Prankard was unusual among Bristol merchants.[50]

It is not easy to assess how large the commercial upper middle class was in the country as a whole. It has been suggested that it numbered around 2,000 in 1700 and 3,500 by 1800. Certainly it was much smaller than the class of inland merchants, the wholesalers. The changing conditions of the eighteenth century suited them. Markets widened; fairs declined to give way increasingly to regular outlets demanding goods more constantly, while transport improved beyond all recognition enabling them to be reached. A man like Abraham Dent of Westmorland could turn over £1,000 a year, but he ran a retail business and was a brewer, bill broker and small landowner as well as a wholesale hosier.[51] These men reached down to the ranks of the shopkeepers proper: the fixed-site retailers. To Defoe:

> all sorts of warehousekeepers, shopkeepers, whether wholesale dealers or retailers of goods, are called tradesmen, or, to explain it by another word, trading men, such are whether wholesale or retail, our grocers, mercers, linen and woollen drapers, Blackwell Hall factors, tobacconists, haberdashers, whether of hats or small wares, glovers, hosiers, milliners, booksellers, stationers and all other shopkeepers who do not actually work upon, make, or manufacture, the goods they sell.[52]

50. Prankard's career is described by J. Bettey in 'Graffin Prankard, an Eighteenth-century Bristol Merchant', *Southern History*, XII, 1990 pp. 34-47. I am grateful to Dr Bettey for the opportunity to preview it.
51. Minchinton, 'Merchants in England', p. 60; Porter, *English Society*, p. 95.
52. Defoe, *Complete English Tradesman*, p. 7.

but of these:

> there is not a man in the universe deserves the title of a complete
> tradesman, like the English shopkeeper.

Defoe justified this by reeling off the breadth of knowledge needed
by a shopkeeper in an age when retailers outside the large towns
rarely specialised. He had to know:

> what goods are generally bought by barter and exchange, and what by
> payment of money, what for present money and what for time; what
> are sold by commission from the makers, what bought by factors, and
> by giving commission to buyers in the country, and what by order to
> the maker, and the like, what markets are the most proper to buy
> everything at, and where and when; and what fairs are proper to go to
> in order to buy or sell, or to meet the country dealer at, such as,
> Sturbridge, Bristol, Chester, Exeter; or what marts such as Beverley,
> Lynn, Boston, Gainsborough and the like.[53]

Just such an unspecialised local shopkeeper, Thomas Turner of East
Hoathley near Lewes in Sussex, kept a diary between 1754 and 1765
which shows him to have been constantly on the move obtaining
supplies of one kind of goods or another. He knew how to keep his
eye on the details which made the difference between profit and
loss: 'This day Mrs Atkins in a manner huffed me pretty much
because I would not cut her a Cheshire cheese at the same price I
sold them whole. Now I affixed a small profit upon my Cheshire
cheese, even only about a farthing a pound.'[54] It was a busy life; as
often as not his wife kept the shop while he rode around between
various suppliers. But when the day was over:

> At home all day; thank God very busy. Oh how pleasant is trade when it
> runs in its proper channels, and flows with a plentiful stream. It does,
> as it were, give life and spirit to one's actions. I think the most
> phlegmatic constitution must feel its pleasing and enlivening charms.[55]

It has been claimed that over the eighteenth century not only did
the number of shops in England substantially increase, but their
keepers were innovative in their business practices and entrepreneurial in their outlook.[56] By 1800 they were everywhere, with petty
shops supplying necessities and decencies in smaller communities
while specialist ones propelled the consumer revolution in larger

---

53. *Ibid.*, p. 9.
54. Vaisey (ed.), *Diary of Thomas Turner*, p. 195.
55. *Ibid.*, p. 233.
56. This is the argument of Mui and Mui, *Shops and Shopkeeping*.

ones. China shops, for example, were widespread, from Wedgwood's front-line showroom in St James's Square, an address shared with several dukes, through the Bridgewater shop which supplied the Reverend William Holland, to the small thatched one drawn by Thomas Rowlandson passing through Farnham in Surrey in 1784. Goods were displayed in glass windows, some even well lit.[57] Grocers at least seem to have known all about 'loss leaders', while the use of trade cards and press advertising was widespread. In 1795, for example, the *Telegraph* was one of more than twenty publications which carried distinctively worded advertisements extolling the virtues of the razor strops patented and sold by George Packwood.

> In the compting-house the smart City blade,
> Before he is dress'd for the shop,
> The razor can flourish, what gives him the aid?
> Why Packwood's ingenious Strop.

> And see my lord's valet his shaving perform,
> With a speed to astonish each gazer;
> While his master is calm, his friends they all storm,
> They are mad to possess such a razor.

> Then to Packwood's repair, and your wishes possess,
> And shave with a good inclination;
> Your beards will come off with great ease and address
> Through the Strop that's the pride of the nation.[58]

The first verse clearly addresses itself to a potential middle-class customer. Only with the second is the message aimed at the real gentleman who doesn't have to scrape his own chin. It is a well-calculated advertisement, for the shopocracy was a middle-class sector brought into being by the significant expansion of middle-class consumers of non-essentials. Had the aristocracy and gentry remained the only significant consumers, then most of their needs could have been bespoken, made to their measure and their taste by tailors, shoe makers or cabinet makers: a 'client' class of tradesmen. As for the labouring people, what they needed and could afford was still supplied largely in the market place and occasionally by itinerant hawkers. No example better illustrates the rise of the shop selling from fixed premises than that of the grocer. In very small towns

57. For the spread of fixed-site shops, see E. Pawson, *Early Industrial Revolution*, pp. 167–8; N. McKendrick, 'Commercialization of fashion' in McKendrick, Brewer and Plumb, *Birth of a Consumer Society*, pp. 78–9.

58. McKendrick, 'George Packwood and the commercialization of shaving', *ibid.*, p. 158.

and in villages the grocer would sell a range of general merchandise, but in the larger towns he was essentially a specialist in the 'new' dry goods of the eighteenth century. Groceries really described imported foodstuffs: tea, sugar, coffee, currants and spices which they bought from the wholesale importers. Manchester had twenty-four grocers in 1772 and even the small Worcestershire town of Bewdley had five by the 1790s.[59]

A full range of specialist shops dealing in groceries, pottery, clothing, ready-made footware, fashion accessories, books and hardware was to be found in London. By 1803 Oxford Street was said to have among its shops as many as 153 which catered for the 'whim-whams' and 'fribble-frabble' of fashion. A Russian visitor in 1789 found 'beautiful shops' everywhere in London, with their windows exhibiting wares 'as in a continuous fair'. Regional centres like Bristol, York and Newcastle followed suit, and so, of course, did the spas and other resort towns. The Liverpool guide of 1797 described a view from the Exchange of a 'spacious street . . . perfectly uniform; all shops containing everything useful and ornamental, to indulge the taste and gratify the necessities'. Once around the corner, however, the visitor was advised, 'the eye should not be turned to either side as it would be offended at the very indecorous practice of exposing the shambles meat in the public street'. Smaller towns followed larger ones, and by the end of the period Jane Austen expected even her village shopkeeper to 'go to Town' to purchase fashion goods for resale.[60]

Over the country as a whole, the retailers of alchohol were easily the most ubiquitous of shopkeepers. While the keepers of squalid gin shops hardly ranked higher than the poor they poisoned, the keepers of inns and taverns were an important commercial group. They provided room for sleeping, eating and meeting, were employers of many and were essential links in the transport network. In 1732 London had an estimated 16,000 drinking places. Most of these were gin or brandy shops or alehouses, but there were 654 inns and taverns as well as 551 coffee houses. Birmingham had 248 innkeepers in 1777, Manchester 140, while smaller towns had them in proportion.[61]

What proportion of the urban population did the shopkeepers make up? On the basis of tax returns from 1798, Dr Schwarz has

59. Pawson, *Early Industrial Revolution*, p. 168.

60. McKendrick, 'Commercialization of fashion', pp. 78–9, 92; Pawson, *Early Industrial Revolution*, pp. 168–9.

61. Pawson, *Early Industrial Revolution*, p. 168.

suggested that the upper middle class of London enjoying incomes of more than £200 a year formed no more than 5 per cent of the metropolitan population, while those on middling income formed a further 25 per cent. Shopkeepers probably formed more than half of this second group; more than a third of all those earning above £75 a year; were 37 per cent of all those paying taxes and between 11 and 14 per cent of London's total population.[62] By most they were clearly placed among the 'useful' classes who increased the national wealth, but their usefulness did not end there. In small towns and villages their experience with accounts, their relative status and income standing and their generally high level of literacy made them natural candidates for those petty offices at parochial level on which the administration of local government depended, such as serving as constables or supervising the administration of poor relief. Thomas Turner, the Sussex village shopkeeper, was churchwarden in 1757–8, 1765 and 1765–6; overseer of the poor in 1756–7, 1762–3, 1763–4 and 1764–5 and surveyor of the highways in 1765. From 1760 to 1766 he collected the window and land taxes. He also served as village scribe, especially in the drawing up of wills.[63] Even in London, social zoning meant that in many parishes in the south and east the lower middle class supplied the only suitable residents to fill such offices.[64]

Defoe was specific on one point.

> On the other hand, those who make the goods they sell, though they do keep shops to sell them, are not called tradesmen, but handicrafts, such as smiths, founders, joiners, carpenters, carvers, turners and the like; others who only make, or cause goods to be made, goods for other people to sell, are called manufacturers and artists etc.[65]

Typically dogmatic, he was asserting a distinction which the everyday language of the eighteenth century hardly recognised. Campbell called his compilation of 1747, which described more than a hundred occupations, *The London Tradesman*, and included all those excluded by Defoe and very many more besides, ranging from merchants through pawnbrokers to coal heavers and chimney sweeps. Consideration of the baker, among the most widespread of urban shops, makes the point. Birmingham had sixty-four bakers in 1777, compared with forty-nine butchers. Not only the master baker but

62. L.D. Schwarz, 'Social class and social geography', pp. 168–77.
63. Vaisey (ed.), *Diary of Thomas Turner*.
64. Schwarz, 'Social class and social geography', p. 182.
65. Defoe, *Complete English Tradesman*, p. 7.

his family, his apprentices and any journeymen he employed lived, made and sold from a single premises, the last named receiving in 1747 five or six shillings a week as well as their board.[66] The master tailors of the West End and of the better quarters of the provincial towns and cities also headed enterprises which both made and re-tailed.

> In a Taylor's shop, there are always two sorts of workmen; first the Foreman, who takes measure when the Master is out of the way and finishes all the work, and carries it home to the customer. . . . The next class is the mere working Taylor; not one in ten of them know how to cut out a pair of breeches: they are employed only to sew the seam, to cast the Button Holes, and prepare the work for the finisher . . .. The master's profit is very considerable . . . and many of them affect to be called Merchant Taylors . . . and would raise estates soon, were it not for the delays in payment among the quality.[67]

Dress makers, mantua makers and milliners similarly directed shops in both the retail and the work sense. Campbell describes the last as having to be both 'a neat Needle-woman' and 'a perfect Connoisseur in Dress and fashion'. The double nature of tradespeople in the garment trade is further revealed when we also learn from him that in all its branches the masters and mistresses took as much of their profit from charging heavily for their materials as well as from the low wages they paid their journeymen and women.[68]

Tradesmen who retailed commodities they made, or at least directed the making of, obviously covered a huge wealth and income range. Francis Place, who began as an apprentice in the late eighteenth century, enjoyed an income of £3,000 from his tailoring business in the 1820s. William Hutton, who had had an even more disadvantaged youth – factory child and then apprentice to the 'starving trade' of stockinger – used the profits from book selling to move backwards into book binding and paper making. He also ventured into the land market and in 1768 was worth £2,000 as well as having property of such a value that part of it destroyed in the Birmingham riots of 1791 was worth £8,000. These were the exceptions that a capitalist economy needs to demonstrate the advantages of opportunity to the greater number who do not make it. Many tradesmen made comfortable livings, including building craftsmen who were able to utilise growing mortgage opportunities and

66. Campbell, *London Tradesman*, Appendix and p. 275; Pawson, *Early Industrial Revolution*, pp. 162–3.
67. Campbell, *London Tradesman*, pp. 192–4.
68. *Ibid.*, pp. 207–8.

mutual inter-employment between the various building crafts to enter speculative house building. Some self-employed workshop traders in small towns were local monopolists and lived comfortably enough. Others gained little but insecurity from their 'independence': men like the poorer shoe makers who were stretched on the rack of credit between the short credit or cash expectations of those who supplied materials and the long credit expectations of their customers. The more skilled of the waged artisans could live more comfortably.[69]

The richest class who mixed manufacturing and merchanting were the putting-out capitalists, who controlled the process of manufacturing in some of the most important textile and metal-working districts. Some of them employed so many home-based workers that they hardly knew their number. The celebrated 'Gentlemen Clothiers of the west-country' perhaps best represent this group. Several from their ranks did move their fortunes into land, but on the whole, like the greater trading merchants of London, they tended to remain distinct. Although Defoe mentions some clothiers who founded landed families, in general he represents them as a wealthy urban class even when possessed of fortunes of £10,000 to £40,000. As Julia de L. Mann demonstrated, there was some regional variation in their status and place in the 'county community'. In Wiltshire clothiers had sat on the bench since the late seventeenth century. There were four on it in 1726 and appointments continued to be made through the century. There was some fear that too many such appointments could be made and in 1751 the locally influential Duke of Bolton was urged to try to ensure that 'Gentlemen only and not tradesmen' were put on to the next Commission, and it was clearly clothiers who were understood as 'tradesmen', for the request continues to describe their exploitation of woollen workers. Yet in Gloucestershire no clothier seems to have been appointed to the bench before the later eighteenth century, and in Somerset not even then.[70]

But what of the 'new style' manufacturers, the coming class over the later eighteenth century, the factory masters? These men were to take over the word 'manufacturer' and change its meaning to cover only the employers of labour on fixed production sites. Andrew Ure assumed the linguistic change was complete, when he

69. Porter, *English Society*, pp. 94–5; J.G. Rule, *Experience of Labour*, pp. 33–4.
70. Daniel Defoe, *A Tour through the Whole Island of Great Britain*, I, Everyman, 1962, p. 281; Mann, J. de Lacy, *The Cloth Industry in the West of England from 1640 to 1880*, Oxford UP, 1971, pp. 116–18.

wrote in 1835: 'manufacture is a word, which, in the vicissitude of language, has come to signify the reverse of its intrinsic meaning, for now it denotes every extensive product of art which is made by machinery, with little or no aid of the human hand'.[71] The shift had begun much earlier. 'Manufacturer' in the modern sense was used as far back as 1752 and became progressively more usual. In 1800 James Watt described his famous Birmingham partner, Matthew Boulton, as a 'manufacturer' without any sense of special usage, while in a question to a witness, a parliamentary committee of 1818 virtually assumes the modern definition: 'By calling yourself a manufacturer, the Committee suppose you mean you are a capitalist employing weavers to that effect?'

Alongside, older words betraying specific origins continued to be used: mill owner, factory or iron master, master spinner. Professor Crouzet suggests that the modern 'industrialist'[72] became current only in the 1860s, and that the absence of the generic reflects the fact that the traditional industry which prevailed before the industrial revolution was 'industry without industrialists'. Gregory King had not even listed 'manufacturer' as a separate category, but working from the 1801 census, Patrick Calquhoun estimated a population of 25,000, although perhaps only a fifth of those were manufacturers in the sense of industrialists.

The Declaration of the General Chamber of Manufacturers, set up in 1784 on the initiative of Samuel Garbett and Matthew Boulton of Birmingham, Josiah Wedgwood and other leading industrialists to oppose William Pitt's Irish Treaty, is often cited as the first self-conscious statement of the group.

> It seems hitherto to have escaped the notice of the manufacturers that whilst the *landed* and *funded* interests, the East India, and other commercial bodies, have their respective advocates in the great council of the nation, *they* alone are destitute of that advantage; and it is probable from this source that many of their grievances have arisen – that they have so repeatedly and inadvertently been oppressed by ministers unacquainted with their real interests, and misled by the designs of interested individuals.[73]

Industrialists tended to remain middle-class. Indeed, far more than the merchant elite, they took pride in this. Few of them made for-

71. Cited in Crouzet, *First Industrialists*, p. 2.
72. *Ibid.*, pp. 3–4.
73. Cited in H.J. Perkin, *Origins of Modern English Society*, p. 29. See W. Bowden, *Industrial Society in England*, pp. 164–93 for an account of eighteenth-century manufacturers' organisations.

tunes comparable to those made in the City. Often their wealth was more fable than fact. When the Dutch loom was introduced into smallware weaving around 1725, the idea that it had made manufacturers who could 'vie with some of the best gentlemen' of the locality met with a scornful riposte: 'I wonder what any country gentleman can be supposed to envy them for! Is it their houses? Which country gentleman has reason to envy the possession of a house of four, five or six rooms of a floor with warehouses under and warping rooms over?'[74]

The highest rungs of gentility were blocked in part by a myth promoted as much by the industrialists themselves as by others. In the nineteenth century the notion of the 'self- made man' was to become one of the justifying myths of industrial capitalism: an asserted counter argument to the view that the system was exploitative. But it was already there in the eighteenth century. Matthew Boulton told an enquiry of 1799 that 'all the great manufacturers' he had ever known 'have begun the world with very little capital'. William Hutton wrote that of 209 Birmingham manufacturers in 1783 worth more than £5,000, 103 'began the world with nothing but their own prudence'. It was a persuasive conceit epitomised in Jedediah Strutt's self-composed epitaph shortly before his death in 1797. He described himself as one 'who without Fortune, Family or Friends rais'd to himself a fortune, family and Name in the World'. Small beginnings were relative. Thomas Williams, 'the Copper King', described as having made a fortune from them, had in fact been a successful county solicitor, well connected with the landed in his vicinity. Crouzet has pointed out that to rise from rags to riches was rare. His analysis of 316 industrialists from 1750 to 1850 shows that at the time they founded a large undertaking only one in ten could be placed in the working class. Distribution of social class by their fathers brings a working-class share of only 7.1 per cent. Combining the middle-class and the lower-middle-class fathers produces 84 per cent. There seems little doubt that considered as a group, industrialists were middle-class in origins as well as in standing.[75]

No rising 'tradesman' received more scornful derision than Richard Arkwright, the inventor of the water frame and the pioneer of the spinning mill, when he gained his knighthood. A 'great *mill-monger* is newly *created* a knight, though he was not *born* a gentleman' was one snide reaction. Arkwright may once have been an

74. Bowden, *Industrial Society in England,* pp. 150–1.
75. Crouzet, *First Industrialists,* pp. 38, 127–43.

itinerant barber, but in 1787 he was performing the role of High Sheriff of Derbyshire with all the expected pomp and ceremony. Robert Peel, founder of the country's leading cotton-printing enterprise, did not see himself raised to a baronetcy; that was to wait for his son, the father of the great prime minister. Honours for successful industrialists were sparse indeed. 'Our landed gentlemen reckon us poor mechanics no better than the slaves who cultivate their vineyards' remarked James Watt in 1787.[76] An appropriate sentiment if a strange image for Britain; it is indicative of a society which certainly esteemed its industrialists, even boasted of them, but offered them little honour within the system. When their supporters labelled them 'captains' or even 'lords' of industry, it had something of the protesting alternative about it, as had had the ironic poem of Manchester's Reverend Thomas Bancroft in 1777.

> Is it then, ye vain lordlings! ye treat us with scorn,
> Because titles and birth your own fortunes adorn?
> What worth to yourselves from high birth can accrue?
> Are your ancestors' glories, entailed upon you?
> And is your lazy pomp of much use to a nation?[77]

76. Bowden, *Industrial Society in England*, p. 155; P. Mantoux, *Industrial Revolution in the Eighteenth Century*, pp. 367, 388, 394–8.
77. *Ibid.*, p. 156.

CHAPTER FOUR
Middle-class Values

CHANGING LIFE-STYLES

Whether commented on by natives or remarked on by foreigners, the English middle ranks were usually first identified materially by the goods and services they purchased and by the status linked to and revealed by that consumption.[1] It was in part a circular definition, for many of the middle classes could also be identified as the providers of the increasing range of goods and services marketed in eighteenth-century England. The piano-ed parlours and poshly educated daughters of the farming middle ranks have already been mentioned. In towns the consumer culture was even more evident. According to their means, the urban middle classes purchased more or less of ordinary or superior quality. Their solid houses were well furnished and were beginning to be loaded with the bric-à-brac that the Victorians turned into a superabundance. Their tables bore richer meats, more imported 'groceries' and wines instead of ale. Their dress became fine and fashionable rather than serviceable, while their recreational aspiration to emulate the urban culture of those higher up provided a broad enough basis for genteel leisure to become commercialised. They were an employing class – not only of those who worked on their farms or in their shops, offices and workshops, but also of the increasing number of domestic servants. These came cheap, although moaning about their scarcity and quality became the standard topic of conversation for those above the lower orders. Only with the decline of domestic service did the English have to invent the weather. The number of servants

1. Only for the early years of the 'vital century', and then only for London is there a comprehensive attempt to reconstruct the material world of the middle classes: P. Earle, *The Making of the English Middle Class.* For the last years there is some coverage in Davidoff and Hall, *Family Fortunes.*

and, even more so, their specialisation was the most obvious gauge of status. According to Defoe in 1726, so many of the tradesmen and shopkeepers of London were keeping blue-liveried servants 'that they are called the tradesmen's liveries; and few gentlemen care to give blue to their servants for that very reason'.[2] He advised the small trading shopkeeper to think hard before considering early marriage. As a bachelor he could get by with a journeyman or apprentice and live over the shop, but with marriage came not only a house to be furnished but 'he must have a formal house-keeping, even at the very first; and as children come on more servants, that is maids or nurses, that are as necessary as the bread he eats'.[3]

Income rises brought extra servants as much for status as from necessity. Defoe created this specimen dialogue between a worried tradesman, of the more comfortable sort, and his wife when business began to turn down.

> Wife: Why first I keep five maids and a footman. I shall immediately give three of my maids warning, and the fellow also and save you that part of the expense.
>
> Husband: How can you do that? You can't do your business.
>
> Wife: There's nobody knows what they can do till they are tried. Two maids may do all my house-business, and I'll look after my children myself . . . . In order to abate the expense of living, I will keep no visiting days; I'll drop the greatest part of the acquaintance I have; I'll lay down our treats and entertainments and the like needless occasions of expense.
>
> Husband: But this, my dear, will make as much noise almost as if I were actually broke.[4]

Defoe's couple were clearly trying to stay on a high rung of the ladder, for no matter how far you climbed, the fearsome heads of long snakes could still be met on the ninety-ninth square. Most persons covered by the wide generic 'tradesman' settled at a more modest height. One of those who did rise high, however, has left a good description of his ladder. James Lackington, the inventor of cut-price book selling, looking back at the end of the eighteenth century, attributed his fortune to '*small profits*, bound by *industry*, and clasped by *economy*'.

> I have for many years expended two thirds of the profits of my trade; which proportion of my expenditure I never exceeded. In the

2. Daniel Defoe, *The Complete English Tradesman*, 1726, rept Alan Sutton, 1987, p. 85.

3. *Ibid.*, p. 97.

4. *Ibid.*, p. 103.

beginning, I opened and shut my own shop, and welcomed a friend by a shake of the hand. About a year after on such occasions I beckoned across the way for a pot of good porter. A few years after that, I sometimes invited my friends to dinner, and provided them a roasted fillet of veal; in a progressive course the ham was introduced, and a pudding was the next addition made to the feast. For some time a glass of brandy and water was a luxury; a glass of Mr Beaufoy's raison wine succeeded; and as soon as two thirds of my profits enabled me to afford good red port, it immediately appeared; nor was sherry long behind.

It was some years before I discovered that a lodging in the country was very conducive to my health. The year after, my country lodging was transformed into a country house; and in another year the inconveniences attending a stage coach were remedied by a chariot.[5]

Lackington may have made his rise visible with status symbols, but his careful phasing of it reveals that other and in a sense contradictory characteristic of the middle classes: the emphasis on the thrifty expenditure of both time and money. Lavish purchase of goods, it was cautioned, was fraught with danger for other than well-established tradesmen. Extravagant expenditure on leisure was even worse, for it wasted time as well as money. As Henry Fielding saw things, it could drag even the middle-class tradesman into the criminal ranks, especially if gambling was involved.

There is no greater degree of shame than the tradesman generally feels at the first inability to make his regular payments; nor is there any difficulty he would not undergo to avoid it. Here then the highway promises, and hath I doubt not, often given relief. Nay, I remember very lately a highwayman who confessed several robberies before me, his motive . . . to pay a bill that was shortly to become due.

Describing the experiences of a 'gentleman' who took his wife and two daughters to a masquerade and found that once the ladies had been satisfied in matters of dress, the total cost of a single night out amounted to three times the four guineas he had paid for the ticket, he continued: 'I am convinced that many thousands of honest tradesmen have found their expenses exceed their computation in a much greater proportion.'[6] Fielding was offering a condescending magisterial view on a matter to which Defoe had earlier directed a plainer homily.

5. From an extract from James Lackington, *Memoirs*, 1792, included in the excellent *Human Documents of Adam Smith's Time*, ed. E. Royston Pike, Unwin, 1974, pp. 100–2.

6. Henry Fielding, *An Inquiry into the Causes of the Late Increase in Robbers, 1751*, in collected works, ed. T. Roscoe, 1849, p. 763.

I know nothing is more frequent than for a tradesman, when company invites or an excursion from business presses, to say, 'Well, come, I have nothing to do; there is no business to hinder, there's nothing neglected, I have no letters to write', and the like; and away he goes to take the air for the afternoon, or to sit and enjoy himself with a friend – all of them things innocent and lawful in themselves; but here is the crisis of a tradesman's prosperity. In that very moment business presents, a valuable customer comes to buy, an unexpected bargain offers to be sold; another calls to pay money, and the like. . . .

The tradesman's pleasure should be in his business, his companions should be his books; and if he has a family, he makes his excursions upstairs and no further; when he is there a bell or a call brings him down.[7]

Changing habits among tradesmen, or 'citizens' as those of London were sometimes known, were commonly presented as a sign of degenerating times. It was remarked in 1796 that forty years earlier, 'a thriving tradesman was almost as stationary as his shop. . . . Born within the sound of Bow Bells he rarely ventured out of it, except perhaps once or twice a summer, when he indulged his wife and family with an expedition to Edmonton or Hornsey.' Things were now different, for the present-day tradesman was 'as seldom found in his shop as at church'. He left his shop to apprentices while he talked politics in coffee shops, and he spent his evenings 'at different clubs and societies'. He took his wife and daughters to a monthly assembly and from time to time to card parties. For two or three months in the summer he rented rooms in Margate or Brighton for his family to stay, 'dressed in every expensive piece of trippery then in vogue'. He over-educated his daughters and wrongly educated his sons. Depending increasingly on credit, the 'gentleman-like tradesman' ended his life in a debtors' gaol. His sons, forced into crime, ended theirs in Botany Bay and his daughters in a brothel.[8]

It is a familar enough parable. Defoe wrote its like seventy years earlier and Hogarth drew it twenty years after that. Both hyperbolic and generalised, its very familiarity over the eighteenth century testifies to a perpetual awareness of the bourgeois consumer. Yet within some writings can already be discerned the elements of a later nineteenth-century view of a virtuous commercial class to whom life was a serious business with expenditures controlled, proportionate and sensible and thrift a maxim. Thomas Turner, the Sussex shopkeeper diarist, represents a characteristic mixture. On his own

7. Defoe, *Complete English Tradesman*, pp. 90–1.
8. Pike (ed.), *Human Documents*, pp. 105–7.

admission he drank too much, usually in the company of the parish curate, but he was assiduous enough in business and efficient and conscientious in carrying out a range of parochial administrative duties. He did not really respect or cherish his wife, but significantly he knew that he ought to have. He never missed the chance to watch a cricket match, but in his prodigious reading he absorbed many titles of which the ghosts of Richard Baxter, Daniel Defoe or Benjamin Franklin would have approved.[9] What needs to be known is why it was the solid and worthy elements within the values of the bourgeoisie, rather than the flighty and extravagant ones, which later came to characterise not only their self-presentation but also the way others saw them.

Many careers in trade reveal an early period in which strict economy was essential, but attach it to a stage of life rather than present it as a continuing way of life. Further, although poverty can be looked back on with complacency or even mythologised into the 'humble origins' of self-made men, at the time it was actually experienced, great lengths were taken to hide it. 'The number of my customers was small, the prices I charged were very low, and what was worse some few got into debt with me and never paid their debts.' Thus Francis Place described the penury when he began to work for himself as a tailor. His wife begged him to return to journeywork but:

> I insisted upon it that I should work myself into a condition to become a master tradesman and should then be able to maintain my family respectably, that no hope of my ever being able to do this in any other way existed, and that nothing should therefore divert me from my purpose.

During this period, however, Place shared knowledge of his poverty only with his fretting wife.

> The few good cloaths we had left were taken great care of, and when out of the house we always made a respectable appearance and were generally considered by those who knew us as flourishing people, who wanted for nothing.[10]

Perhaps even more poignant was the hidden poverty of a West Country shoe maker setting up on his own in 1787. His sister, who kept house for him, recalled 'the distressing privations' of the first year.

---

9. D. Vaisey (ed.), *The Diary of Thomas Turner.*
10. M. Thale (ed.), *The Autobiography of Francis Place*, pp. 158–9.

. . . He obtained a great many genteel customers, and was obliged, in some degree, to keep up a creditable appearance. This frequently added to our difficulties. Towards the end of the first year, business increased so much, that he was compelled to employ a journeyman. He could not pay him board wages, and therefore the man was to live with us. We had two rooms, and but two beds; one I occupied, and in the other my brother and his apprentice slept. It was at length, after much reluctance on my brother's part, agreed to place my bed in his room for the man, and substitute mine by a bundle of straw. I used to carry on a little business of my own as a seamstress, and had many female acquaintances calling to see me; but after getting my straw bed, I would never admit them to my room, lest they should discover 'the nakedness of the land', and prejudice my brother's business.[11]

'Creditable' largely overlapped in meaning with 'creditworthy'. Defoe compared a young tradesman borrowing upon interest to 'a man going into a house infected with the plague'. It was a caution to some purpose in an age when the calling in of debts could bring not just the collapse of business but imprisonment. For as small a debt as £2 on the oath of a single creditor a small master or shop-keeper could be removed from his business and his family. Defenders of imprisonment for debt always stressed that it was protection of the small businessman from careless or inveterate non-payers that the law sought to provide. But it was a fine wire to tread. To obtain the imprisonment of a man for a debt, unless it was a matter of grudge, hardly improved the prospects of repayment while it much increased the general insecurity of the small and middling trading classes. As John Brewer has put it, 'To be in a man's debt was to be in his power, for it was he, in effect, who determined when the credit that he had extended transmuted itself into a debt for which one had legal liability.'[12]

Perhaps a fraught dependency on interest-bearing formal loans could be avoided at the beginning by borrowing only from friends or relatives and by making maximum use of any portion a well-chosen wife might bring, but everyday business for the trader or manufacturer was enmeshed in a matrix of credit, even if only in the simple form of book debts owed to suppliers and, usually, longer-standing ones due from customers. In London and other urban centres mutual trust, tolerance and assistance between trades-men kept things going so long as there was some hope. As a writer

11. J.H. Drew, *Samuel Drew, M.A. The Self-taught Cornishman*, Ward & Co., 1861, pp. 69–71.

12. J. Brewer, 'The commercialisation of politics' in McKendrick, Brewer and Plumb, *Birth of a Consumer Society*, p. 211.

commented in 1788: 'Distressed tradesmen in general form a connection in keeping open their shops, by drawing bills upon one
another, in being bail for each other, and having an attorney to
defend all actions brought against them.' There were formal ar-
rangements, especially mortgages, through which small masters in
the building trades and more widely obtained finance to continue
or increase their businesses, but much more widespread was a world
of private agreements and allowances largely unrecoverable by the
historian. Where journals or similar writings have survived they document a world of intricate and widespread credit. The northern
shopkeeper Abraham Dent, for example, extended credit on
around half of his sales to customers who included clergymen, shoe
makers, lawyers, medical men, building tradesmen and publicans.[13]

There seems a measure of agreement among its historians that
the interacting combination of attitudes which has defined the
nineteenth-century middle class, or at least that section of it sometimes described as 'businessmen', became increasingly evident in
the last years of the eighteenth century and that from then and
over the first quarter of the nineteenth, the middle class in its modern sense was born. According to Professor Perkin:

> At some point between the French Revolution and the Great Reform
> Act, the vertical antagonism and horizontal solidarities of class emerged
> on a national scale from and overlay the vertical bonds and horizontal
> rivalries of connection and interest. That moment saw the birth of
> class.[14]

One might well wonder about 'moments' in social history, but the
suggested dating is appropriate for the middle class at least. Perkin's suggestion, that the articulation of a middle-class interest *separate* from that of the upper class was inevitably delayed by a shared
fear of a revolutionary working class so long as the French wars
were in train, is a reasonable explanation of the delayed emergence
of a middle-class consciousness despite its increasing economic
power.[15] Asa Briggs in an influential article also saw a middle class
revealed by 1815: 'Between 1776 and 1815, however, the numbers
and wealth of the "owners of capital" increased and both their
public grievances and their public claims were advocated with en-
ergy and persistence.' A sense, perhaps exaggerated, of the burdens
they had borne during the French wars helped. Pitt's income tax

13. *Ibid.*, pp. 207–8.
14. H.J. Perkin, *Origins of Modern English Society*, p. 177.
15. *Ibid.*, pp. 194–5.

was a major contributor here. As the *Monthly Magazine* asked in 1809, why should there be rejoicing in the continuing war 'while the burden of taxation presses so heavily on the middle classes of society, so as to leave the best part of the community little to hope and everything to fear'? Very soon statements representing the 'position' of the middle class were about more than grievances, and had begun to stress the middle class as the dynamic progressive element in the nation; high self-estimation was becoming a characteristic, making a common use of language anticipated by the *Monthly Magazine* in 1798 when it pronounced the middle ranks to be those in which 'the great mass of information, and of public and private virtues reside'.[16]

The most recent historians of the middle class agree that it was the crisis of the last decade of the eighteenth and early years of the nineteenth century which 'brought out common interests and drew its disparate membership together' and point out that the process of class identification was more apparent in the provinces than in the capital.[17] If based only on a perception of shared interests and an increasing awareness of economic power, then middle-class consciousness would have had little ideological force or sense of legitimation. Total belief in the market as arbitrator and justifier would not in itself have been sufficient. Even Adam Smith's metaphor of the 'invisible hand', which ensured that the commonwealth benefited from the unchecked pursuit of individual self-interest, smacks of the theological, and it was to be the religious idiom provided by the evangelical revival which offered a belief system. It could not only support a rational outlook on life, eschewing superstition as well as indulgence, but could coexist with the rapacity often involved in the active pursuit of commerce and the not-noticeably Christian values of the market place.

THE ROLE OF RELIGION

Doctors Hall and Davidoff join Professor Perkin in seeing the role of religion as crucial in that it was growing nonconformity as well as an autonomous desire for independence which, by the end of the eighteenth century, was breaking down the many affinities which

16. A. Briggs, 'Language of class', pp. 53–4.
17. Davidoff and Hall, *Family Fortunes*, p. 18.

the middle ranks had previously shared with the landed upper classes. Perkin has described religion as 'the midwife of class'. In a sense it had to be so, for dissent from the established Church was the most significant manifestation of opposition in the 'old' society. William Pitt was speaking for his class, apart perhaps from a small and low-profile group of Catholics, when in 1796 he declared the established Church to be 'so essential a part of the constitution that whatever endangered it would necessarily affect the security of the whole'. This negative view of dissenters displaced among many of the ruling class the previous toleration. It reflected the insecurity of the French Revolutionary years as well as both the growth of religious dissent and its increasing concern to remedy its position of legal disadvantage and political exclusion.[18]

There is a beguilingly simple sociological view of eighteenth-century religion which sees the Anglican Church as that of the landed ruling classes and their dependants from tenant farmers through custom-dependent tradesmen to 'tied' labourers, as well as of the large numbers to whom religion did not matter a great deal. It also sees Methodism as the church of the increasing population of mining and manufacturing workers who could be independent in many cases of squirearchical constraint. Dissent, for Methodists in the eighteenth century were not nonconformists, is viewed as largely confined to the middle ranks, whether wealthy Quaker manufacturer or staunch tradesman Baptist. It serves as a starting point. Most Methodists were from the lower orders, and few dissenters came from other than the middle classes. What it must not suggest, however, is that most of the lower orders followed John Wesley, or that most of the middle ranks were to be found outside the established Church. In all social groups *most* people were at least nominally Church of England. Nor was there any marked trend away from this situation of a very general conformity until the last years of the century.

The importance of Methodism will be considered in the next chapter. Here it is the role of dissent in defining a middle class which is our concern. By the time of the Hanoverian succession, Protestant nonconformity had experienced both an absolute decline in numbers and a contraction of its social base. On the one hand the aristocracy closely followed by the gentry withdrew, while on the other there was precious little recruiting from the lower

18. Perkin, *Origins of Modern English Society*, pp. 196, 207; Davidoff and Hall, *Family Fortunes*, p. 23.

orders. In a sense, therefore, dissent became bourgeois by default and it became so in both senses: predominantly middle class and over-whelmingly urban. Falling numbers hardly went with serious preten-sions of challenging the domination of the established Church. Protestant nonconformists of all kinds had numbered around 300,000 in 1700, about 5 per cent of the population. By 1740 there were only half as many, and of these perhaps only 50,000 were no-ticeably committed. The main legacy of post-Restoration tolerance was not the rise of nonconformity as the result of allowing the dedi-cated to worship in their own way, but declining church attendance as the indifferent interpreted tolerance not so much as the right to alternative worship but as the right to stay away. An Oxfordshire rector pointed out in 1738 that more people went nowhere than went to the dissenting chapels.[19]

Nonconformity was therefore dominated by the urban middle ranks, from successful merchants and manufacturers down to seri-ous tradesmen. It is true that the Act of Toleration applied only to worship and removed none of the civil disabilities which still ex-cluded dissenters from attendance at university and from govern-ment at national, county or civic level. Dr Porter has suggested that those on the rise who could 'stomach the farce of occasionally tak-ing Anglican communion' could still go far. Mid-eighteenth-century parliaments usually contained around forty such men, and more than that achieved corporate office, even to the point of becoming mayors of major cities like Nottingham. If there was a trend it was away from nonconformity rather than into it as successful business-men like Ambrose Crowley, the Barclays and after a couple of generations the Darbys became Anglicans to facilitate their accept-ance into county society.[20] Most successful men would not have had to make that recantation, for as Professor Minchinton pointed out of eighteenth-century merchants, the importance of dissent has been exaggerated: 'most merchants like most Englishmen adhered to the Established Church'. Dissenting merchants were, however, noticeable in several leading ports. In Bristol in the 1760s and 1770s half of the merchants engaged in the Atlantic trades were Presby-terians, as were several leading merchants of Whitehaven. At Liver-pool and Exeter Unitarians were more prominent, and examples of Quaker merchants can be provided for several ports from Falmouth to Liverpool. But Anglican merchants were also plentiful: at Bristol the Hobhouses, the Frekes, Henry Cruger, John Noble and George

19. A.D. Gilbert, *Religion and Society* p. 11; R. Porter, *English Society*, p. 195.
20. Porter, *English Society*, p. 187.

Daubeny; at Liverpool Bryan Blundell and the Cunliffes; in Whitehaven the Kelsicks, while at Hull there were practically no dissenters
among the leading merchants, although the port did become a
centre of Anglican evangelicalism, symbolised today by the prominent statue of William Wilberforce.[21]

Why, then, has the idea of a strong link between nonconformity
and business success played such a large part in explanations of the
growth of enterprise in eighteenth-century England? In the first
place because some very important merchants and manufacturers
did come from their ranks and because some dissenting sects, for
example the Quakers, did provide entrepreneurs in numbers out of
proportion to their populations. This sect, which was in fact in decline and numbered only 20,000 by 1800, half the level of 1700, was
especially prominent in the metal industries with ironmasters like
the Darbys and Wilkinsons and the dominant London Lead Company, as well as bankers like the Peases and Barclays. The roll of
successful Quaker businessmen would be a long one, justifying the
claim that they formed 'a muster of undissipated industrial talent
unmatched elsewhere in the eighteenth century world'. The Quakers were exceptional and indeed the mutual support, especially financial, available within their small world had as much to do with
their success as any special attitude, education or motivation. The
assumption that because they were excluded from state employment, able dissenters had to seek success in other spheres is logical,
as is the related argument that being excluded from the universities, they received a more relevant education at dissenting academies. Both doubtless are justified by reference to a number of life
histories, but in fact only a small number of successful merchants
exhibit them. Minchinton has pointed out that of 361 listed in the
Dictionary of National Biography, only forty-four were educated at dissenting academies, significantly fewer in fact than those who went
to public schools. Interesting case studies apart, the dissenting tradition hardly seems to have been a *sine qua non* for the economic
development of Hanoverian England.[22]

In the second half of the eighteenth century the number of dissenters, Quakers excepted, increased significantly. Especially after
1790 there was 'an ominous growth of extra-Establishment religion'.
Congregationalists, Independents and Baptists expanded hugely, although Presbyterians less so. Licensing figures for places of worship

21. W.E. Minchinton, 'Merchants in England', p. 66.
22. Porter, *English Society*, pp. 198–9; Minchinton, 'Merchants in England', p. 65.

show that whereas only 95 Independent Baptist congregations were formed from 1700 to 1749, 269 were established between 1750 and 1799 with a further quickening in pace after 1800. In 1808 there were 532 Baptist churches compared with 200 in 1751. In general the practice of Old Dissent had been hardly more demanding than that of Anglicanism, but New Dissent, the dynamic force in the latter part of the century, was much more enthusiastic and preached for conversion. It also had a wider social appeal, recruiting especially strongly among the lower tradesmen and the artisan ranks of the working class. It is this growth which has been seen as an essential precondition for the emergence of class society. The quiet, small-scale nonconformity of the early eighteenth century had posed no threat, but even though the number of truly radical Rational Dissenters like William Price or Joseph Priestley, who did explicitly link religious with political agitation, was small, the sheer increase in the population of those who had overtly rejected the Church of England, by law established, amounted to a fundamental and irreparable rupture of the dependency system of the *ancien régime*. And a ruling class prepared to ferment destructive 'Church and King' mobs against the likes of Priestley and Price was well enough aware of this. From at least 1790 there could not even be the pretence that England was a 'confessional society'.[23]

The alienation of so many, although not the majority, from the Church of their rulers was a breach in the vertical consciousness of eighteenth-century society, but the growth of nonconformity, along with that of Methodism, which despite all the protestations of its leaders was never considered by many of the landed ruling classes as other than a form of dissent, had a more positive dimension. As well as being a form of emancipation and, inherently, a form of social protest, it inculcated values which endorsed the aspirations and enhanced the confidence of middling persons from merchants and manufacturers to shopkeepers and tradesmen. Central to their emerging value system was an emphasis on domesticity and on the 'private' world of the home. 'Home life' came into being with the middle class.

23. Gilbert, *Religion and Society* p. 35. That England before the end of the second decade of the nineteenth century was both an '*ancien régime*' and a 'confessional society' is the controversial view put forward in J.C.D. Clark, *English Society*.

MIDDLE-CLASS WOMEN

Several historians have discerned a trend over the eighteenth century for middle-class wives to retreat to the home front. The numbers actively participating in the family business declined. Keeping a wife in a home separate from the shop became a mark of status, an emulation of 'gentility' affordable by the rising incomes of increasing numbers.[24] Early in the century, Defoe had seen things differently. For him one of the main purposes of employing domestic servants had been to free the wife for business and he bemoaned an increase in wages which might mean that an ordinary tradesman's wife, 'who might be useful in his shop or business, must do the drudgery of household affairs'. Not that he saw marriage in purely functional terms. He valued domesticity and would not have wished the 'Complete English Tradesman' to disdain the comfort and pleasure of sitting before the fire with his wife and children.

> That tradesman who does not delight in his family will never delight long in his business; for as one great end of an honest tradesman's diligence is the support of his family, so the very sight of, and above all, his tender and affectionate care for his wife and children is the spur of his diligence.

But this fireside was upstairs, over the shop, with a bell to allow prompt recall to business. He was aware that there were wives who 'scorn to be seen in the counting house, much less behind the counter', while 'as to business, she shall not stoop to touch it'. Defoe was especially concerned that unpractised wives would be unable, if widowed, to carry on the business until sons were of age to take over. In fact the directories of most towns reveal that widows carried on a wide range of businesses, not only in retail. If growing wealth and spreading ideas of refinement did bring the increasing confinement of middle-class women to the home, it was a trend which became pronounced only in the last decades of the eighteenth century and characteristic only in the early decades of the nineteenth. Keeping the wife at home was, for most of the eighteenth century, an aspiration centred on considerations of status and on pretensions to gentility. It later became something much more than that.[25]

As the eighteenth century drew to an end, the middle-class world

---

24. For example I. Pinchbeck, *Women Workers and the Industrial Revolution 1750–1850*, Cass, 1969, Chapter 12.

25. Defoe, *Complete English Tradesman*, pp. 91, 204.

– one as assertively distinct from that of the upper classes as it was from that of the lower orders – was beginning to develop. Critical to this emerging sense of class identity was the acceptance of a division between the 'private' and the 'public' and the organisation of sexual difference to correspond to it. The family emerged as the crucial unit of mediation between the two worlds. As Doctors Davidoff and Hall have put it: 'The apparently autonomous individual man celebrated in both political economy and evangelical religion, was almost always surrounded by family and kin who made possible his individual actions.'[26]

Evangelical religion, especially in the socially conservative Anglican form through which the likes of Hannah More linked piety and duty to the world of place and rank, presented a 'holy' family in which the domestic role and subordinate position of the woman was not only appropriate but ordained and proper. It was as important in this as in other respects in forwarding the growth of a nineteenth-century middle class which prided itself on domestic moderation, displacing an eighteenth-century one which had sought to emulate the aristocratic style of lavish display and highly conspicuous consumption. The 'separate spheres' for men and women became more rather than less emphasised as middle-class men began to seek greater political participation at the national level. In their agitation for the vote, middle-class radicals did not dispute the view expressed by the greatest upper-class radical parliamentarian of the late eighteenth century, Charles James Fox in 1797, that women should not have the vote because both nature and convention had made them dependent on men and therefore 'their voices would be governed by the relations in which they stand to society'.[27]

POLITICAL CHANGE

In this matter the eighteenth-century historian must be reticent in his claims, for he discerns only the beginnings of a cultural formation far from general and far from mature. Equal reticence is called for in considering the political situation of the middling people, for it has become increasingly agreed that in so far as the Great Reform

26. Davidoff and Hall, *Family Fortunes*, p. 33.
27. Catherine Hall, 'Private persons versus public someones: class, gender and politics in England, 1780–1850' in C. Steedman, C. Unwin and V. Walkerdine (eds), *Language, Gender and Childhood*, Routledge, 1985, p. 15.

98

Act of 1832 enfranchising the male middle class was a political landmark, it was one reached after only a short period of widely supported agitation of surprisingly low intensity until the very eve of
reform. Even then the force came from the working-class reformers,
while the spoils went to the bourgeoisie. The two related aspects of
parliamentary reform were the recognition of the growing economic power of the middle class and the representation of their
urban strongholds, like Manchester and Birmingham, which still
sent no members to Westminster. Yet eighteenth-century manufacturers have been described as 'indifferent in respect to reform'.
When Pitt's unsuccessful motion for reform was being debated in
1783, considerable embarrassment was caused to its proponents
when it was discovered that Manchester and Birmingham were not
among the petitioning towns. 'What horrid sound of *silence* doth
assail mine ear?' sneered Lord North.[28]

Most eighteenth-century historians would agree with E.P. Thompson's
view that for most of the eighteenth century the growing middle
class posed no real challenge to the aristocratic domination of the
political system.

> Such a class did not begin to discover itself (except, perhaps in
> London) until the last three decades of the century . . . we can find
> no industrial or professional middle class which exercises an effective
> curb upon the operations of predatory oligarchic power.[29]

Even Christopher Wyvill's Association Movement for reform in the
late 1770s was essentially a *county* movement, not one organised by
the urban bourgoisie.

True as this may be, that they did not contest for power does not
mean that the middle classes were either without political influence
or that they were politically ineffective. We must also ask *why* the
middle classes were 'content to submit'. Part of the answer, as we
have seen, lies in the middle-class deference to aristocratic values
and cultural leadership. The other part, however, is the governing
class's acceptance of what are usually considered the 'bourgeois'
values of the market and its willingness to recognise the importance
to the nation of trade, especially in employment-creating manufactures. When eighteenth-century Britain went to war it did so for
commercial rather than dynastic reasons. With no opposing ideology to defeat, the men of commerce and manufacturing sought to
advance their interests through contact, petition and pressure.

28. W. Bowden, *Industrial Society in England*, p. 162.
29. E.P. Thompson, 'Eighteenth-century English society', p. 143.

While the trading interests of London and the great incorporated towns had a parliamentary presence, it was not one which intended to form a 'party' in its own right; rather it acted from time to time as an in-house pressure group – or rather groups, for mercantile interests represented were diverse and sometimes contending. When the General Chamber of Manufacturers of Great Britain was formed following the initiative of Josiah Wedgwood and Matthew Boulton, it aspired to the same kind of influence that it considered merchants had long possessed. It came into being in a particular situation – apprehension from the proposed freeing of trade with Ireland and France – and it came in the wake of several more local organisations, such as that of the Yorkshire worsted manufacturers in 1777 which sought enhanced powers to suppress embezzlement by weavers.[30] The Manchester 'committee for the protection and encouragement of trade' represented the cotton, linen, silk and smallware manufacturers from 1774; Birmingham's manufacturers, stung to action by a legislative threat to its brass manufacture, organised themselves from 1783, and there is evidence of other manufacturers' organisations appearing in this period among Staffordshire potters and the ironmasters of several Midland counties.[31]

Boulton was generally sympathetic towards parliamentary reform but seems to have been far from eager to push the claims of Birmingham because he feared the tumults associated with contested eighteenth-century elections would be good for neither order nor business. A letter writer to the *Leeds Intelligencer* in 1792 shared this view.

> It is notorious that elections promote profligacy, immorality and indolence; it is equally notorious that those manufacturing towns (such as ours and Manchester) which delegate no Members are in a more prosperous condition than those which elect their Representatives.[32]

Wedgwood, a one-time supporter of the American Revolution, insisted that he never 'intermeddled' in politics unless the interests of himself and his fellow industrialists were threatened by government. Any tendency away from operating an interest in politics *within* the system towards strong support for radical reform of the constituencies and of the franchise was postponed by the fear of an emerging political consciousness among the lower orders which dominated

30. Perkin, *Origins of Modern English Society*, p. 29.
31. Bowden, *Industrial Society in England*, pp. 164–93.
32. C. Emsley, 'Revolution, reform and British elites *c.* 1780–1832' in Emsley, *British Elites 1750–1870*, Open University, 1974, pp. 14–15.

the French Revolutionary years. A serious and more widely supported middle-class reform movement emerged only after the war. Even a campaign in 1811–13 to revoke the Orders in Council and end the monopoly of the East India Company succeeded through employment of the old methods. The great fear of *popular* radicalism was much assuaged by the victory of conservative Europe celebrated at the Congress of Vienna in 1814, while the Corn Law of 1815 served as the most blatant of reminders that, however accommodating to the needs of commerce and manufacturing the unreformed parliament might be most of the time, it would still put the landed interest first.

That the middle-class drive for parliamentary reform did not gain momentum until the second and third decades of the nineteenth century does not mean that earlier developments were without importance. As Dr O'Gorman has recently shown, for every unrepresented town of size and for every 'closed' borough constituency enjoyed without challenge by its patron, there were several where electoral success depended upon an electorate that was usually from 50 to 60 per cent middle class. The unreformed electorate was approaching a million by the early eighteenth century, and well past it by 1831. Historians have noted that, even so, few borough elections were contested after the early eighteenth century, but that does not mean that electors of the 'middling sort' could be taken for granted. To make sure of success the landed interest was forced, in this field at least, to associate with men of that rank and if there were few contests, then that is a measure of their ability to harmonise interests.

> . . . the close identification between the landed order and the merchant/manufacturing class prevented, or at least delayed, the emergence of a potential rival. More broadly an electoral system in which the middling orders could play such an indispensable political role also enabled their ideas in politics both local and national, in religion and in economics, to gain acceptance and legitimacy. The transition from one political and electoral system to another was effected in 1832 with such little disruption, largely because of the capacity of the unreformed system to make accommodations and compromises with the middling orders.[33]

The influence of manufacturers on county elections in the west Midlands has been demonstrated by Dr Money.[34]

33. F. O'Gorman, 'The unreformed electorate of Hanoverian England: the mid-eighteenth century to the Reform Act of 1832', *Social History*, XI, 1, 1986, p. 52.

34. J. Money, 'Birmingham and the West Midlands'.

Historians of the conservative tendency have ever since Namier's assertive work on the structure of Hanoverian politics been prone to understate the pre-1832 electoral importance of this growing group. But as important for the development of their nineteenth-century political consciousness was the increasing sense of *independence* displayed by the eighteenth-century middle classes. We have already noted that one important manifestation of this was a large increase in dissent in the latter part of the century, but it was not the only one. John Brewer has perceptively noted that the widening of the consumer market was bound to weaken the clientage ties of important sections of the bourgeoisie to the aristocracy and gentry.[35] This was a precondition for the support of John Wilkes at the polls and in the streets in 1766 and 1768. Nor was the Wilkes incident a wholly isolated example of the engagement of the lower middle class in electoral politics in the early Hanoverian years. In the Westminster constituency so close to the seat of power, the ruling Whig faction only just scraped home against strongly and noisily supported popular candidates in 1741 and 1749.[36]

While all this qualifies the image of an eighteenth-century society as deferential in politics as in manners, it does not make such contesting typical. But the support of the electorate in the four out of five constituencies which were boroughs was no simple matter of deference to the 'rule of the landed'. To secure or maintain their control, the gentry had to perform considerable services in parliament, especially in securing private improvement acts. The real contribution of the eighteenth century to later electoral reform was the establishment of the prerequisite 'independence' from the patronage and power of the establishment. Manifested in the astonishing late-century growth in dissent and in the expansion of the market which first reduced and eventually marginalised the 'client economy', it would sooner or later seek recognition in fuller membership of the political nation. It was a matter of worth. As Joseph Priestley, the Birmingham dissenter and reformer, put it, a successful man needed 'a constant feeling of his own power and importance'. When, after the delaying interlude of the war of 1793–1815, middle-class reform agitation revived, it was not because interests were at stake but because self-esteem demanded it.[37]

Middle-class political power was more evident in town than in

35. Brewer, 'Commercialisation of politics', pp. 197–9.
36. N. Rogers, 'Aristocratic clientage, trade and independency: popular politics in pre-radical Westminster', *Past and Present*, **61**, 1973, pp. 70–106.
37. Hall, 'Private persons versus public someones', p. 16.

national government. They participated locally at many levels. In the administration of urban parishes middle-class professional and commercial men played the role in supervising the Poor Law and in acting as key officers, such as constable, as did the farmers in the countryside. As Dr Schwarz has pointed out in respect of London, the social composition of some parishes meant that even the lower middle class were the natural fillers of their responsible offices. Professor Minchinton considered that locally the merchant class often displayed a degree of cohesion which enhanced their role as civic leaders, while as mayors and senior aldermen they provided the urban magistracy. The growth of civic ritual brought ceremony to enhance their power. In London the Court of Aldermen, twenty-six in number, was a small elite, more of an urban aristocracy than a bourgeoisie, but they shared power with the Court of Common Council which was made up of 234 freemen elected annually from the great livery companies who probably amounted to 10,000 voters. In the incorporated provincial towns the corporations exercised much power and even more influence. They levied rates, controlled parliamentary elections, regulated trades and markets, managed considerable urban property, administered charity and tried as hard as they could to perpetuate themselves. This last tendency to close ranks was, as the century progressed, much offset by the mushroom growth of Improvement Acts, through which parliament gave considerable powers to specified commissioners to sit alongside the old corporations in the regulation of building, paving and cleansing and in setting rates for these purposes. When the Southampton Commissioners were appointed in 1769, a leading citizen protested that it was 'an encroachment upon the right and privilege of the magistracy of this town', yet the archives reveal no disharmony between the specific commissioners and the town's common council. Southampton had deliberately followed the example of neighbouring Portsmouth and as one town followed another more than 300 individual acts were passed in the eighteenth and early nineteenth centuries. This widespread movement has been described as 'an important step towards what might be termed urban collectivism'.[38]

38. For local urban political structures and roles, see J. Walvin, *English Urban Life 1776–1851*, Hutchinson, 1984, pp. 68–9; Porter, *English Society*, pp. 140–2. For improvement acts see P. Corfield, *Impact of English Towns*, pp. 157–8; M. Falkus, 'Lighting in the dark ages of English economic history: town streets before the industrial revolution' in D.C. Coleman and A.H. John (eds), *Trade, Government and Economy in Pre-industrial England*, Weidenfeld, 1976, pp. 248–73. For the Southampton episode, see J. Stovold (ed.), *Minute Book of the Pavement Commissioners for Southampton 1770–1789*, Southampton UP, 1990, p. 4; E.L. Jones and M.E. Falkus, 'Urban improvement and the English economy in the seventeenth and eighteenth centuries' in P. Borsay, *Eighteenth-century Town*, p. 132.

In the growing commercial centres, many of which, like Birmingham, were not encumbered with the oligarchical ossification that incorporated status could bring, a vigorous urban middle-class 'club' culture was emerging which reinforced the ties of commercial interest. At least it did so for men, for the development of middle-class institutions and organisations tended to increase the marginalisation of women. The role of tavern or coffee-house clubs and lodges in the politics of the Wilkes era in London has been emphasised by Professor Brewer, but it was not confined to the capital. After 1780 especially, as Dr Morris has indicated, the urban middle class came to control through their domination of voluntary societies a whole range of aspects of urban life from poor relief, hospital and dispensary provision and administration, moral reform, public order, the diffusion of science and culture and the organisation of leisure. For the most part the gentry provided only a limited and occasional patronage. Morris has seen this development as forming a middle-class identity and as serving 'a vital function in developing the informal web of association that gave urban society a measure of coherence and community'.[39] In such associations, in clubs, in the debating societies stimulated by the American Revolution, in lodges as well as on corporations and chambers of commerce, through involvement in parish administration and as trustees of chapels, the urban middle class was finding its voice – auditioning, as Dr Porter has put it, 'for the national theatre of politics to come'.[40]

39. Brewer, 'Commercialisation of politics', p. 201; Hall, 'Private persons and public someones', pp. 16–19; R.J. Morris, 'Voluntary societies and British urban elites 1780–1850: an analysis' in Borsay, *Eighteenth-century Town*, pp. 338–66. See also Borsay's Introduction, p. 13.

40. Porter, *English Society*, p. 98.

CHAPTER FIVE

The Lower Orders

The 'lower orders' made up the bulk of the population. Describing them in more specific terms is a social historian's nightmare. The 'common people' has been popular but is no less general. The 'labouring poor' covers the majority who did work and who were less than comfortably off, but the truly poor were usually so because they could not work or could not get enough work, while many skilled journeymen earned more than small-holding freeholders. 'Working class' is anachronistic in implying a stage in class formation and consciousness which had hardly been reached even by 1815. Its plural, 'working classes', allows for differentiation and even hierarchy among the lower orders but still reflects nineteenth- rather than eighteenth-century usage. In a book spanning the years 1750 to 1850, the present writer opted for 'labouring classes'. It is still my preference.[1] For the most part the lower orders depended on selling their labour. For an artisan elite it was skilled labour power sold at a premium, but for most men and almost all working women it was unskilled labour. Only a small fraction would elude this category if we accept that, contrary to much contemporary opinion, paupers were largely made up not of a delinquent or a wilfully dependent population but of those who could not work either through incapacity or age, or who could not, in the vagaries of the labour market, find work.

Of the divisions of English society suggested by Defoe in 1709 –

> The great, who live profusely
> The rich, who live plentifully
> The middle sort, who live well
> The working trades, who labour hard, but feel no want

1. J.G. Rule, *Labouring Classes*. For contemporary usages and a demonstration that 'class' was increasingly used by the late eighteenth century, see P. Corfield, 'Class by name and number', pp. 38–61.

> The country people, farmers, etc. who fare indifferently
> The poor who fare hard
> The miserable, that really pinch and suffer want.[2]

– we are concerned with all but the first three, as he clearly meant poor small-holders by 'farmers' in his fifth category. Defoe provided a further, more useful categorisation in 1728.

> Those concerned in the meaner and first employments are called in common, working men or labourers, and the *labouring poor* such as the mere husbandman, miners, diggers, fishers and in short, all the drudges and labourers in the several productions of nature or of art. Next to them, are those who, though labouring perhaps equally with the other, have yet some art mingled with their industry, and are to be particularly instructed and taught how to perform their part, and those are called workmen or handicrafts.
>   Superior to these, are the guides or masters, in such works or employments, and those are called artists, mechanics or craftsmen; and in general all are understood in this one word mechanics; such are clothiers, weavers etc. handicrafts in hardware, brass, iron, steel, copper etc.[3]

'Mechanic' was not the only term used to describe skilled workmen. 'Artificer' was then used more widely than in its later application to the royal dockyards and the Navy. 'Artisan' could embrace many independent craftsmen trading in their own product from their own shops, but it usually covered as well those skilled manufacturers dependent on work put out by merchant capitalists and wage-earning journeymen on employers' premises. In short, those who claimed possession of a trade. What proportion of the labouring classes did they comprise?

In 1759 Joseph Massie estimated that 228,000 families were supported by metal, wood and textile manufactures. He estimated that below them were 462,000 families of labourers and cottagers, 60,000 dependent on the earnings of common seamen and 18,000 on those of common soldiers. This would suggest that around 30 per cent of the 'living-out' labouring classes were to some extent skilled, but if living-in servants of all classes are included the proportion would shrink to a quarter and if unskilled 'manufacturers' are removed, we can conclude that at least a fifth of the men of the labouring classes of the eighteenth century were more or less skilled, that is had something other than 'common' labour power to

2. Cited in P. Earle, *The World of Daniel Defoe*, Weidenfeld & Nicolson, 1976, p. 164.
3. Daniel Defoe, *A Plan of the English Commerce*, 1728, rept Blackwell, 1928, p. 3.

offer on the labour market.[4] The true fraction is higher, but no eighteenth-century listing distinguished between specialist and general farm labourers. The number of shepherds, stockmen, etc. is simply not known, but it is still the case that employed artisans made up a significant proportion of the urban male population. Dr Linebaugh has discovered that around 40 per cent of those hanged at Tyburn in the middle years of the eighteenth century had completed apprenticeships and a further 20 per cent had at least begun one (see pp. 230–1) Even in London, the greatest centre of artisan manufacture, not all apprenticeships led to a skilled trade – the unfortunate climbing chimney boys for example – but it would seem reasonable to suggest that around half of the working men of the capital were to some degree skilled, in the sense of selling specialised labour. They are the fraction of whom we know most. They were more literate, more organised, more articulate and more regularly employed. We know less of common labourers and less again of working-class women.

The fully independent craftsman owning the materials on which he worked and selling the product of his own labour was much in a minority by the middle of the eighteenth century. There are, however, other degrees of 'independence'. The control of the out-working artisan or small-workshop craftsman over the rhythm and intensity of his working week was one which survived, for the most part, until the factory age. But by a proud assertion of 'independence', an eighteenth-century artisan more likely would have been referring to his ability to maintain a wife and family at a proper standard without recourse to charity or poor relief. When, in 1808, the cotton weavers were forced to work a sixteen-hour day for a subsistence wage, they complained bitterly: 'there never was a time before the present when the workman could not live by his trade'. Living by his trade meant more than surviving. It meant the ability to educate and supervise his own children rather than be driven to place them in the mill, and to preserve a customary lifestyle. The compositors put the matter clearly in 1810.

> The profession of a man should always be equal to the support of himself and family in a decent way. They should be supplied with not

---

4. See P. Mathias, 'The social structure in the eighteenth century: a calculation by Joseph Massie' in P. Mathias (ed.), *The Transformation of England*, Methuen, 1979, pp. 171–89.

merely what will preserve animation, but what custom has rendered necessary for their comfort.[5]

When crisis hit the watch-making trade in 1817, the distressed watch makers looked back on prouder days when, if misfortune did befall one of their number, the 'trade' not the poor rate would have taken care of him.

> [Around 1800] persons . . . were enabled by their skill and industry to maintain themselves and families in a state of comfort and respectability; and to keep their own houses and pay taxes, scot and lot, and contribute towards the maintenance of other persons in their profession, who were either sick or in distress, so that it was scarcely known that any person in this trade ever applied for parochial relief.[6]

THE 'ARTISAN CULTURE'

Clearly, any notion of a distinctive 'artisan culture' is a conditional one. As a description of a life-style and material standard it is applicable to times of normal and good earnings but may lose its distinctive characteristics in trades under pressure of falling incomes and growing insecurity. This was not simply from poverty but also because such times were often associated with longer hours of working, which pressurised leisure. It was leisure as well as material gain which marked the 'golden ages'. Radcliffe's description of the period 1788–1803 for Lancashire cotton weavers mingles experience and myth but conveys something of the style of the good times: 'Their dwellings and small gardens clean and neat – all the family well clad – the men each with a watch in his pocket, and the women dressed to their own fancy – the church crowded to excess every Sunday – every house well furnished.'[7]

Samuel Bamford's father was a muslin weaver at the time. He was full of book knowledge and interested in mathematics and astronomy. He could play the flute and compose verse. Bamford remarks that such talents were 'not often possessed by men of his condition in society' at that time and that he stood 'far above his rustic

---

5. *Report of SC on Petitions of Several Cotton Manufacturers and Journeymen Cotton Weavers*, II, BPP, 1808 (177), p. 6; E. Howe, *The London Compositor, 1785–1900*, Oxford UP, 1947, p. 391.

6. *Report from SC on the Petitions of the Watchmakers of Coventry*, VI, BPP, 1817 (504), p. 73.

7. Cited E.P. Thompson, *Making of the English Working Class*, pp. 304–5.

acquaintance in the village'. Before experiencing a Methodist conversion, Bamford senior had been a noted drinker and wrestler, but even at that time had had a taste for books. He may have been unusual, but that would lie in the range of his talents rather than in possessing any individual one of them. During such periods of high earnings weavers could allow their children an education. It has been suggested that literacy levels in these weaving villages were higher than they were to be in the industrial towns of south Lancashire a generation later.[8]

It is certainly possible to talk of an 'artisan culture' characterised by 'independence', by leisure interests which could embrace the 'improving', high levels of literacy, general awareness and a mutuality expressed though trade societies and a variety of clubs. William Hutton in his account of Birmingham published in 1781 described the 'low amusements' of the 'humbler class': the wakes – 'completely suited to the lowest of tempers' – bull baiting, skittles and ale. He also describes 'perhaps hundreds' of clubs among the artisans, including building and capital clubs as well as book clubs. Francis Place described a similar situation among London's artisans. Such life-styles were, however, fluctuating in two senses. For any particular trade a period of bad times could change things, and secondly, some trades could experience a permanent decline, leaving members with only a fading memory of better times. Professor Hobsbawm's argument for an 'aristocracy of labour' among nineteenth-century skilled workers depends upon the kind of material and cultural conditions and status assumptions which can certainly be found in the cases of some eighteenth-century crafts, but fluctuations in fortune make the idea less firmly applicable.[9]

If a 'respectable' artisan culture was emerging in late eighteenth-century England, was it coming about by a process of separation from a more embracing 'culture of poverty' which included the unskilled and casual labourer, the unemployed, the vagrant and the criminal? The culture of deprivation and poverty, of violence, crime and prostitution was an evident feature of eighteenth-century London, but how far removed from it were the city's artisans? Some trades were better than others, 'honourable' as opposed to 'dishonourable', and within some trades there were differences between a quality and a poorer end. The West End/East End distinction in

8. Samuel Bamford, *Early Days*, rept Cass, 1967, p. 2; M. Sanderson, 'Literacy and the industrial revolution', pp. 304–5.

9. William Hutton, *A History of Birmingham*, 1781, pp. 130–9; Francis Place, *Autobiography*, p. 106; E.J. Hobsbawm, *Labouring Men*, p. 273.

trades like shoe making and tailoring was well established by the end of the eighteenth century. Francis Place was the very type of the journeyman striver after independence and status, but he held off less reputable associations at only arm's length. His father had been something of a rough diamond, barely literate and excelling in 'drinking, whoring, gaming, fishing and fighting'. The young Francis had been educated with the sons of the better class of tradesmen. These youths were the friends and companions of his apprenticeship years. 'The class to which I belonged was by no means the lowest. The boys with whom I associated would not keep company with Journeymen excepting in their workshops, nor with lads whose fathers were not housekeepers.'

They considered themselves above parish apprentices, yet of the fellow members of the cutter club with whom he rowed on the Thames, Place recalled that the stroke was hanged for a murder he did not commit, not being able to provide an alibi as he was committing a burglary at the time, while the cox was transported for a robbery. Both of these young men had been printers. Most of the other apprentices robbed either their masters or other persons. This club was 'no better than many others'. Place's first master had three daughters who were prostitutes, a son who picked pockets and another who was a different sort of thief. His sister married a butcher who was a member of a family which kept a shop as a front for dealing in stolen goods. This brother-in-law was eventually hanged for highway robbery.[10]

Place believed that only since his youth in the 1780s had London's artisans begun to improve into a more 'respectable' class. He warned those who read his recollections:

> The circumstances . . . I have mentioned relative to the ignorance, the immorality, the grossness, the obscenity, the drunkenness, the dirtiness, and depravity of the middling and even of a large portion of the better sort of tradesmen, the artisans, and the journeymen tradesmen of London in the days of my youth, may excite a suspicion that the picture I have drawn is a caricature.

Subsequent improvement he attributed to better policing, education, including Sunday schools, stricter moral values and the availability of cotton underwear. He was sure, too, that drunkenness had declined, remarking of the tailors:

> I should say, they like all other journeymen, are greatly improved in morals. Twenty years ago few tailor shops were without a bottle of gin:

10. Place, *Autobiography*, pp. 17, 40, 71, 73–4, 121–2, 133–4.

the men drank as they liked; one kept the score, and the publican came at certain times to replenish the gin bottle. I suppose there is not a shop in London that has one now.[11]

'Now' was 1824 and Place was not the only witness before a select committee in that year to make this point. Print workers too were said to have improved in character: 'a printing office was like a public house on a Monday when I was an apprentice, and now we have no drinking at all'. The engineers were also said to have become better dressed, improved in their conduct and manners and much less given to drink: 'they are decidedly better men'. There was a dissenting opinion on the hatters but, from another source, William Lovett, we learn of a delayed improvement among the cabinet makers. Place was further of the opinion that what he described for London went for the country as a whole. While artisans certainly had better opportunities than had most of the lower orders, it is probably unwise to insist that a very wide behavioural gap separated them from the 'crowd', at least until the last years of the eighteenth century.[12]

To write of male artisans is tautologous. In the eighteenth century working-class women worked. In the Bedfordshire village of Cardington in 1752 the activity rate among females of age to work was a very high 82 per cent. But skill was a gendered concept. The evidence strongly suggests that it had become increasingly so since the seventeenth century. Campbell's survey of London trades in 1747 lists only a handful of female crafts all paid wages well below male trades. Two of them, mantua-making and millinery, he explicitly linked with prostitution.[13] Several new female occupations which emerged in the eighteenth century, such as the hand-decorating of china or hand printing of cottons, demanded great dexterity and control. They were well paid for women's work, but brought neither the status nor pay of male artisans. Bridget Hill has headed her chapter on women's work in the eighteenth century: 'Ignored, unrecorded and invisible.' It is a fair enough summary of what we know about the working lives of most women.[14]

11. *Ibid.*, pp. 14–15; *Report of SC on Artisans and Machinery*, V, BPP, 1824 (51), First Report, p. 25, Second Report, pp. 46, 55.

12. *Ibid.*, Second Report, p. 86; William Lovett, *Life and Struggles in Pursuit of Bread, Knowledge and Freedom etc*, 1876, rept MacGibbon and Kee, 1967, p. 25.

13. R. Campbell, *The London Tradesman*, 1747, rept David & Charles, 1969, pp. 208–9, 227–8.

14. B. Hill, *Women, Work, and Sexual Politics*, p. 148.

Women were important to the economy in general and especially so in manufacturing. In textiles more women were employed than men. However the modish concept of 'proto-industrialisation' (above pp. 4–5) has led to a dominant image of women's work as having been hidden because in rural cottage manufacturing it, as with the work of children, was subsumed in a family unit of production in which it was neither separately waged nor described. This pattern has come to be considered as something of a pre-industrial norm. It was, after all, to be found not only in textile manufacture, but in nailmaking and some branches of the metal smallware trade. These are the areas of manufacture to which the proto-industrialists have largely confined their researches. In fact many, almost certainly most, working-class women worked other than in their husband's employment. They contributed small earnings to supplement the husband's main wage. They were contributors to a family wage rather than independent earners, but they were not members of a family unit of production.

The vast majority of working-class women worked, but not in an occupation shared by husbands or fathers. Even when they worked in the same industry they were often employed in quite different processes: in copper mining for example at the surface not underground, and were separately waged. A study of women's occupations in London for the period 1695 to 1725 has found only 26 from a sample of 256 women who shared the occupation of their spouse and these were usually involved in retailing. The working-class wives of early eighteenth-century London earned from charring, laundry, nursing, making and mending clothes, hawking, silk-winding and in the catering and victualling services:

> The great majority of women were unable to work in male trades and, since nearly three quarters of women wanted to or had to work for a living, they necessarily competed intensely for the work which was left, much of it of a casual nature and none of it organised by gilds and livery companies.[15]

Few apart from servants and those running retailing shops would have expected to have been employed the whole year through. A description of 1678 is so close to the kind of situation which Mayhew would give of London in the mid-nineteenth century, that it must be taken as applying just as much to the eighteenth:

> a poor woman that goes three days a week to wash or scoure abroad, or

15. L. Earle, 'The female labour market in London in the late seventeenth and early eighteenth centuries', *Econ. H.R.*, XLII, 3, 1989, p. 342.

one that is employed in nurse-keeping three or four months in a year, or a poor market-woman who attends three or four mornings in a week with her basket, and all the rest of the time these folks have little or nothing to do.[16]

The problem was almost certainly worse and more rapidly deteriorating in the countryside, for most towns offered a greater range of casual opportunities and some offered special localised employment, such as glove making in Worcester or Ludlow. The larger households in town and country seem to have had washdays, not weekly, but even monthly, as Parson Woodforde did. Heating water etc. to cope with large quantities of laundry made for a periodic need to bring in extra labour over that maintained in the household. The wife of a Sussex shopkeeper paid a woman 18d (7.5p) in 1760 for coming in for two days, while Eden in 1794 reported that Lincolnshire women who went out to wash earned 6d to 8d (2.5 to 3p) a day. Such women would almost certainly have evaded recording in any listing of 'occupations'.[17]

Most commonly young women entered, and so long as they remained unmarried, stayed in domestic service. They and male servants were 'hidden' in a real sense. Neither Gregory King, Joseph Massie or Patrick Colquhoun listed living-in servants as a group. They were enumerated in the 'families' of those they served from the aristocracy through the gentry and middle class to the farmers and shopkeepers. In 1767 Jonas Hanway thought that one in thirteen of London's population was a domestic servant. He revised this to one in eight in 1775, a population of 80,000. In 1806 Colquhoun thought there were were 910,000 in England and Wales of whom 800,000 were female. For the young woman it was the obvious choice. As Sir John Fielding put it in 1758:

> The infinite variety of professions, trades, and manufactures joined to the army, navy and services, leave few men idle, unless from choice; whilst women have but few trades, and fewer manufactures to employ them. Hence it is, that the general resource of young women is to go to service.[18]

Increasing demand was largely met by country girls. The daughters of small farmers were best esteemed, but they were declining and the supply was made up from the cottages of artisans, shopkeepers and labourers. Servants were of course boarded. Higher servants

16. Cited *ibid.*, p. 342.
17. B. Hill, *Women, Work and Sexual Politics*, pp. 157–9.
18. *Ibid.*, pp. 126–8.

might get £10 a year on top but the lower servant girls only £2. Over 60 per cent of female servants in a London sample 1750 to 1760 received between £3 and £6. Rates outside London were lower. A considerable proportion, perhaps around a quarter in London, stayed in domestic service to rise up the steps of the profession. The cost, or perhaps the choice, was to stay unmarried. For most domestic servants though, the occupation was a temporary life-cycle one. Of a sample of 696 women derived from London settlement examinations 1750 to 1760, almost 60 per cent were between 15 and 29 years old, with only 10 per cent in their forties. Some married well, but most married back into the working class from which they had come. Many after all had served in households not much better than their own, for servant-keeping reached well down the social scale. Two-thirds of the London sample were employed in the homes of artisans, publicans and victuallers. Most were hired annually, and the employment did give young women a measure of choice and relative economic independence. Employers were changed regularly.[19]

Those who left service for marriage were as often as not entering an economically less secure situation: rarely one in which they could expect to be 'kept' in comfort. They were advised in 1743:

> You cannot expect to marry in such a manner as neither of you shall have occasion to work, and none but a fool will take a wife whose bread must be earned solely by his labour and who will contribute nothing towards it herself.[20]

Engels was to remark that since property was not a consideration, only the proletariat could marry for love. They could and often did, but that does not mean that practical considerations could be ignored: as a line in one of John Clare's poems has it: 'Love without money brings winter for life'. Even small dowries mattered. A young Cornish shoemaker married at the time he was setting up on his own: 'his wife's immediate fortune was ten pounds – a sum to him at that time, of great importance'. That does not mean he would not otherwise have married a woman, in whom, according to his son, 'he found an efficient substitute for his sister's domestic management, and a helpmate ready to second all his exertions'. This autobiography has nothing to say of courtship, but that, as Dr

---

19. D.A. Kent, 'Ubiquitous but invisible: female domestic servants in mid-eighteenth century London', *History Workshop Journal*, **28**, 1989, p. 115.
20. Cited in I. Pinchbeck, *Women Workers and the Industrial Revolution*, pp. 1–2.

Vincent has suggested, could well be because working-class autobiographers did not judge it a subject their readers wanted to know about, and many of them in any case lacked the command of an emotional language to describe their feelings. Samuel Bamford, the Lancashire weaver, has plenty to say of both serious romance and of dalliance in his youth at the beginning of the nineteenth century. He wrote love-letters for his less literate friends, as did William Lovett growing up in a fishing village at the other end of England. Both of these well-known working-class autobiographers wrote of courtship and its rituals. There is no reason at all to suppose they are unrepresentative in this respect.[21]

There is strong evidence to believe that Bamford was representative in another respect: their first child was present at the wedding. On the basis of an 8-month marriage to baptism gap in the parish registers, it has been estimated that more than 40 per cent of eighteenth-century brides were pregnant. Locally levels could be even higher. The prevalence of sexual intercourse before marriage is clearly indicated.

Historians have not suggested that this implies promiscuity. Rather it suggests that intercourse was normal once a couple began to 'keep company' and considered each other 'promised'. Pregnancy thus determined the timing rather than the fact of marriage. That is, assuming formal church marriage was intended at all. Bridget Hill has remarked that what constituted marriage among the eighteenth-century lower orders was 'anything but clearly defined', especially in the first half of the century before the passing of Hardwicke's Marriage Act. It seems clear that a wide range of liaisons, some permanent, others later resolved one way or the other, existed in both rural and urban areas. Nor is it clear that increasing sophistication, defined by literacy, or increasing religiosity, as brought for example to some communities by Methodism, made much difference in this respect.[22]

---

21. J.H. Drew, *Samuel Drew, M.A.: The Self-taught Cornishman*, Ward & Co., 1861, p. 85; D. Vincent, *Bread, Knowledge and Freedom: A Study of Nineteenth-century Working-class Autobiography*, Methuen, 1982, pp. 39–46; Rule, *Labouring Classes*, pp. 195–6.

22. Rule, *Labouring Classes*, p. 196; and especially P. Hair, 'Bridal pregnancy in rural England in earlier centuries', *Population Studies*, XX, 1976, pp. 233–43: B. Hill, *Women, Work and Sexual Politics*, p. 202.

POVERTY AND THE POOR LAW

By later standards and by those of their middle- and upper-class contemporaries, most labouring people were poor. But how many were unable to exist on their earnings without some degree of supplementation from poor relief? Obviously this population was not constant. The price of bread cereals, on which labouring families spent a vast proportion of their wages, fluctuated wildly. Using the most fundamental measure of poverty, the 'breadline', Professor Hay has estimated that over the years 1760 to 1802 in a normal year around 10 per cent of Staffordshire families would have been unable to buy sufficient bread over the year even if they had spent their whole earnings on it. In years of high prices 20 per cent would have been in this situation, while in extremely hard years, such as 1801, the proportion would have exceeded 40 per cent. This takes no account of other basic living costs like housing, clothing and medical care. Average cereal prices were seriously higher after 1760 than they had been in the early eighteenth century so there was less fluctuation around the breadline in the first half of the century, but the relief-dependent population was even so probably not much below 10 per cent in most parishes in most years and capable of rising much above that from time to time in localities affected by short- term unemployment of the kind that manufacturing slumps could bring even to the pre-industrial economy.[23]

Only a small section of the labouring poor was wholly or permanently dependent on poor relief, predominantly the old, the sick and the orphaned who made up the 'impotent' as opposed to the 'able-bodied'. Even quite elderly people, male or female, could often earn something towards their maintenance, while the practice of assisting low-wage earners with large families of young children was widespread. Gregory King, in his description of the population at the end of the seventeenth century, made a famous distinction between those who 'increased' and those who 'diminished' the wealth of the kingdom. Into the latter category, embracing all those groups whose *annual* expenditure exceeded their earnings, he put more than half of the population. But the average degree of deficiency was relatively small. For labouring people and out-servants the average income per head is given as £4 10s (£4.50) against an expenditure of £4. 12s (£4.60), while for cottagers and paupers, whom he considered to make up almost a quarter of the popula-

23. D. Hay, 'War, dearth and theft', pp. 131–3.

tion, the respective figures are £2 and £2 5s (£2.25). It has recently been suggested that King overstated the numbers of the really poor because he used too large a multiplier for family size, and that perhaps their proportion of the population was nearer to a seventh in most years. But at least a quarter lived in some kind of poverty, even if the degree of their deprivation stopped short of actual destitution.[24]

Women were more likely than men to be dependent on poor relief. In 1724 the Vicar of Piddletown in Dorset listed the inhabitants of his village house by house.[25] As well as noting occupations, he made occasional comments on specific instances of poverty. In one house lived a 'maiden' of seventy along with a 'poor and lame widow' and two sisters of sixty-five and fifty-nine. They were 'all poor and maintained by the Parish'. In another house lived two widows, one with a daughter of twenty-eight and the other with one of nineteen. This household is described as 'very poor'. In a third house lived a deserted woman – 'her husband lives from her'; she had two children out at service but had five still living at home. She was described as a 'poor woman'. Her family is described as 'infirm', and this may explain why even with two of her daughters grown women in their twenties the family was able to earn little, although it may also reflect the fact that earning opportunities for women were so poor that even able-bodied spinsters could not wholly maintain themselves. Old age and infirmity could come to men and women alike. A household consisting of a seventy-year-old man, his sixty-three-year-old wife and a thirteen-year-old grandson was described as poor, as was that of Thomas Stumey, 'an ancient man and a cripple'. Life-cycle poverty was a condition not confined only to the old. The first years of marriage with dependent infants and according severe earnings restrictions on wives were commonly difficult until the children were old enough to contribute. A carpenter and his wife with five children aged from three to fifteen are described as 'poor', as was the family of a miller – an occupation not usually associated with poverty – who had four children in a similar age range.

Seventy years later an even more detailed survey of another

---

24. King's calculations have been summarised and appended to several textbooks, for example to Porter, *English Society*, pp. 386–7; T. Arkell, 'The incidence of poverty in England in the later seventeenth century', *Social History*, XXII, 1, 1987, pp. 23–47.

25. The survey has been edited by C.L. Sinclair Williams, *Puddletown, House, Street and Family*, Dorchester, 1988.

Dorset town was made.[26] It confirms the pattern of poverty, although its level would seem to have risen significantly. In Corfe Castle women employed in the local out-work manufacture of knitting stockings could expect to earn only around a shilling or one shilling and sixpence (5–7½p) a week. This survey made in 1794 reveals that out of a population of 1,239, 370, almost a third, received some form of parish pay. Women again figure prominently. In one house three spinsters, all younger than fifty, earned only 4s 6d (22½p) between them, but presumably gained something from the rent paid by their lodger, a clay worker on 10s (50p) a week. Jane Webber, a sixty-six-year-old spinster, was the keeper of another house; she earned a shilling a week but had eight lodgers. They can have afforded her little in the way of rent. They comprised a widowed mason with two daughters, who was himself dying of consumption, and a widow of forty with four daughters aged from two to fourteen. Their combined earnings were 3s 6d (17½p). Clearly this entire composite household was dependent on poor relief. So too was Hannah Trent, who inhabited another cottage. She was only twenty-eight, but, having been deserted by her husband and left with children of one and two years old, she could earn only 2s 6d (12½p) a week by taking in washing.

As in Puddletown seventy years earlier, large families needed income supplementation. A clay cutter who earned 10s (50p) a week, to which was added a further 5s 6d (27½p) from his two teenage sons, still needed some supplementation as he had three young daughters to support. William White was the mole catcher, but he was seventy-three and earned only 3s (15p) a week from his occasional and rather specialised occupation. He received parish supplementation, even though he lived with a clay worker son, a bachelor on 10s (50p) a week.

Investigations of this kind reveal something of the structure of poverty by indicating those who were kept going by the poor rate, the only eighteenth-century tax which was redistributive. They do not reveal as much about the value of the relief received, or the degree of willingness with which it was paid. There is a high level of consensus among historians of the eighteenth-century Poor Law that relief in general was neither ungenerous nor ineffective. Research has markedly redressed the unfounded and ill-wishing treatment of it dished out by the zealots seeking to bring about the

26. The Corfe survey can be found in printed form only in the 1796 edition of G. Hutchins, *History and Antiquities of the County of Dorset.*

hardened approach to poverty eventually enacted in the harsh workhouse-based act of 1834. Before rising population and inflating prices for necessaries began to increase the burden on rate-payers from the last third of the century, the relief of the village and small-town poor seems to have been based on humane assessment of need and sufficient relief. From its Elizabethan origins, the Poor Law had based responsibility firmly on the parish. This had one obvious limitation. It made coping with locally severe unemployment difficult, since only the resources of the rate-paying parishioners could be drawn on. Slumps in manufacturing brought problems for this reason. Writers like Defoe were apt to stress the value of manufacturing in bringing extra employment, for women and children as well as for men.

> In the manufacturing counties you see the wheel going at almost every door, the wool and the yarn hanging up at every window, the looms, the winders, the combers, the carders, the dyers, the dressers, all busy; and the very children, as well as women constantly employed.
>
> As is the labour so is the living; for where the poor are full of work, they are never empty of wages; they eat while the others starve, and have a tolerable plenty.[27]

But there is another side. As Lord Townshend recognised in 1730, the availability of poor relief was in fact a subsidy to rural manufacturing which allowed cheap wages. 'Were it not for what they receive out of the tax . . . they would not knit or spin for so small wages, as they receive for that work, because they would starve by it.'[28] But it was not only in this way that the poor rates assisted manufacturing. The rationale of the putting-out system was that it enabled the merchant capitalist to draw on only as much labour as he needed at any given condition of the market. Faced with a slump in orders, or with any problems over the supply of raw materials, he simply could not employ many of those he needed in brisker times. Even the employer operating from his own premises often took it for granted that if his advantage dictated it, the parish must take the strain. In 1773 when raw silk was difficult to obtain, the owner of a throwing mill in Sherborne wrote:

> . . . having discharged many of my hands which are either starving, or are become burdensome to the town, others are incessantly crying for a little work and could they obtain but a morsel of Barley-bread they are happy, they very often go days with little or no nourishment . . . the

---

27. Defoe, *Plan of the English Commerce*, p. 67.
28. Cited in C. Hill, *Reformation to Industrial Revolution*, Penguin, 1969, p. 259.

continued cries of the poor people complaining for want of the
necessaries of life as well for want of employment is shocking indeed .
. . . and what is worse the overseers are not so bountiful to the
necessitous as I could wish.

Two years later he was again dismissing a third of his hands in a
mid-winter lay-off.[29]

Manufacturing workers were aware of this situation, and at times
of dispute with their employers sometimes attempted to use it to
gain support from the landed rate-payers who, correctly, believed
that, compared with land, the assets of manufacturers were significantly under-assessed. In a petition of 1756 the weavers of the West
Country pointed out the consequences of wage reductions being
imposed by their employers: 'insomuch that weavers cannot get
above fourpence for sixteen hours labour . . . whereby their
families are thrown upon and become burthensome to the parishes'. The cotton weavers of Lancashire made a similar point in
1799 when claiming that piece rates had been more than halved
since 1792. 'No wonder the poor rates increase when people are
situated in this manner. A little reflection will show how matters of
this kind affect the landed interest.'[30]

On the credit side, the local base of the Poor Law meant that it
operated in a face-to-face world where people and their problems
were known. National pamphleteers remote from the social relations of the villages might rant on about the idle and undeserving
poor, but relief at local level was in the hands of the annually
elected parish overseers supervised by the vestry meeting, and they
knew their own poor well enough. Indeed, sickness, ill fortune or
even old age could reduce even a former overseer to a needy situation. In the Corfe Castle listing of 1794, one of the relief recipients, in his seventies and with a large family from a younger wife,
is described as a labourer, but a marginal note informs us that he
had once been a farmer and overseer of the poor. It has been suggested by Dr Henriques that parish poor relief in small communities provided 'a personal service in which the pauper was
relieved in familiar surroundings. . . . The small parish provided
for its poor without frills; but it provided on the basis of personal
knowledge of immediate needs.' This generally approving judgement has characterised work on the Poor Law up until about the

29. M.E. Weinstock, *Old Dorset*, David & Charles, 1967, p. 90.
30. W.E. Minchinton, 'The petitions of the weavers and clothiers of Gloucestershire in 1756', *Trans. Bristol and Gloucs Arch. Soc.*, LXXIII, 1954, p. 218; A. Aspinall,
The Early English Trade Unions, Batchworth, 1949, p. 23.

time of the American Revolution. In her pioneering study Dorothy Marshall wrote that the main abuses were to be found in the 'crowded and impersonal' urban parishes, a view echoed recently by Professor Malcolmson.

> . . . for all those unfortunate and aged people the institution of the poor law did provide some genuine relief, especially in small communities where the poor were personally known and acknowledged to have a legitimate claim on the assistance of their neighbours.

But he joins others in considering that this happier state of affairs deteriorated well before the end of the century. Up until then the labouring people may have enjoyed only basic material fare, 'but most of them were able to support their families in an average year without having to resort to the parish for relief'.[31]

It has been argued by Dr Snell that the fact that overseers were often of humble stock themselves was crucial for the social order of rural communities in that it 'facilitated agreement and mutual respect between the ranks and orders of parish society'. He argues further that the parish vestry and its officers, the churchwardens, overseers and constables, could cut across divides of wealth and were a means by which the gentry and rural middle class secured positions which would have been more precarious without the respect they received by fulfilling certain customary expectations of relief. Until about 1780 these expectations were met largely by a relief system which was 'generous, flexible and humane'. The poor's entitlement to relief depended upon their having a *settlement* in the parish. If they had, they could view relief as a right to be called upon when necessary. A claimant had a right of settlement in only one parish, originally in his or her father's place of birth. But events in one's life history could change this. Marriage brought a woman on to her husband's settlement. If a person completed a year's hiring in a parish, or served a full period of apprenticeship, then the right of settlement shifted to that parish. It also did so if a property was rented for a qualifying period. Bastards took settlement rights in the parish of their birth. The problems and abuses connected with the laws of settlement will be discussed below; for the moment we are concerned to stress that persons with a settlement in a parish had a real claim to relief should misfortune or simply age overtake them, or indeed if they could find no work or

---

31. U.R.Q. Henriques, *Before the Welfare State*, p. 11; D. Marshall, 'The old poor law, 1662–1795' in E.M. Carus Wilson (ed.), *Essays in Economic History*, I, Arnold, 1954, p. 299; R.W. Malcolmson, *Life and Labour*, p. 80.

even none at wages sufficient for the support of the family. Snell has suggested that this sense of right was sufficiently marked to make expectations from the Poor Law part of the 'moral economy' which Edward Thompson has applied to the poor's expectation that corn would be sold to them at 'just' prices.[32]

The readiness of the poor to appeal over the heads of overseers to the magistrates suggests this. In drawing up his list of inhabitants of Corfe Castle in 1794, the compiler justified his efforts by claiming that it would not only help the overseers keep in touch with actual and potential needs, but would 'enable the magistrates to form an opinion on the propriety of applications for parochial relief on the one hand, and of the refusal of it by the parish officers on the other'.[33]

The general regulation of the Poor Law was the responsibility of the justices at quarter sessions, but under an act of 1691 individual justices sitting out of sessions could overrule the overseers on appeal and order relief to be given. How often did they do so? It is very hard to know for the simple reason that very few records of justices' out-of-sessions activities survive, and although sometimes these cases were heard by two or more justices at petty sessions, even the records of these hearings are scarce and incomplete. Complaints from the side of the parish officers suggest it was not uncommon. George Crabbe in his poem of 1802, 'The Parish Register', writes of the village paupers as 'Those who take from our reluctant hands / What Burn advises, or the Bench commands'. Richard Burn was the author of the standard reference work on the Poor Law.

A Somerset vicar of the time complained in his diary:

> The law is too lenient to the poor in this Kingdom. They summon the
> overseers before the magistrates for not complying with their
> unreasonable demands and though they do not always gain their ends
> yet it teases and harasses the overseers and takes up their time which is
> a great hardship. They should be subject to punishment if their
> complaints were found to be vexatious and without foundation.

He recorded again a short time later:

> The overseers are harassed to death and summoned everyday before a
> justice, this will never do. . . . The Justices attend to every complaint,
> right or wrong, and every scoundrel in the Parish crowd to make their
> complaints.[34]

32. K.D.M. Snell, *Annals of the Labouring Poor*, pp. 104–7.
33. See note 26 above.
34. J. Ayres (ed.), *Paupers and Pig Killers*, pp. 26, 47.

Thomas Turner, a shopkeeper, served as overseer in an east Sussex parish in 1757. In his diary he records several incidents. 'This day Dame Vinal brought me a summons from Mr Courthope to appear before him, to show cause why we use the poor so hardly.' Turner attended and convinced the magistrate that 'we were not hard on our poor'. The woman was reprimanded for 'a heap of lies' and told she was entitled to nothing unless 'we liked to give her daughter's child a pair of shoes'. A draw perhaps?[35]

On another occasion an out-of-work blacksmith came and said that 'if the parish would not find him a shop to work in, he would make his complaint to a justice'. The smith was invoking the part of the Elizabethan Poor Law which required the parish to assist the able-bodied to work. A special vestry was called and resolved 'to hire a shop as soon as they could'. Arthur Young in 1795, pointing out in a year of extreme hunger that it was against the law to starve in England, included in his argument: 'Parish officers are bound to provide . . . and if they do not do their duty, there is an appeal to the justice, who will force them to its performance.'[36]

Evidence from the justices is scarce. Petty sessions throw up a few cases, but not many. Yet in 1800 a Gloucestershire JP reckoned that he spent the greater part of his mornings dealing with Poor Law disputes. Probably he was including bastardy and settlement cases, at least as much as complaints against overseers. That is, he was more often issuing summonses on behalf of than against overseers. The few surviving justices' diaries give conflicting impressions. One which has been reprinted, that of Richard Wyatt of Surrey, covers 224 cases between 1767 and 1776 among which are 58 bastardy examinations and many settlement ones, but there is no record of any complaints against overseers. In contrast, the diary of William Hunt of Wiltshire covering the years 1744 to 1749 records fifteen cases against overseers covering ten parishes. In all but one he found for the complainant. Even in that case it was the third complaint from a woman who had had her previous two met. Whether this justifies the conclusion of Esther Moir that 'The most that can be said is that on and off the bench, the Justices interposed between the parish overseer and his helpless victim' is uncertain. A pamphleteer opposing a 'too generous' Poor Law in 1786, noting that paupers were too easily allowed to build cottages on the waste and install themselves to become eventual burdens on the rates,

35. D. Vaisey (ed.), *The Diary of Thomas Turner*, pp. 91–2.
36. *Ibid.*, pp. 92–3; cited in R.A.E. Wells, *Wretched Faces*, p. 288.

remarked, 'Happily the justices of the peace have no legal authority to augment the number of our cottages. There can be no compulsion in this case'. This leaves no doubt of his feelings about justices' powers in other areas of poor relief.[37] Among the appellants assisted by Hunt was George Wiltshire, 'for to find him labour or to relieve him'. The parish officers promised to find him work. Another man appealed against the denial of relief for his sister. He made the officers on another occasion agree to give a woman 6d (2½p) a week, 'touching in particular her being a poor sickly woman, as also her husband having no work to do'. Another woman was awarded relief for her bastard child, 'upon their appearing and not showing why they should not'. A labourer complained, 'touching in particular the said churchwardens and overseers of the poor, not finding a house and providing labour or work for the said William Ashton to do in the parish'. The officers appeared and agreed to relieve the pauper.[38]

We will turn later to the question of finding work for the unemployed able-bodied. What must strike the modern reader is the very small amounts of out-relief involved in such cases. What was the cost of basic subsistence in the first part of the eighteenth century? In 1697 John Locke, commissioned by the Board of Trade to survey the problem, concluded that a labouring man and his wife could support just two dependent children on the common country wages: 'The children of labouring people are an ordinary burden to the parish. A great number of children giving a poor man a title to an allowance from the parish.' Joseph Hanway in 1766 observed that the 'mass of people' lived on less than £5 a year, and considered that when provision prices were 'moderate', husbandmen supported a family of three or four children on 1s to 1s 6d (5–7½p) a day. Defoe in 1730 had considered a poor man in constant work could earn from 4s to 5s (20–25p) a week, 'which will barely purchase bread and cheese and clothes for his family, so that if he falls sick or dies his wife and children infallibly come to the parish for relief, who allow them a small pittance or confine them in a workhouse'. If a family of, say, five could in years of normal food prices be almost supported on 4s 6d a week, then a payment of 6d

---

37. E. Silverthorne (ed.), *Deposition Book of Richard Wyatt, JP, 1767–76*, Surrey Record Society, 1978; E. Crittall (ed.), *The Justicing Notebook of William Hunt 1744–1749*, Wiltshire Record Society, 1982; E. Moir, *The Justice of the Peace*, Penguin, 1969, p. 97; J. Townshend, *A Dissertation on the Poor Laws*, 1786, rept University of California Press, 1971, p. 48.

38. Hunt, *Notebook*, entry nos 180, 214, 222, 223, 272, 340, 355, 377, 399, 436.

or 1s, either to a single pauper or as a supplement to the earnings of a large family, was indeed significant, especially if it was combined with occasional relief payments for tools, clothing, towards rent or for medicine.[39]

Viewing the accounts of parish overseers with their detailed entries of small payments for a range of needs, some historians have found it possible to write approvingly of a Poor Law which was sensitive to local needs and did not deal in bread alone. To Dr Porter, 'in a multitude of small ways, the poor law served as a thoroughgoing system of support' which was in the first half of the eighteenth century 'quite generous in their paternalist supplements to domestic income'. The examples he provides, of 'dribbling payments of a shilling or two' for house repairs, funerals, clothes, tools and medicines and for tiding over occasional hard times, can be multiplied from a number of local studies. Recipients like the widow of Oswestry who in 1788 got an allowance of 3s (15p) a week for three years supplemented by occasional special payments – 1s to hedge her garden, 3s (15p) for seed potatoes and even £1 for thatching straw – are far from uncommon. When her children needed clothing she received doles for shoes, stockings and shoe repairs, but at least as grateful was the woman in Leytonstone who in 1740 received one to redeem her stays from pawn. Dorothy George, after describing the 'roastbeef' of old England, retained her rose-coloured spectacles as she went on to an extraordinarily generous view of the Poor Law.

> All this made for contentment, and the greater part of the century was a time of content, though a bad harvest invariably meant serious food riots. Even the poor law, in spite of the inconceivable hardships which it brought to individuals, and its disastrous social consequences in certain directions, gave a sense of security and well being which was new in England. There was a seventeenth-century ballad now known only by tradition as the name of a tune called 'Hang care the parish is bound to save us'. In sickness and old age, as well as when he had a number of young children, poor relief was the accepted, inevitable and unresented lot of the labouring man. His settlement he regarded as his birthright or his freehold.[40]

Henry Fielding was one of those who was annoyed by the poor's presumption in this regard. Noting the same ballad in 1751, he argued that the Elizabethan Poor Law had given:

39. M.D. George, *England in Transition*, pp. 22–3.
40. R. Porter, *English Society*, pp. 143–4; George, *England in Transition*, pp. 28–9.

a new turn to the minds of the mobility. They found themselves no longer obliged to depend on the charity of their neighbours, nor on their own industry for a maintenance. They now looked upon themselves as joint proprietors in the land, and celebrated their independency in songs of triumph.[41]

The parishioner could expect relief 'in sickness, infirmity and in old age, in unemployment or inadequate wages'. He could expect to be 'buried, his children to be apprenticed, his wife to be assisted in childbirth and his daughter helped to recover payments from the putative father of her illegitimate child'. But, as Dr Henriques has remarked, 'he was secure of this only in the parish where he had established a settlement'. In short, popular expectations ran parallel, in this case, with the law. There is little indication that parishioners much opposed the removal from *their* parish of strangers who might become chargeable or, when the act of 1795 had changed the situation, after they had actually become chargeable. The harassing of those caught out by need where they had no settlement was the dark side of the eighteenth-century Poor Law with its associated evasive strategies such as hiring for less than a year, pulling down cottages on the wastes, apprenticing pauper children beyond the bounds and hustling unwilling couples into marriage to avoid the maintenance of a bastard. If the poor asserted a 'right', it was an exclusive one.[42]

The right to be relieved in one's parish, perhaps as much as aversion to the workhouse as an institution, lay behind riots in Suffolk in 1765 where a practice of building large workhouses to serve several parishes had been developing since a private enabling statute had been obtained in 1756. This transferred overall authority from the parish vestry to a board of directors drawn from substantial land-holders. A mob of 400 labourers on Nacton Heath told the magistrates that 'they came to fight for their liberties'. They were dispersed by soldiers but reassembled to attack another workhouse at Bulcamp. There was a drought at the time, and the crowd declared that 'God would not suffer it to rain till Bulcamp Hell was pulled down'.[43]

Most opposition was produced, however, by the notion that the purpose of the workhouses was to 'imprison' the poor, who 'should range at liberty and be their own masters'. When, ten years later, neighbouring Norfolk set afoot proposals to follow suit, its two MPs

41. Cited in R. Palmer, *The Sound of History: Songs and Social Comment*, Oxford UP, 1988, pp. 253–4.
42. Henriques, *Before the Welfare State*, p. 11.
43. George, *England in Transition*, pp. 98–9.

were petitioned by the small-holders and labourers of the hundreds concerned to use their influence to prevent:

> that imprisonment of our persons, that separation from our children, that destruction of our race, that loss to the kingdom, and that curse from the Almighty which must attend establishing a poor house upon the specious fallacy of providing for our comfort, by the breaking of our hearts.

As Dr Digby has pointed out: 'That a freeborn Englishman had the right to be relieved in his own home and should not be imprisoned in a workhouse was to be a recurrent theme in East Anglian popular protest.' It was certainly the theme of a protest against the building of a workhouse in 1785 which argued that it threatened 'our liberty and laws'. It was an argument which had point. The Workhouse Act of 1723 had empowered parishes to apply a workhouse test by denying relief to those who refused to enter. It was not wholly unreasonable for the protesters to view this as 'imprisonment' without trial. Parson Woodforde, visiting a Norfolk warehouse containing 380 poor in 1787, found they did not look 'either healthy or cheerful'. He also commented on the high death rate. But it is likely that loss of liberty was more often held against the workhouse than the belief that the subsistence provided was lower than that available from out-relief.[44]

Popular opposition was not unimportant among the factors which prevented the workhouse system from becoming general throughout East Anglia, despite the considerable interest shown in that region. But how important generally were workhouses in the relief of poverty in the eighteenth century? The answer is not very. Only one in nine of Oxfordshire's parishes had one in 1777, although one-third did in Essex. Official figures suggest that there were around 2,000 in 1775, a large number in itself, but then there were 13,000 parishes. It is also true that there were moments, like the 1720s, the 1780s and to a lesser extent the 1750s, when their establishment was especially noticeable, but even where they existed, large numbers of claimants were still relieved at home. Sometimes this was easier and cheaper, especially as increasing population could outpace workhouse provision; sometimes it was because the parish officers discriminated in their application of the 'test' and did not apply it to all kinds of claimant. An estimate for 1802 suggests that only a twelfth of relief recipients were inmates.[45]

44. A. Digby, *Pauper Palaces*, pp. 34–6.
45. P. Clark, 'The old poor law' in *Poverty and Social Policy 1750–1870*, Open University, 1974, p. 13; Snell, *Annals of the Labouring Poor*, p. 106.

By then the name 'workhouse' was in any case inappropriate. The original intention that the poor could be put to work for their own support, or even show the country a profit, was one which developed out of the Elizabethan founding idea of the 'parish stock'. It was attractive but fantastic in its assumption that such employment could be provided in an age of widespread rural underemployment heightened by occasionally severe local unemployment. Run by the parishes or by groups of parishes, workhouses never produced an output which even repaid the purchase of raw materials, nor did they meet the vaunted secondary objective of training the poor in the 'habits of industry'. When let out to private contractors, corruption and harsh treatment of the paupers was too often added to failure. It is difficult to know how far they were a significant deterrent to claiming relief, but over the long term there is little to suggest that any parish maintained the lowering of its poor rate which sometimes accompanied the initial operation of a workhouse. Perhaps the majority of the 'workhouses' still so called in the last third of the eighteenth century were in no real sense distinguishable from 'poorhouses', that is from places where the impotent poor, through age or infirmity, could be lodged either until death or more temporarily. Pregnant single women, for example, were often taken in until after the birth. The more the inmates came to consist of the impotent or temporarily incapacitated, the greater became the gap between intent and reality.[46]

Following the pioneering incorporation of the Bristol workhouse in 1697, these institutions were more readily adopted in urban than in rural parishes. In part this was a reflection of the great strain on small financial resources which building, maintaining and perhaps in time enlarging workhouses imposed, but it also reflected the greater difficulty in an effective and controlled administration of out-relief in the more anonymous and densely populated towns. In extreme cases they became simply receiving institutions for classes of paupers with little hope. Orphaned or abandoned children were especially vulnerable. The 168 children out of 2,339 received into London workhouses between 1750 and 1755 who survived hardly over-exercised the parish authorities in seeking out apprenticeships on their behalf. Workhouse building, despite the permitting of parishes to combine for the purpose in 1723, was until 1750 largely an urban phenomenon, for in the countryside out-relief was proving itself a more flexible and still not frighteningly expensive option. In

46. See Porter, *English Society*, pp. 147–8.

fact Gilbert's Act of 1782, remembered mostly as one which permitted parishes to unite for Poor Law purposes without undergoing the expensive process of incorporating through a private act of parliament, was equally significant in its effective sanctioning of the subsidising of wages from the poor rates for the able-bodied who were to be removed from workhouses and found work. The workhouses could be made more fitted for the accommodation of orphans, the sick and the aged poor.[47]

For a while the increasing national cost of poor relief after mid century did not bring with it harsher attitudes. Officially collected statistics provide the figures in Table 5.1.

Table 5.1 National poor relief expenditure 1748/9 – 1803

1748/9	£689,971	1783/5	£1,943,649
1776	£1,496,129	1803	£4,077,891

Whether there was a clear trend before the mid 1790s is uncertain. Bad harvests or trade slumps could still make enormous differences either way between one year and the next, while some parts of the country, notably the South and East, experienced much sharper increases than others. Recently historians have been reasserting the view that the social consequences of parliamentary enclosures included a local increase in poverty. Before the 1790s higher spending on poor relief, although it convinced many contemporaries that the incidence of poverty was increasing, probably did not, except in particularly bad years, reflect much other than the increase in population and in food prices. Since right up until the first census in 1801 the increase in population was not generally perceived, much contemporary comment was not qualified by this relationship. The sharper increase in relief expenditure once the boom of the early 1790s gave way to the food crises of the mid 1790s, with only brief respite before the hyper-crisis of 1800–1, is unmistakable even if the wartime inflation from 1793 is taken account of. Expenditure on the eve of the French wars of 1793–1815 had already passed £2,600,000; by 1812 it was almost £8 million.[48]

The failure of the Younger Pitt's Poor Bill of 1797 perhaps marks the end of a period of 'sympathetic paternalism' towards the poor.

47. *Ibid.*, p. 147; Henriques, *Before the Welfare State*, pp. 17–18.
48. Henriques, *Before the Welfare State*, p. 19.

That proposal would have more generally introduced the system of the wage-allowance scheme to the able-bodied, most famously (or perhaps infamously) associated with the decision taken by Berkshire's justices meeting in 1795 at the Pelican Inn in the Berkshire village of Speenhamland. Historians of the Poor Law have discerned a more sympathetic attitude towards the settled poor and even in respect of removal proceedings. As well as kinder practices at parish level there was a more marked emphasis by reformers on finding alternative methods of helping the poor, for example in facilitating the setting up of friendly societies, the most popular vehicle for self-help. Their funds were given special protection by an act of 1793 and by 1803 their number in England had reached 9,672. The aggregate membership of 704,350 was 8 per cent of the population, but few of these were recruited from the poorest and most vulnerable class of rural labourers.[49]

It was they whom the justices at Speenhamland had in mind in a year of extreme hunger when they produced their system of allowances in aid of wages determined by the ruling price of bread and by family size. In some areas the birth of a child might add a shilling or more a week to the wage, leading to some pessimistic projections of runaway demographic increase, notably by followers of Thomas Malthus whose 'Essay on Population' of 1798 was the most important ideological underpinning for the views of those who were beginning to urge a much harsher attitude towards the poor as the cost of their relief surged. The demographic evidence on this matter has been examined above and found wanting as an explanation of population growth. Its contemporary influence on social policy was nevertheless significant. The Speenhamland proposals were not wholly novel, but as a response to an extraordinary surge in cereal prices their direct tying of relief to a bread scale was a major factor in a widespread adoption of wage supplementation.[50]

The proponents of the radical reform of the Poor Law which was to result in the workhouse-based act of 1834, with its hated principle of 'less-eligibility', ensured that the wage-allowance system was presented in the worst possible light. Until Professor Blaug shattered that polemical myth in the early 1960s, historians tended to follow the reformer's selective use of evidence and defective reasoning to argue that out-relief payments to the able-bodied demoralised the labourer into a 'dependency culture', divorcing subsistence from

49. Rule, *Labouring Classes*, pp. 165–6.
50. For developments after 1795, see Marshall, *Old Poor Law*.

a direct relationship to labour output. Thanks to the 'parish subsidy', they argued, farmers could offer lower wages and employ on a casual rather than regular basis. At the same time the linking of allowances to family size encouraged feckless marriage and carefree breeding which in turn added to rural population and turned the labour market even more strongly against the rural poor. Much of this adverse criticism also drew attention to the usual association of the allowance system with some form of 'make-work' scheme. Typically this involved rotating the unemployed around the rate-paying farmers. It was assumed that parishes, very largely the agricultural villages of the southern and eastern cereal regions, who were using Speenhamland-like systems of poor relief, had placed themselves on a vicious spiral of soaring poor rates and were progressively increasing the very poverty they sought to relieve.[51]

The old Poor Law had always provided instances of parishes making allowances to able-bodied parishioners unable to secure work or, more commonly, unable to secure work at adequate wages. But such supplementary payments were regarded as short-term expedients, payable in extraordinary years of high prices, to relieve temporary unemployment, typically seasonal, or paid to families at difficult points in the life-cycle. In so far as the situation changed in the 1790s it was to the extent that such payments became systematised both as a *regular* basis for relieving poverty and in being tied to a scale of bread prices. To some extent this is not surprising. High cereal prices were not at all 'extraordinary' in the years of the French wars from 1793 to 1815. There were only three abundant harvests between 1793 and 1818 and fourteen which were deficient to some degree including some which were extraordinarily bad. The crises of 1795–6 and 1800–1 have been described as 'famines', while that of 1813 was also severe.[52] There is no doubt either that despite the fact that wartime needs generally produced a slight upward trend in money wages, the usual earnings of rural labourers in the South and East, especially when periods of unemployment are taken into account, fell short of need. It has been pointed out by Dr Baugh that if rising levels of poor-relief expenditure are expressed in per capita terms and related to wheat prices, the *real* level of poor-relief spending was fairly constant from the early 1790s to 1814. He concludes that high relief was essentially a response to

51. M. Blaug, 'Myth of the old poor law', is reprinted in M.W. Flinn and T.C. Smout (eds), *Essays in Social History*, Oxford UP, 1974, pp. 123–53. Page references are to this text. Blaug, 'Poor law report re-examined', references to *Jn. Econ. Hist.*
52. See Wells, *Wretched Faces.*

high food prices rather than to perception of a chronic employment problem. In coming to this conclusion he makes two important observations. Firstly that, since the trend of relief expenditure follows that of wheat prices, it does not indicate any tendency to lower wages, although it equally clearly denies any strong upward wage trend. This supports the view expressed, for example, by Professor McCloskey and derived from economic theory that given the constant labour demand of the war period, the poor-relief system could not have resulted *both* in falling wages and in falling amounts of labour. The second of Baugh's observations seems to me especially important. Given the rate of inflation of food prices, *all* forms of relief expenditure would have become considerably more expensive. The infirm, the old and the illegitimate or orphaned young, however, as well as the inmates of workhouses, would all have cost more to feed. Further, a widespread parish response to famine-level prices was to purchase supplies of wheat or substitute foodstuffs and re-sell them at subsidised prices to the poor. This too would have raised expenditure irrespective of whether or not a Speenhamland system existed.[53]

All this suggests that the allowance system was a response to rather than a cause of the relief burden. Blaug presented his argument with a rather different emphasis. Remarking that 'Speenhamland counties' is to a great extent another way of describing the agricultural parishes of the wheat-growing regions, he noted that the upward trend in relief expenditure was similar in non-Speenhamland counties. Levels in the former group were higher because they compounded a greater burden which already existed by 1795. This leads him to see the growth of the wage-allowance scheme as a response to problems of unemployment and underemployment which, while they became more visible in years of high food prices, were inherent in social and economic changes taking place in the Speenhamland counties. Among these in some counties was the parliamentary enclosure of open fields and of common lands. It is true that much of England had already been enclosed by 1760, but in some areas, notably in the south and east Midlands in counties like Northamptonshire, Cambridge and Oxfordshire, more than half of enclosures took place after 1760 under acts of parliament.[54] Increasing levels of poverty were a likely outcome. For many years the view of J.D. Chambers in 1953 that earlier historians like the Hammonds had seriously misrepresented the links between enclo-

---

53. Blaug, 'Myth of the old poor law', p. 148.
54. Blaug, 'Poor law report re-examined', p. 243.

sure and poverty became the orthodoxy. He argued that the evidence from Nottinghamshire suggested that enclosures both increased the total demand for agricultural labour and the regularity of employment. In recent years this orthodoxy has crumbled. Better-designed and applied investigations have largely reinstated the views of the Hammonds. Professor Crafts has shown that in the Midlands, far from retaining labour, recently enclosed parishes experienced considerable out-migration. Dr Snell has shown that when land was enclosed for arable farming, both male and female employment became *less* regular, especially the latter, with severe effects on family earnings. He has also discovered a strong correlation between the extent of enclosure and high per capita levels of poor relief in the first decade of the nineteenth century.[55]

It was not only that enclosures forced some small-holders into the ranks of the landless and into wage-dependency for the first time; it was also the case that many who had been able partly to support themselves from small-holdings supplemented by access to common grazing for a beast or two lost that element of independence. Up to enclosure, according to Professor Malcolmson, 'an economy of self-reliance and an economy of wage dependence could be linked together'. As the Reverend David Davies put it in 1795, 'depriving the peasantry of all landed property has beggared multitudes'.[56] Enclosure may not have been the only or even the most potent of the forces increasing and impoverishing the rural proletariat in the southern and Midland counties, but it was important in bringing many to a *total* wage-dependency. The loss of access to even a small plot in the open fields affected many, but far more were affected by the loss of common rights. Perhaps the most widespread loss was fuel. The huge number of prosecutions for wood stealing supports the views of most commentators on the South and East that scarcity of fuel was a major aspect of the poor living of rural labourers.[57]

A second factor in the South and East was the decline in rural manufacturing employment, in particular the loss of hand spinning in cottage households. A third was the rapid fall in the numbers of

55. J.D. Chambers, 'Enclosure and labour supply in the industrial revolution', 1953, reprinted in E.L. Jones, *Agriculture and Economic Growth in England 1650–1815*, Methuen, 1967, pp. 94–127; Snell, *Annals of the Labouring Poor*, pp. 138–66, 168–79, 194–5; N.C.R. Crafts, 'Enclosure and labour supply revisited', *Explorations in Economic History*, XV, 1978, pp. 177–82.

56. R.W. Malcolmson, *Life and Labour*, pp. 24ff.

57. Snell, *Annals of the Labouring Poor*, p. 168. For wood stealing, see R.W. Bushaway, *By Rite*, pp. 207–33.

boarded farm servants, and a fourth the very high seasonal reduction in the demand for labour associated with wheat growing, even where the change to cereal from mixed or pastoral farming was not associated with recent enclosure. All these factors were intensified by rural population growth, although it was not in itself caused by the family-based allowance scheme.

> We can hardly resist the conclusion that the parish officers only had recourse to the policy of subsidizing wages wherever the attraction of urban industry made itself felt too weakly, leaving a pool of surplus manpower and substandard wages.[58]

Without this 'attraction' it was hardly to be expected that rural labour markets could clear themselves through falling wages, since they were already so close to the level of subsistence that a further lowering would have reduced the productivity of labour via its depressing effect on the calorific value of workers' diets which would no longer have sustained the same work effort. As a response to this situation, Blaug concludes, the wage-allowance system was criticised by the reformers on the basis of arguments which would 'equally condemn most modern welfare legislation'.

Was the poor relief paid to able-bodied workers over-generous to the extent that it not only created a dependency culture by reducing the incentive to work, but put a premium on early marriage and on childbirth? There is a suggestion that farmers were inclined to discriminate in favour of married labourers, since they would otherwise have been a greater burden on the parish rate of which the farmers were the main payers. This may have been so, but it is unlikely to have become significant until the post-war depression in cereal prices, the adverse influence of demobilisation on labour supply and the accumulating impact of the rising birth rate began to exert a combined effect after 1816. Allowances under the Berkshire scale of 1795 began with a 'gallon loaf' at 1s (5p) and increased with each penny rise up to 2s (10p). A single man was guaranteed 3s (15p) a week, and a married one an extra 1s 6d (7½p) for each dependant. Thus in cheap years a family with three children were guaranteed 9s (45p), while the doubling of the bread allowance in dearer ones would bring this up to 12s (60p). In 1795 a single labourer in the Midland and southern arable regions could, with supplements in kind, earn the equivalent of 10s (50p) a week.

---

58. On these matters, see especially D.A. Baugh, 'Cost of poor relief', pp. 50–68.

If unemployed, the scale would have given him 5s (25p) a week. A married man and his wife who could between them earn 15s (75p) and had one child would, out of work, have received 10s (50p). If, however, a married man had children young enough to keep his wife at home, then during the high-price years he could not have earned enough to support his family without supplementation. But it was an allowance on top of wages. He was expected to earn as much as he could; that was the point of the 'roundsman' system. The Berkshire justices had made it clear enough that the scale was payable to 'every poor *and* industrious man'. In the still face-to-face world of the agricultural village the character of the claimants was easily known. The existence of the bread scale was to guarantee subsistence at a very low level. It seems more than likely that with parishes concentrating on basic food needs, the other kinds of discretionary payments, which had been a feature of the eighteenth-century poor, were made less often and with declining generosity. It may also have been the case that magistrates were less willing to overturn the appeals of disappointed claimants, since they were well enough aware that the increasing burden of relief was being thrown on to a decreasing number of shoulders as the proportion of the village populations either needing assistance or at least no longer able to pay poor rates increased. In general the move towards wage supplementation in the rural South and East enabled the old Poor Law just about to cope with the problem of subsisting the poor in a period of unprecedentedly high bread prices, during which some years can only be described as desperate. The last act began only when the deep-seated problems of the southern rural economy intensified to produce an endemic rural poverty that persisted even after the wartime prices had ended.

MIGRATION

Contemporaries differed in their view of the overall effect of the Settlement Laws on the mobility of the labouring poor. They saw things from different perspectives. For Adam Smith in 1776, laying down the philosophical system which was to become the ideological underpinning of the market economy, they were the greatest obstruction placed on the movement of labour for they affected even common labour, while the regulations of guilds and corporations restricted the movement only of artisans. Henry Fielding in 1751 saw the matter from the perspective of a London magistrate, linking vagrancy to crime. For him the laws of settlement hardly prevented the 'idle poor' from wandering and a stricter enforcement of vagrancy laws would 'compel the poor to starve or beg at home; for there it will be impossible for them to steal or rob without being presently hanged or transported out of the way'.[59] Whatever personal suffering the laws caused – and there is no doubt they caused a great deal – there is little to suggest that the development of the eighteenth-century economy was frustrated by an unusual level of institutionally produced labour immobility. There is also much evidence from a variety of sources that the labouring poor moved a great deal in search of employment, if usually not over very great distances.

Most people did not spend their whole lives in one place. A study of some West Riding parish registers has found that in the late eighteenth and early nineteenth centuries, farming was the only occupation where more than half of sons remained in their fathers' places of residence. Another analysis of a sample of sixteen English parishes has shown that in only one case did the number of males married between 1721 and 1750 who could also be found in both the baptism and burial records exceed 50 per cent (in that case it was 51 per cent). The proportions for women were even lower.[60] It was the argicultural parishes which produced the smallest percentages. Villages where rural manufacturing enhanced employment possibilities, like the framework-knitting villages of Shepshed and Gedling, had 36 and 51 per cent of their male sample with a 'complete' registration. For the same reason the coal-mining parish of Earsdon also had a more stable population. Such measures of absences from parish registers are the crudest of indicators, but other evidence points in the same direction. On the evidence of church court depositions, Professor Clark has suggested that in the early eighteenth century six out of ten males moved at least once in their lives. Country rates were higher than those of the towns; in the former case the ratio was seven out of ten. Women were even more mobile, reflecting perhaps the large proportion who at some time

59. Henry Fielding, *An Inquiry into the Causes of the Late Increase of Robbers*, 1751, Section VI: 'Of laws relating to vagabonds'. For an assessment of the impact of the Settlement Laws, see J.S. Taylor, 'Impact of pauper settlement', pp. 42–74.

60. M. Long and B. Maltby, 'Personal mobility in three West Riding parishes, 1777–1812', *Local Population Studies*, **24**, 1980, p. 18; D. Souden, 'Movers and stayers in family reconstitution populations', *ibid.*, **33**, 1984, pp. 11–28.

of their life entered service and married extra-parochial partners. Three out of four country women moved at least once.[61]

Mobility was closely linked to the life-cycle: men and women moved while they were young. Farm service and apprenticeship, two especially common reasons for relocation, were obviously related to young persons. In general only a very small proportion moved much after their twenties. In the case of the Bedfordshire parish of Cardington in 1782, only 57 per cent of boys aged fifteen to nineteen who had spent their childhoods there in their parents' home were still residing in the parish. At the ages of twenty to twenty-nine only 35 per cent were. In fact, if the children aged thirty and above are considered as the second generation of adults, then three-quarters of the men and two-thirds of the women were living in parishes other than Cardington. London was only 45 miles away and seems to have drawn significant numbers of young men and women, more than Bedford which was only 2½ miles away.[62]

For the most part, however, the labouring classes did not move very far. Clark found that around half of his sample had travelled only 10 miles or less and only a tenth 40 miles or more, with women tending to move over shorter distances than men. By the eighteenth century the long-range hunger-driven mobility which had provided Tudor and Stuart governments with their problem of vagrant beggars had become insignificant. It seems likely that the Settlement Laws were not so much preventing migration as inhibiting distance. This, plus strengthening of the laws against vagrancy in 1714, 1740 and 1744, meant that many of the lower orders found it more difficult and more risky to move over long distances. There is, however, a more positive dimension. If the parish-based Poor Law was operating as well for the settled poor as modern historians seem to suggest, then more generous relief and serious attention to the provision of work and cottages may well have led to a decline in subsistence-driven migration. There were still to be found on the roads a vagrant population of Celtic wanderers from Scotland or Ireland, and those who followed the travelling occupations like chapmen, pedlars and itinerant entertainers, as well as the true travelling people, the gypsies and tinkers. The largest group on the

---

61. These are among the conclusions of P. Clark, 'Migration in England during the late-seventeenth and early-eighteenth centuries', *Past and Present*, **83**, 1979, pp. 57–90.

62. The Cardington findings are in R.S. Schofield, 'Age-specific mobility in an eighteenth-century rural English parish', in P. Clark and D. Souden (eds), *Migration and Society*, pp. 253–66.

roads, especially following an outbreak of peace, were soldiers and sailors; they made up, for example, a third of all migrants passing through Lichfield in 1692.[63]

There was a variety of different patterns of 'local migration'. Nearby towns drew in labour for service or apprenticeship. Of a sample of immigrants in Stratford on Avon in 1765 examined by Dr Martin, a third had come only 4 miles or less from neighbouring villages, while only a fifth had come from more than 20 miles. An examination of settlement certificates confirmed this pattern, with three-quarters coming from within 10 miles. Farm service also produced a local pattern. The majority of farm servants stayed only the one year with their master after the annual hiring, but they moved only into the service of other farmers drawing labour from the same hiring fair. Accordingly their mobility, though constant, was roughly constrained by a circle of 15 miles around the relevant town.[64]

The rapid rise of copper mining in eighteenth-century Cornwall certainly expanded the population of the western parishes, but at the expense of the non-mining parishes in the eastern parts of the same county. Against an overall county population increase of 22 per cent between 1672 and 1744, the western mining parishes of Gwinear, Illogan, Gwennap, Camborne and Kenwyn and Kea all increased by more than 70 per cent; the last named by 400 per cent, although the county as a whole was still losing part of its natural increase to out-migration. Cornwall is no exception. It seems clear that the labour needs of the growing mining and manufacturing districts were not significantly met by long-distance migration, although by the end of the period Irish immigrants were contributing, especially to the factory towns of the North. Professor Clark is probably correct in seeing in eighteenth-century mobility, not a development constraint but a 'steady but flexible labour response to economic change' which assisted an 'orderly progress' towards early industrialisation. There is a further sense in which the Settlement Laws assisted the building up of labour forces in manufacturing. It has been pointed out that the intent of the act of 1691 which allowed settlement 'earned' from an apprenticeship, a period of qualifying employment or householding, was constructive. Its preamble stating that persons chargeable in their parish 'merely for want of work' could in another place find 'sufficient employment as

63. Clark, 'Migration in England', pp. 68, 86–7.
64. A.S. Kussmaul, 'The ambiguous mobility of farm servants', *Econ. H.R*, XXXIV, No. 2, 1981, pp. 222–35; J.M. Martin, 'The rich, the poor and the migrant in eighteenth-century Stratford-on-Avon', *Local Population Studies*, **20**, 1978, pp. 38–47.

to be able to maintain themselves without being burthensome'. As for the certificate system whereby a parish acknowledged its responsibility to relieve holders who became chargeable while working in other parishes, that may well have helped industrial employers for they received the labour while the risk of having to relieve in cases of unemployment or sickness was underwritten by the parish of settlement. By the late eighteenth century it was increasingly common for rural parishes to remit payments to their poor who had become temporarily chargeable elsewhere, rather than have them delivered back. In effect poorer parishes with too little employment available paid a form of subsidy to those with expanding economies.[65]

The working conditions of the labouring classes were considered in an earlier chapter and in the companion to this volume, *The Vital Century*. Their standard of living will be assessed in Chapter Seven. In the following chapter we will examine several aspects of their lives and attitudes, some of which are often loosely grouped by historians as 'popular culture'.

65. This is the argument of J.S. Taylor, 'Impact of pauper settlement', especially pp. 64–70.

CHAPTER SIX
Popular Education, Religion and Culture

LITERACY AND SCHOOLING PROVISION

> Gentleman, this is to quaint you all of you cor Serning the Billing of this workhous think to starve the poore theare Stephen Wite Stratford Lews of Barfield Wile of TataSon Loyd hintlesham but let them tak care of thin Selves for farit that is hap on shall there Brains be Blown out and that as sure as death and fail not and the hous shall not be bilt a toyle for theare shall be 500 planted soon and will di all it and pull Wiles hous down.[1]

This warning was sent to persons involved in the building of a work-house at Tattingstone in Suffolk in 1765. For all its defective syntax and idiosyncratic spelling, its message is clear. Perhaps we could re-gard it, along with very many other anonymous letters expressing the grievances of the poorer sort, as an example of 'functional liter-acy'. At least it is a reminder that eighteenth-century England was a society in whose popular culture literate and oral means of creating and transmitting ideas coexisted. This did not depend on majority let alone mass literacy. By the final quarter of the seventeenth cen-tury literacy among the adult males of the labouring poor was prob-ably around 30 to 40 per cent, depending on occupation and location. For women it was only half as high. Apart from some nar-rowing of the gender gap, this situation largely persisted through the eighteenth century. Over its last two decades, slight improve-ment in some areas may well have been offset by a measure of de-cline in industrialising areas like the west Midlands and south

---

1. Cited in P. Muskett, 'A picturesque little rebellion? The Suffolk workhouses in 1765', *Bulletin of the Society for the Study of Labour History*, No. 41, 1980, p. 28. For anonymous letters as a form of protest, see E.P. Thompson, 'The crime of an-onymity', D. Hay *et al.*, *Albion's Fatal Tree*, pp. 255–344.

Lancashire.[2] Literacy rates among artisans and shopkeepers was much higher: 80 per cent or more would seem a reasonable approximation for the level reached by the late seventeenth century and persisting through most of the eighteenth century. The petty bourgeoisie of shopkeepers and self-employed tradesmen needed to keep accounts even if only of a primitive kind, but the growing fraction of permanent journeymen among the artisans grew into a more literate as well as more skilled elite section of the labouring classes. Some journeymen employed their literacy in their everyday work, compositors in the print trade being an obvious example, but many others had their books of prices. Hardly any had written manuals for their work. Even among the skilled the 'mystery' of the trade was still conveyed largely through the apprenticeship system with its on-the-job training and induction into the particular culture of the workplace.

Trade-union development did, however, impart a literary dimension for all its continued employment of ritual and symbolism. The tramping system had to be organised (see below, p. 207). Records of membership, subscriptions and payments had to be kept, and at times of dispute, petitions and other statements of grievances were drawn up and presented from at least the beginning of the eighteenth century. Devonshire serge weavers, for example, were presenting their case to parliament in 1725, while the journeymen tailors of London had done so in 1720. Apprentices were probably among the significant consumers of the popular literature of chapbooks, broadsheets and the Newgate 'confessions' of condemned malefactors.

Even for many artisans mensuration was probably a more necessary skill than writing, and for the unskilled working class the low occupational functional value of literacy is the most feasible explanation of the stagnation in levels after the seventeenth-century surge. Dr Schofield, from a study of the marriage registers of 274 parishes, found no significant improvement in overall male literacy levels between 1754, when marriage registers began to require signature, and 1815. The large majority of the illiterate labouring classes had sufficient access to the written word through the mediation of literate family members, friends or workmates. Just about the only humble occupation which derived from having the ability to read and write was that of teaching it to working-class children, and at that level school teaching was often the resort of widows, cripples and those generally unable to find better-paid work. In

2. See D. Vincent, *Literacy and Popular Culture*, Cambridge UP, 1989, pp. 12–13; M. Sanderson, 'Literacy and the industrial revolution', pp. 75–104.

John Cleland's novel of 1749, *Fanny Hill*, the heroine describes her north-country parents as 'extremely poor'. Her father, a net maker, earned a 'scanty subsistence' which was 'not much enlarged by my mother's keeping a little day-school for the girls in her neighbourhood'. She did not teach much, for Fanny describes her own educational level as 'no better than very vulgar reading; or rather spelling, an illegible scrawl, and a little ordinary plain work'. The mistress of the church school in a Somersetshire parish in 1805 was not a widow but still sufficiently poor for her ten-year-old son to be killed working in a coal mine.[3]

The best that can be said for the education available for the children of the eighteenth-century poor is that it managed to maintain the levels of the later seventeenth century. Even the much-vaunted 'Charity School Movement' of the early decades seems only to have helped stop a poor level becoming worse. While the numbers taught by their parents without any formal schooling is unknowable, there is still bound to be a close relationship between the availability and take-up of schooling and the literacy level. Since provision of education for the lower orders was largely dependent on local initiative and attendance was usually a matter of parental inclination, both were haphazard. Towns were generally better off than villages, but within the same county variations even between towns could be marked. A study of Kent has illustrated this. In 1660 provision was very limited, especially in the rural parishes. By 1811, with the addition of a modest number of new subscription-based schools designed for the poor, things had improved although the geography of provision remained very uneven. Almost half of the county's 172 parishes had a school of some kind by 1807, including almost all of those with a population of a thousand or more. There had been a surge in provision between 1710 and 1725, indicating the influence of the Charity School Movement on a county adjacent to London, but by mid century this had given way to a pattern of augmentary endowments to already established schools and there was no fresh surge until 1780–90. By 1811 only some rural parishes were without any provision, while most of them had registered some improvement over the seventeenth century. Improving village schooling may, however, have done no more than keep the total proportion of Kent's children receiving schooling constant, for

3. Vincent, *Literacy and Popular Culture*, p. 52; L. Stone, 'Literacy and education', pp. 69–139; John Cleland, *Fanny Hill or Memoirs of a Woman of Pleasure*, Penguin, 1985, pp. 39–40; H. and P. Coombs (eds), *Journal of a Somerset Rector 1803–1834*, Oxford UP, 1984, p. 25.

there is also evidence of a deteriorating situation in some of the towns. Examples like Keston and Milsted where 50 per cent or more of poor children were enrolled in non-classical schools were exceptional. In the worst urban examples the figure was as low as 5 per cent.[4]

Day schooling was received by only a minority of children from the labouring classes, in some parishes a very tiny one. There was no association of elementary education with a prescribed period of childhood. Those who did receive schooling did so for perhaps a year or two, often much less, at some point in their childhood, with hardly any attending school beyond the age of ten or eleven. Even within these short periods attendance was irregular. Of schooling in the East Riding in the 1790s, it was later recalled:

> When the labourers' children could obtain employment from the farmers, the school was abandoned, and the youthful pupils were sent to cut weeds in the cornfields in the spring; to frighten away the birds from the standing corn; then to assist in harvest operations; and next to glean the fields which had been reaped.[5]

The poet John Clare's father was a country labourer in Northamptonshire who managed to secure for his son around three months' schooling a year.[6] Manufacturing and mining made just as heavy demands on child labour, although here the problem was not seasonal but one of whether parents could afford to buy a brief period of schooling before the child entered full-time employment. A Cornish miner later recalled of his late-eighteenth-century childhood:

> When I was eight years old my parents sent me to a raiding school kept by a poor owld man called Stephen Martin. My schoolin cost three a'pence a week. I was keept there for seven months, and so my edication was worth no less than three shillin and sixpence – there's for 'ee! When my edication was finished, as they do say, I was took hum, seven months larning being all that my poor parents cud afford me, but I shall have to bless God to aull etarnity for that edication.[7]

Charity schools had a negligible impact in areas where child employment opportunities were widespread. It was suggested more

4. R. Hume, 'Educational provision for the Kentish poor, 1660–1811', *Southern History*, 4, 1982, pp. 123–44.
5. T. Jackson, *Recollections of My Own Life and Times*, Wesleyan Conference Office, 1873, p. 19.
6. D. Vincent, *Bread, Knowledge and Freedom: A Study of Nineteenth-century Working-class Autobiography*, Methuen, 1982, p. 98.
7. S.W. Christophers, *Foolish Dick: An Autobiography of Richard Hampton*, Haughton & Co., 1873, p. 16.

than fifty years ago by M.G. Jones that the setting up of charity schools with common objectives between 1710 and 1730 under the leadership of the Society for Promoting Christian Knowledge (SPCK) amounted to a 'movement'. She saw it as one of the major manifestations of eighteenth-century philanthropic puritanism. Schools affording hundreds of thousands of places were set up to bring some form of education to the children of the poor. The 'movement' combined passion and responsibility in the firm purpose of instilling correct behaviour and moral reformation. The driving impulse was the fear of the development of a 'dangerous class' in the cities where children were growing up ill disciplined and ill exampled by their parents. To counteract such baneful influence, they should be removed from it into an educational programme designed to instil a proper sense of their place in society, of the duties attached to it and of the importance of attending to the teachings of the established Church. In the vital years before a child was apprenticed he or she could be captured from the streets, confirmed in God-fearing ways and inoculated against those habits of sloth, debauchery and irreligion which propelled so many of the lower orders to crime, prostitution and heathenism.[8]

This was a distinct motivation from that which had offered free places in the old endowed grammar schools and which had allowed a small measure of upward mobility for the bright working-class child. The schools lacked any concept of educational advancement and were not providing a popular education as the basis of a common citizenship nor as a matter of occupational utility. The conviction that the general education of the poor was economically unsound and unnecessary remained. Instead of the ambitions of the grammar school, the curriculum was confined to the 'plain accomplishments' which were the only ones needed by the 'generality of the people'. There was no step up to higher things, but a system complete in itself under which poor children were to receive just that modicum of education which would enable them to become useful and content in their inevitable station as hewers of wood and drawers of water. Such a conditioning would save not only their souls but their necks.

This was certainly the most sustained attempt to reach the children of the lower orders before the Sunday School movement towards the end of the century, but its extent and consistency have been questioned by historians, some of whom doubt that it was a

8. M.G. Jones, *The Charity School Movement: A Study of Eighteenth-century Puritanism in Action*, Cambridge UP, 1938.

'movement' at all. Its momentum was flagging by 1730 and even its constrained educational objectives were being criticised as a step too far. Many saw little utility in teaching reading rather than instilling labour discipline more directly. This strand urged instead the workhouse school, the school of industry, where useful accomplishments like spinning would fill up the time. However, for the first half of the century the offerers of the catechism still led the way. Charity schools were inexpensive and could be readily supplied in the boom years, while even such an early champion of the bourgeoisie as Defoe could approve their attack on sloth and indiscipline as going to the heart of the problem of the labouring poor. It was also to many a crusade defending Anglican Protestantism against irreligion, popery and even the Jacobites. Miss Jones had argued that it was the coordinating activities of the SPCK which made charity school provision a movement. The Society was certainly an initiator and active propagator, and when it turned its attention more towards foreign missions, the loss of momentum was noticeable. But it did not manage the schools and outside London and several other cities, such as Bristol, it had little strength. In rural districts and in manufacturing towns charity schools could expect to make little progress against the competition of child employment and complaints of this came repeatedly from clothing and mining districts. Within a diocese charity schools were more likely to be found near the cathedral city than in outlying regions. Exeter saw a strong movement, but in Cornwall, then part of that see, it was practically non-existent.[9]

If there are substantial doubts as to whether the provision of charity schools was ever sufficiently widespread, directed or differentiated from earlier, or later, efforts to have constituted a special movement, there is none that school provision for the poor in the middle and later years of the century remained uneven and spasmodic. Professor Stone's assertion that there was 'an upsurge of literacy' after 1780 'underlying the process of industrialisation' seems over-confident in view of evidence that the ratio of school places per capita actually declined in places as distant as Lancashire, Leamington, Cornwall, Devon and the East Riding.[10] This is not

9. F.L. Harris, 'Education by charity in eighteenth-century Cornwall', *Jn. of the Royal Institute of Cornwall*, IX, Part 1, 1982, pp. 30–52. The strongest critique has been made by Joan Simon; see her letter in *Bulletin of the Society for the Study of Labour History*, **31**, 1975, pp. 11–13 for her own summary of her argument.

10. L. Stone, 'Literacy and education' pp. 87, 92, 130–1, 137; Sanderson, *Education, Economic Change and Society*, p. 13.

surprising since there was little perception of a functional link between popular education and economic development. The phrase
'factory system' was already entering the language when, in 1807,
Davies Gilbert MP, a distinguished scientist, declared:

> However specious in theory the project might be of giving education to
> the labouring classes of the poor, it would in effect be prejudicial to
> their morals and happiness: it would teach them to despise their lot in
> life, instead of making them good servants to agriculture and other
> laborious employments to which their rank in society had destined
> them; instead of teaching them subordination, it would render them
> factious and refractory, as was evident in the manufacturing counties.[11]

Significant developments were taking place in the early nineteenth century. Even as Davies Gilbert spoke, discussions were beginning which led to the setting up in 1808 of the British and
Foreign School Society. Originally non-sectarian, it intended to
maximise school places by using Joseph Lancaster's monitorial system under which older pupils passed on their lessons to younger
ones. Conservative Anglicans, unable to endorse its open approach
in matters of religion, founded a rival organisation in 1811: the National Society for the Provision of Education for the Poor on the
Principles of the Established Church. It adopted a similar monitorial system, developed by Andrew Bell, and set about providing 'National' schools to rival the 'British' schools of the BFSS. These were
just beginnings. Neither made a significant provision before 1820,
and their rivalry still persisted in the 1830s when the government
began at last to assist them with grants. It was a beginning, but 1815
was reached with not much to acclaim in day-school provision for
working-class children and with no national policy as yet in prospect.[12]

From the closing decades of the eighteenth century Sunday
schools began to make a contribution, but how significant a one?
Their appearance was quite sudden. As A.P. Wadsworth expressed
it: 'In the early eighties, quite suddenly, the Sunday school movement flashed over the country. One wonders whether any social reform movement had ever before spread with equal rapidity through
England.'[13] The 'kindling spark' was Robert Raikes, the printer and
proprietor of the *Gloucester Journal*, who in 1780 was moved to start a
school to keep the unruly child workers from the city's pin manu-

---

11. *Hansard*, 13 July 1807.
12. See J.S. Hurt, *Education in Evolution 1800–1870*, Paladin, 1972, pp. 11–38.
13. A.P. Wadsworth, 'The first Manchester Sunday schools', p. 102.

factory from breaking the sabbath. The publicity he gave to the idea in his paper was taken up by other newspapers and the example of Gloucester was followed all over the country. By 1783 John Wesley was writing from Yorkshire, 'I find these schools springing up wherever I go.' They took off especially rapidly in manufacturing south Lancashire. By 1786 the magistrates of Salford were much impressed with their influence.

> If these Institutions should become established throughout the
> kingdom, there is good reason to hope they will produce an happy
> change in the general Morals of the People, and thereby render the
> Severities of Justice less frequently necessary.[14]

Their great merit was that they 'schooled' the children of the lower orders without interfering with the need for them to be at work on weekdays, hence their great appeal in manufacturing and mining areas. The Bishop of Chester saw them as the solution to the problem of reconciling 'manual labour and spiritual instruction' in a way so 'as not to interfere with or obstruct each other'. Estimates of total enrolment vary, but it seems unlikely that there were less than 100,000 Sunday school pupils by 1800. Far from all of these were eager seekers after learning, secular or religious. Vicars bribed with halfpennies and were known to pressure parents about what was expected before someone became an appropriate recipient of charity.[15]

Certainly Sunday schools had the opportunity to advance working-class literacy, but that was not seen as their main purpose. That was perhaps best defined by a Manchester committee: 'They call in a sense of religious obligation to the aid of industry.' It was also claimed that 'The improvement of these children in learning has been wonderful; in religious knowledge still more surprising.' It did not take long for moral earnestness to clash with secular utility. The issue was that of teaching writing on the sabbath, which was being described as a 'growing evil' by 1786. The original impulse had been non-denominational, but by the late 1790s the Anglican Church was drawing apart to go its own way, fearful that Methodism especially was gaining converts and even, as the Bishop of Rochester expressed it in 1800: 'Schools of Jacobinical religion and Jacobinical politics abound in this country in the shape of charity schools and Sunday schools.' The schools of the established Church banned the teaching of writing for this kind of reason as much as the Methodists did

14. *Ibid.*, pp. 100, 104.
15. *Ibid.*, p. 108.

for sabbatarian ones. There is simply no way in which to measure the contribution to popular education made by Sunday schools. Hardly anyone can have learned both to read and to write and probably few learned even to read just by attending Sunday classes. But for those who could receive a smattering of instruction at home, or who had spent a short while at day schools in their infancy, they may well have nourished a plant that might otherwise have ceased to grow, or even withered.[16]

POPULAR RELIGION

Looking back from 1826, a Cornish vicar wrote:

> Within my remembrance, there were conjuring parsons and cunning clerks; every blacksmith was a doctor, every old woman was a witch. In short all nature seemed to be united – its wells, its plants, its birds, its beasts, its reptiles, and even inanimate things in sympathising with human credulity; in predicting or in averting, in relieving or in aggravating misfortune.[17]

Oral tradition played a major part in transmitting and passing down this culture of superstition. Samuel Bamford, the son of a Lancashire weaver, recalled:

> My poor aunt Elizabeth no more doubted these things, than she did the truth of every word betwixt the two backs of her Bible. Often when on a winter's night we youngsters were seated round the hearth . . . would she set her wheel aside, take a pinch of snuff, hutch her chair towards the other hob, and excite our curiosity and wonder by strange and fearful tales of witches, spirits, and apparitions, whilst we listened in silence and awe, and scarcely breathing, contemplated in imagination, the visions of an unseen world, which her narratives conjured up before us.[18]

The reference to her Bible suggests two things: firstly the oral and the literary could exist side by side, and secondly that religion and superstition were not necessarily perceived as contesting forms of popular belief. The most popular form of reading among the literate poor was, as Dr Vincent has pointed out, one which told much

---

16. *Ibid.*, pp. 110–11. For a view which qualifies the idea that Sunday schools were imposed on the working class, see T. Laquer, *Religion and Respectability*.

17. R. Polwhele, *Traditions and Recollections*, II, 1826, p. 605.

18. Samuel Bamford, *Early Days*, 1549, repr. Cass, 1967, p. 162.

the same tales as did the oral tradition. John Bunyan wrote of the reading of his youth: 'Give me a ballad, a news-book, George on horseback, or Bevis of Southampton; give me some book that teaches curious arts, that tells of old fables; but for the holy Scriptures I cared not.' His *Pilgrim's Progress* was by far the most popular book in the cottages of the poor, and in Apollyon he had conjured up a monster fit for any fable: scaled, bear-footed, dragon-winged and breathing fire and smoke from a lion's mouth. Next in popularity were the various almanacs Professor Harrison has described as having 'catered to the needs of a great part of the nation, and their peculiar form served to keep alive the ancient traditions of folk astrology'.[19]

Bamford wrote of his parish church in the eighteenth century: 'every one in those days admitted that there was not a rood of earth around it which was not redolent of supernatural associations'.[20] It was a form of association which had not been unremarked by several of the socially better placed. An early nineteenth-century parson wrote:

> In the last age some of the rusticated clergy used to favour the popular superstition, by pretending to the power of laying ghosts etc. etc. I could mention the names of several persons whose influence over their flocks was solely attributable to this circumstance.[21]

More tersely, a lawyer noted in his diary in 1795: 'Superstition is gone, and refinements there on have made the people very irreligious.'[22]

It was a significant symbiosis, central to any discussion of what constituted the popular religious experience or pattern of beliefs. In recent years several historians, some influenced by social anthropology, have revealed the large gap which existed between 'official' and popular religious perceptions. Dr Obelkevich in a detailed study of rural Lincolnshire has shown that the 'religious realm' of the rural poor reached beyond Christianity to 'encompass an abundance of pagan magic and superstition' which was integrated with a Christian doctrine itself not left unchanged as it passed from church to cottage. In Cornwall, which was to grow into one of

19. Vincent, 'The Decline of the oral tradition in popular culture', in R.W. Storch (ed.), *Popular Culture and Custom*, p. 47; J.F.C. Harrison, *The Common People: A History from the Norman Conquest to the Present*, Fontana, 1984, p. 167.
20. Bamford, *Early Days*, p. 162.
21. Polwhele, *Traditions and Recollections*, loc. cit.
22. Cited in J.G. Rule, 'Methodism, popular beliefs and village culture in Cornwall, 1800–1850' in Storch (ed.), *Popular Culture and Custom*, p. 63.

Methodism's early strongholds, the teachings of John Wesley were absorbed only through a haze of superstitious beliefs and practices. It has been suggested that the starkness of early Wesleyan theology made for a rather close match, with local preachers assuming something of the role of conjurer.[23]

Dr Gilbert has pointed out that when the evangelist Hannah More remarked in 1789 on the existence of whole village populations no less estranged from the services of the Church than were heathens, she was belatedly recognising something which Wesley and Whitefield had been proclaiming for decades.[24] The established Church failed to keep up either with the growth of the population or with the changing geography of its distribution. It has been noted that early Methodism took root most significantly where the Church was weak.[25] It did not so much contest with the establishment as succeed in areas like the mining districts of Cornwall, Kingswood and around Newcastle, where there was no contest in the sprawling villages which were growing out of the reach of a moribund parish structure. This structure would in any case have presented problems of adaptation, but it was much worsened by the prevalence of pluralism with its associated non-residence. In 1812 almost one parish in ten was not served even by an underpaid and indifferent curate. All these manifest problems intensified the effects of a creeping indifference on the part even of the southern rural poor. A sample of thirty Oxfordshire parishes shows a progressive decline in the number of communicants from 911 in 1738 through 896 in 1759 to 682 by 1802. By 1801 the number of Anglican communicants nationally on Easter Day was 535,000, only around a tenth of the population of age to be confirmed.[26]

Overwhelming evidence of less than staunch religious attachment to the established Church does not, however, deny that its reach was embracing in other respects. Dr Clark has written of the eighteenth-century Englishman:

> The agency of the State which confronted him in everyday life was not
> Parliament, reaching out as a machinery of representative democracy
> . . . but the Church, quartering the land not into a few hundred
> constituencies but into ten thousand parishes, impinging on the daily

23. J. Obelkevich, *Religion and Rural Society: South Lindsey, 1825–75*, Oxford UP, 1976, pp. 258–61; Rule, 'Methodism, popular beliefs and village culture', pp. 61–7.

24. A.D. Gilbert, *Religion and Society*, p. 7.

25. R. Currie, 'A micro-theory of Methodist growth', *Proceedings of the Wesley Historical Soc.*, XXXVI, 1967, pp. 65–73, 26.

26. Gilbert, *Religion and Society*, p. 27.

concerns of the great majority, supporting its black-coated intelligentsia, bidding for a monopoly of education, piety and political acceptability.[27]

Although the rapid decline of the church courts into virtual desuetude over the eighteenth century removed the only institutional form of church control over the moral behaviour of the lower orders, they could hardly be unaware of the continuing power of the parson operating both through the vestry and through areas of personal control such as that over charity and at the vital moments of baptism, marriage and burial. By the last decade of the eighteenth century there is evidence that the wider powers of the Church, even in rural England, were weakening rather than enhancing its spiritual authority. Professor Evans has shown how rapidly the Church not only lost the attachment of the rural populace but aroused its hostility as tithe gathering became more rapacious and as clerical justices became increasingly common.[28]

The decline of the Anglican Church as a purveyor of religion has often been seen by historians as related to the rise of Methodism, while positive aspects have hardly been noted. Nevertheless the efforts of conservative historians, although they have done much to restore the image of the Church of England after 1830, have done little to qualify the depiction of the period from the early eighteenth century to that date as a 'phase of prolonged, rapid, and disastrous decline'.[29] To write, as one historian has recently, that 'a sign of the vitality and strength of Orthodox churchmanship in the eighteenth century was its capacity to put forth new branches: Methodism and Evangelicalism' is to make one point while obscuring another. It is indeed the case that both of these 'new branches' professed an orthodox Arminian theology and regarded themselves as movements within rather than against the Church of England. However, they originated in the vitality of *some* churchmen motivated by what they considered their Church's general *lack* of vitality.[30]

John Wesley directed his mission towards the poor, whom he considered spiritually deprived and ignored. That his theology was orthodox and that his support for the monarch and the political establishment was unswerving are important. However, movements

27. J.C.D. Clark, *English Society*, p. 277 .

28. E.J. Evans, 'Some reasons for the growth of English rural anti-clericalism *c.* 1750–1830', *Past and Present*, **66**, 1975, pp. 92–104.

29. Gilbert, *Religion and Society*, p. 29.

30. J.C.D. Clark, *English Society*, p. 235.

often develop in directions unintended by their founders. There *was* a significant challenge to the establishment inherent in Methodism's message, its organisational novelties and its presumption of spiritual equality. Those of the gentry and clergy who perceived this may have been driven by instinct and may have over-reacted. They may have seen some dangers in Methodism which were not in fact there. It was in no sense a revival of the *political* dissent symbolised by Cromwellian puritanism. But there is truth in the telling of Wesley by one gentleman: 'You are the most disturbing dogs in the nation.' A warrant was issued by one justice against a preacher in the name of 'A person, his name unknown who disturbs the peace of the parish'. John Wesley was a reluctant convert to open-air preaching – 'I would have thought the saving of souls almost a sin, if it had not been done in a church' – but at Bristol in 1739 he followed the example of George Whitefield and 'submitted to be more vile, and proclaimed in the highways the glad tidings of salvation'. He was no more eager to accept local lay preachers; but he overcame his reluctance and these two developments became Methodism's most visible and challenging features.[31]

Charles, John Wesley's brother, co-itinerant and best-known hymn writer, noted the appearance of 'exhorters', as local preachers were first known, in west Cornwall as early as 1746. His reaction was a very guarded welcome.

> I advised and charged them not to stretch themselves beyond their line by speaking out of the [local] society, or by fancying themselves public teachers. If they keep within their bounds as they promise, they may be useful in the church.[32]

In the following year John Wesley examined the qualities of eighteen exhorters who had emerged in the Cornish Societies. Three of them he thought had special gifts but five were 'dangerous'. The remaining ten might be useful 'when there was no preacher in their own or neighbouring societies provided they would take no step without the advice of those who had more experience than themselves'.[33] There were around forty exhorters in England by this time, so their growth does seem to have been especially marked in Cornwall. John Wesley could admire the correctness with which 'an

---

31. John Wesley, *Journal.* There are so many editions available including several useful abridgements that date of entry rather than page numbers will be cited. Entries for 9 September 1745, 29 March 1739, 2 April 1739, 19 June 1745.

32. Charles Wesley, *Journal,* entry dated 30 June 1746.

33. John Wesley, *Journal,* entry dated 7 July 1747.

unlearned tinner speaks extemporare', but more typical of his class was the reaction of one of his opponents in a letter to the Bishop of Exeter. He described the 'teacher' of the local Methodists as 'no better than a mean illiterate tinner, and what is surprising, but a boy of nineteen years old'. Here was Dr Johnson's fundamental reaction to lay preaching as 'utterly incompatible with social or civil society'.[34]

With much irritation the Duchess of Buckingham, who was after all the illegitimate daughter of a deposed king, wrote to the Countess of Huntingdon, an unusually high-born follower of George Whitefield:

> I thank your ladyship for the information concerning the Methodist preaching; their doctrines are most repulsive, and strongly tinctured with impertinence and disrespect towards their superiors, in perpetually endeavouring to level all ranks and to do away with all distinctions, as it is monstrous to be told that you have a heart as sinful as the common wretches that crawl on the earth.[35]

Persons of rank hardly needed anything as manifest as an active involvement in lay preaching on the part of the poor to resent the impropriety of an assertion of spiritual equality. When John Wesley asked 'a little gentleman' why a Methodist tinner had been arrested, he was told: 'Why the man is well enough in other things, but his impudence the gentlemen cannot bear. Why sir, he says he knows his sins are forgiven.'[36]

For the converted and those seeking to become so, the necessary support and pressure came from membership of the Society and participation in the regular local 'class meetings' into which it was divided. As class leaders as well as local preachers, persons of humble birth had the opportunity to play a responsible role in their communities. Confidence gained and abilities thus discovered, for example in organising or in public speaking, could be harnessed for wider purposes. In his biography of John Wesley the by then very conservative Robert Southey warned:

> Perhaps the manner in which Methodism has familiarized the lower classes to the work of combining in associations, making rules for their own governance, raising funds, and communicating from one part of

34. *Ibid.*, entry dated 4 September 1757; O. Bekerlegge (ed.), 'The Lavington Correspondence', *Proceedings of the Wesley Historical Soc.*, XLII, Part 6, 1980, pp. 175–6.
35. H.R. Niebuhr, *The Social Sources of Denominationalism*, Meridian, New York, 1957, p. 61.
36. John Wesley, *Journal*, entry dated 25 June 1745.

the kingdom to another, may be reckoned among the incidental evils which have arisen from it.[37]

Southey's life was published in 1820 and even then its tone was rather more prophetic than a reference to an 'evil' which already existed. Following what has become known as the 'Halévy thesis', historians have more readily seen Methodism as a force for stability against 'the threat of revolution' than as one which worked for it. In the apprehensive 1790s hostility towards Methodism certainly increased. Partly because it was increasing in numbers; more particularly because it was seeking to gain a foothold in the rural parishes which had thus far been largely impervious to its appeal and especially because, in the era of the French Revolution, anything which seemed to pose a threat to the Church of England established by law was suspect. Despite their protestations of loyalty, Methodists could not escape being associated with Jacobinism by some.[38]

Those who tend to see the eighteenth century as above all 'the Age of Wesley' usually bring a good deal of retrospectivity to their view of the rise of Methodism over a period at the end of which Methodists were still not especially numerous in the nation as a whole. Wesleyan membership in 1816 was 189,777 to which the breakaway New Connexion added only 8,146. Even if we multiply this by three to allow for the greater number who considered themselves adherents although they had not joined the Society, and then increase the resulting 200,000 to half a million to allow for more casual 'hearers', this is still not a large fraction of a population of 10 million. At the time of the American Revolution in 1776, when Wesley took great pains to publicise the 'loyalty' of Methodists, there were only 30,875 members. John Walsh has written of Methodism earlier in the century when it was still painfully experiencing instigated mob hostility that it is 'improbable that infant Methodism was strong enough to have much overall effect as an emollient to industrial disturbance, let alone prevent a general revolt'. Eric Hobsbawm has similarly written off its significance in explaining why Britain escaped revolution. He has pointed both to its overall lack of numbers and to the fact that some of the areas where it was strong, west Cornwall for example, were not in any case likely locations for revolutionary agitation.[39]

37. Robert Southey, *Life of Wesley*, Frederick Warne, 1893 edn, p. 522.
38. The clearest statement of the thesis is in the first volume of E. Halevy, *History of the English People in the Nineteenth Century*, rept. Ernest Benn, 1961.
39. J.D. Walsh, 'Elie Halevy and the birth of Methodism', *Trans. of the Royal Hist. Soc.*, XXV, 1975, pp. 1– 20; E.J. Hobsbawm, *Labouring Men*, pp. 23–33.

It has been suggested that Methodism generally produced an attitude of mind and sense of resignation as well as the habits of order and 'industry' which combined to reinforce in the proletariat the necessary submission to the disciplinary imperatives of industrial capitalism. Edward Thompson in particular has stressed this effect, writing of Methodism's late-eighteenth and early-nineteenth-century leaders:

> They weakened the poor from within by adding . . . the active
> ingredient of submission; and they fostered within the Methodist
> Church those elements most suited to make up the psychic component
> of the work-discipline of which the manufacturers stood most in
> need.[40]

Methodism was in an unusual position to do this. For although the great mass of its membership was working class, it also embraced an increasing section of the industrial bourgeoisie. The effect of Methodism in increasing the acceptance of harsh working conditions by its working-class adherents was remarked by William Beckford on a visit to a Cornish mine as early as 1787.

> Piety as well as gin helps to fill up their leisure moments. . . .
> Methodism has made a very rapid progress, and has been of no trifling
> service in diverting the attention of these sons of darkness from their
> present condition to the glories of the life to come.[41]

There is little doubt either of the 'extraordinary correspondence between the virtues which Methodism inculcated in the working class and the desiderata of middle-class Utilitarianism', or of the fact that through the process of religious conversion and its reinforcement through the spiritual discipline of the Methodist system of regular 'class' meetings, these attitudes were deeply instilled. All this gives it some importance in bringing the workforce to acceptance of the new work disciplines of the industrial revolution. But how much importance, as with the question of its role in averting revolution, depends upon an assessment of Methodist strength. Of the minority of the working classes who were Methodists by 1815 even after the growth surge which began in the 1790s, most were not members of the forming industrial proletariat. Miners apart, artisans have been shown by Dr Field to have been the group most closely associated with Methodism. Around two-thirds of its eighteenth-century membership were 'manufacturers' in the sense of

---

40. E.P. Thompson, *Making of the English Working Class*, p. 390.
41. Cited in A.K. Hamilton Jenkin, *The Mines and Miners of Cornwall*, VI, Barton, Truro, 1963, pp. 5–6.

the time, that is working craftsmen like weavers and tailors. While it established centres of strength in many of the growing industrial towns of the Black Country, the West Riding and south Lancashire, it was, *relative* to the population, stronger in the manufacturing and mining *villages*. The hand-loom weaver on the eve of his long decline was much more likely to have been a Methodist than was the mule spinner of the new generation proletariat. Methodism also became and remained strong in some urban centres of old-style manufacturing such as Norwich and the Potteries.[42] In an interesting but rather elusive study of Methodism, which sees it as 'the English counterpart to the democratic revolution', the critical dynamic in a 'modernisation' of English society which bypassed the need for revolution, Professor Semmel writes that Wesley primarily addressed his message to 'The poor of the nascent proletariat of England's growing factory towns'. To present Methodism as essentially an urban phenomenon is seriously misleading. Wesley made little progress with agricultural labourers because they were tied into the rigidities of the traditional social order, although he blamed it on the stolid stupidity of the peasantry, but in many mining and manufacturing villages Methodism throve. Probably many urban employers in the new forms of manufacture would have liked more of their workers to have become self-disciplined Methodists, but it was the employers of the village-dwelling miners who could already appreciate the benefits by the beginning of the nineteenth century.[43]

The phase of Methodist growth which began in the 1790s was not marked simply by the addition of numbers. The revivalist excitement of the early years reappeared. Revivalism also began to appear in the parallel growth of some of the dissenting churches and, most extremely, in the emergence of extraordinary movements of popular messianism and millenarianism. Edward Thompson has placed the fervent nature of popular religious outbursts in the excited years of the French Revolutionary wars into a pattern of oscillation with the peaks of popular radicalism, serving as the 'chiliasm of the defeated and the hopeless'. The defeat of British Jacobinism at the end of the 1790s was the starting point of an effervescence of fringe religious movements. The best known was that which followed the Devonshire prophetess Joanna Southcott. She first recognised her call in 1792 at the age of forty-two and at her death in 1814 was still

42. Dr Field's findings are cited in D. Hempton, *Methodism and Politics*, p. 14. Dr Hempton's study is more wide-ranging than its title perhaps suggests.
43. B. Semmel, *The Methodist Revolution*, Heinemann, 1974, pp. 72–3.

announcing that she was to bear a saviour child, the 'Almighty Shiloh'. Her disciples kept her body warm for several days, expecting a resurrection. The child she could not present, but at least 100,000 people believed in her. She had once been a warm Methodist and so too, probably, had been most of her followers. For those who see Methodism only through the solid shopkeeper image of Victorian times, this may seem a strange assertion. That safe and quiet Methodism had little in common with the revived excitement of the wartime years. Methodism then, as Southey remarked, made of religion 'a thing of sensation and passion, craving perpetually for sympathy and stimulants'.[44] Cornwall was particularly prone to revivals, so much so that their occurrence suggests their functional role was one of periodic recruitment to and consolidation of the membership. That of 1814, however, became known as the Great Revival and it was much more than simply a recruitment phenomenon. So striking was the experience that many were said to believe it was preparatory to the end of the world.

> Such a sight as the chapel of Redruth afforded, and the other towns and parishes in succession was never witnessed here. Men crying with loud and bitter cries, till the anguish of their souls had opened every pore of the body, and produced a perspiration which fell from their face to the ground. From this you may form some idea of their distress, and the holy violence used in entering the strait gate. Almost all temporal business was at a stand, and the shops mostly shut up. When market day came there was scarce any buying or selling, for all were 'labouring for the bread which endureth to eternal life'. The cries for mercy were not confined to the chapel, but extended to the streets, and men and women were seen . . . in the streets, supported on each side from the chapel to their houses, for they could neither stand nor walk, and were not ashamed to, 'cry to Him who is able to save'. In the Redruth circuit alone . . . they have added two thousand to the society.[45]

Excitement indeed! and it even caught up a sober and spiritually distanced Quaker who could not 'find words sufficient to draw it in colours strong enough' but has left a useful description of a phenomenon which seems to have lasted for several weeks, 'when the great noise subsided, but the fire still existed'. He found words

44. E.P. Thompson, *Making of the English Working Class*, pp. 419–31; A. Smith, *The Established Church and Popular Religion 1750–1850*, Longman, 1970, pp. 43–4. See also J.F.C. Harrison, *The Second Coming: Popular Millenarianism in England 1780–1850*, Routledge, 1979.

45. Anon., *Account of the Remarkable Revival of the Work of God in Cornwall*, Dublin, 1814, pp. 5–6.

strong enough to describe a 'torrent' which 'bore down everything in its way', a 'great current' and 'an extraordinary agitation'.[46]

Cornwall was no centre of radicalism, so one would not look there for a pattern of oscillation, but a detailed study of the Great Yorkshire Revival of 1792–6 has led its author to the conclusion that Thompson's speculative idea gains some support from the experience of the North. In any case any pattern of interaction between popular radicalism and revivalism, whether oscillating or of any other kind, could not be discerned in a period bounded by 1815. It would need to look at least at the two following decades.[47]

POPULAR RECREATIONS

Methodism may not have been 'puritan' in the challenging sense of the seventeenth century, but it was so in its behavioural attitudes. From the beginning it confronted the secular 'idle' pastimes of the labouring poor, prohibited them to its followers and generally opposed the 'forces of revelry'. Towards the end of the eighteenth century Anglican evangelicalism reinforced the attack, but it operated *on* the poor; Methodism did that and worked *in* the hearts and minds of the poor. What both opposed was a vital popular culture, which had in the eighteenth century entered on a vigorous phase. The pastimes of the 'plebs' included rude sports such as wrestling, cudgelling, football, quoits, bear and badger baiting and cock fighting. Such activities revolved around the agricultural calendar, village feasts, markets and hiring fairs, or, in the case of manufacturing workers, traditional holidays including 'Saint Monday'.

Edward Thompson maintains that for a variety of reasons traditional pursuits were strongly resilient through the eighteenth century and were weakened only by forces which developed in the nineteenth. His view of a robust plebeian culture embraces more than recreation, although the forms this took played an important and integrated role in a popular culture which represented a whole way of life. It was the 'comparative freedom' of the common people which invigorated this popular culture. 'This is the century which sees the erosion of half-free forms of labour, the decline of living-in, the final extinction of labour services and the advance of free,

46. Hamilton Jenkin, *News from Cornwall*, Westaway Books, 1951, p. 179.
47. J. Baxter, 'The great Yorkshire revival 1792–6: A study of mass revival among the Methodists', *Sociological Yearbook of Religion in Britain*, VII, 1974, pp. 67–8.

mobile, wage labour.'[48] Capitalism, if the labour market was to operate, needed a workforce which was both mobile and wage responsive, and this meant an interim period in which old forms of control were eroded before newer and more appropriate forms of social and industrial control had fully emerged to take their place. Henry Fielding perceived this in 1751 when he wrote:

> . . . the commonality by degrees shook off their vassalage, and became more and more independent of their superiors. Even servants, in process of time, acquired a state of freedom and independency unknown to this rank in any other nation; and which, as the law now stands, is inconsistent with a servile condition.
>
> But nothing hath wrought such an alternation in this order of people as the introduction of trade. This hath indeed given a new face to the whole nation, hath in a great measure subverted the former state of affairs, and hath almost totally changed the manners, customs, and habits of the people, more especially of the lower sort.[49]

The great novelist, here writing as a criminologist, was evidently seeking to describe a social accompaniment of the transition to a capitalist mode of production, which to him as a magistrate was most evident as a problem of order. Changes in hiring forms and in master-to-man relationships tending towards the predomination of the wage form in both agriculture and manufacturing resulted in only a part of the labourer's life, his working hours, being under the control of his employer. As other forms of control and influence, such as that of the lower clergy, diminished, the people were given a space in which to make their own culture. This freedom did not necessarily find expression in forms which were in conflict with the ruling patrician elite. In fact the country gentry were able to patronise popular leisure to some extent in a paternalist extension of their own authority, since no change in the status system was involved. There is, for most of the century, no simple suggestion of a dominant class resisting a popular culture and attempting to supplant it with a preferred alternative, but rather a willingness not only to tolerate it but to accept a functional involvement.

This was not new in the eighteenth century. Peter Burke has shown how in early modern Europe the gentry had enjoyed participation in many of the recreations of the poor, but in the eighteenth century their role in patronising and encouraging certain popular

---

48. E.P. Thompson, 'Patrician society, plebeian culture', pp. 382–405.

49. Henry Fielding, *An Inquiry into the Causes of the late increase of Robbers etc.*, 1751, p. xi.

activities served broader purposes. Through the manipulation of doles in times of dearth, the putting up of prizes for sports and the supplying of beer for calendrical and special festivities, together with an elaborate and conscious 'social theatre' of ceremony, the gentry were able to rule *and* distance themselves from the consequences of their own exploitation. Reciprocation is inherent in a relationship which is an act of giving from above and of receiving from below. Thus the poor were not slow to demand (perhaps as a crowd, with its own forms of theatre and symbolism) recognition of what they considered their 'rights'. In such practices the links, for example, between food rioting for 'just prices' and persisting in lighting bonfires in public places on 5 November even if they were regarded as 'nuisances' by authorities, are evident.[50]

Robert Malcolmson's pioneering researches have placed eighteenth-century recreations sociologically with a thoroughness and insight which can hardly be equalled in a general textbook. He has described the vulgar pastimes of football, bull baiting, etc. and revealed the extent of gentry encouragement and patronage. He has also noted the importance of publicans as profit-minded promoters of plebeian events. How far can their involvement be viewed as a counter tendency, i.e. one working towards commercialisation of working-class leisure? This is an important consideration, but for the moment it can be noted that the activities of the drink sellers took place within existing recreational forms. They were an adjunct to and lubricant for existing activities rather than part of the supplanting of a traditional culture.[51]

In the countryside the timing of feasts, festivals, fairs and wakes was determined largely by the farming calendar and there was a degree of integration between the rhythms of work and those of leisure, leading Thompson to suggest some degree of anachronism in the use by historians of the word 'leisure'. Much recreation was associated with occasions which served to bind the community and emphasise its cohesiveness. Malcolmson has shown that fairs had special significance in terms of courtship and sexual activity for the young as well as allowing participants the chance of winning status and prestige among their peers. The older villagers mainly watched, but by so doing at least attached themselves to and reinforced the validity of the actions of the young. As important as any of the func-

---

50. P. Burke, *Popular Culture in Early Modern Europe*, Temple Smith, 1978, p. 25.
51. R.W. Malcolmson, *Popular Recreations*, pp. 71–4.

tions of popular recreation was the simple element of 'carnival' introducing moments of release into hard and humdrum lives.[52]

Group solidarity was the cornerstone of plebeian activity, for it was as a group that the poor both sported and, on occasion, demanded their rights, fair prices or customary access. It was as a group that they could in 'counter-theatre' mock, mimic and remind their social superiors of their presence as well as discipline offenders against their community norms through charivaris or similar folk forms of expressing displeasure. As a crowd they had power as well as anonymity. In the detailed researches of Malcolmson and others there is ample illustration of the vigour of recreational forms which were an essential part of a plebeian culture, consideration of which is central to an understanding of the social relations of the period.

A different perspective on eighteenth-century leisure has been offered by Professor Plumb. He has seen in the later eighteenth and early nineteenth centuries the emergence of a commercial 'leisure industry' responding to a bourgeois desire to emulate the existing minority culture of the elite. He has illustrated the expanding provision of leisure opportunities for a growing middle class and offered a convincing account of, for example, the spread of newspapers and periodical literature and the complex of activities associated with the remarkable rise of the leisure towns. Indeed, their growth, which Dr Borsay has described as a key dynamic in an 'urban renaissance' between 1680 and 1760, is central to his argument for an expanding leisure industry. However, although Professor Plumb suggests the participation of 'better-off' tradesmen he clearly sees the leisure industry as catering mostly for the expanding and increasingly prosperous middle class. But is there a possibility that it reached further? Plumb, though he mentions horse racing, with working-class spectators, and prize fighting, is really talking about a culture dependent on literacy, not about traditional sports, and about an added dimension to bourgeois life. Thompson is concerned to place plebeian recreations into a popular *mentalité* which remained active through the eighteenth century. The leisure industry was an urban phenomenon at a time when most of the population did not live in towns. For urban artisans the receiving of a handed-down leisure product is at least plausible, but in the

---

52. *Ibid.*, pp. 53–5; R.W. Bushaway, *By Rite*, pp. 34–63, for the role of calendar customs. See also D.A. Reid, 'Interpreting the festival calendar: wakes and fairs as carnivals', in Storch (ed.), *Popular Culture and Custom*, pp. 125–53.

countryside where no significant group mediated between patrician and pleb, it is much less so. Professor Plumb has suggested that commercial leisure was beginning to squeeze popular as well as 'high' culture. Thompson, on the contrary, has drawn lines which link the plebs with the patricians to form a deference/patronage model making sense of many aspects of social relations in a century in which the space between an old paternalist (master/servant) relationship and the coming discipline of the industrial economy was filled with a plebeian culture of evident vitality.[53]

Perhaps a commercial squeeze on popular recreational forms can at least be seen in London and possibly other growing urban centres. Henry Fielding wrote of the capital in 1751: 'What an immense variety of places has this town and its neighbourhood set apart for the amusement of the lowest order of the people.' By the time Francis Place was serving his apprenticeship in the 1780s he and his fellows were avid consumers of leisure. Apprenticeship was, however, a youth as much as a class phenomenon, and although Horace Walpole might remark of Vauxhall pleasure garden that everybody from 'the Duke of Grafton down to children out of the Foundling hospital' went there, an admission fee of 2s 6d a head was a considerable barrier, though some women from the lower orders went there in the way of business.

In a challenging analysis Hans Medick has pointed to the increasing output of gin as indicating greater working-class *expenditure* on leisure. Gin was, after all, commercially produced and consumed only by the lower orders. Thompson's work has emphasised a tradition-based resistance to emerging capitalism but, Medick suggests, concentrates on only one dimension of the relationship between plebeian culture and the expansion of capitalist markets. The other dimension, he argues, is found in an everyday life which was to some extent in harmony with the market economy – in consumption, in fashion and especially in changing forms of plebeian drinking. In this dimension the lower orders did invest *money* as well as 'emotional capital' in leisure. Despite low incomes they had not switched priority to the long-term needs of their households. Instead, conditioned by the nature of the family economy inherited from days of lower wage-dependency, they regarded earnings above those necessary for a customary material standard of living as a sur-

53. J.H. Plumb, 'The commercialisation of leisure', in McKendrick, Brewer and Plumb, *Birth of a Consumer Society*, pp. 265–85; P. Borsay, 'The English urban renaissance: the development of provincial urban culture', *Social History*, II, 2, 1977, pp. 581–603.

plus which could be spent on leisure, festivities and luxuries. This suggests that the constant complaints of their social superiors, that the poor's expenditure was irrationally related to their incomes, were not simply class prejudice. There was clearly a rising consumption of gin which was equally clearly a capitalist product. Indeed, initially favoured by the government to soak up excess cereal production, it was one which linked agricultural, manufacturing and commercial capitalism before it reached its proletarian consumers. Consumption increased sixfold between 1700 and 1743, suggesting that to some degree traditional culture was being undermined by changes in the demand for and taste in leisure – a chosen indulgence on the part of the lower orders.[54]

Medick has posed an important question, but his English examples are narrowly drawn. How representative was *London's* 'Gin Age'? The rise of spirit smuggling, gin, rum and brandy, reflects an increase in national consumption, but we do not know enough to suggest that the drinking culture was changing in the countryside and in the small towns. The beer and cider which lubricated the great festivities of the rural calendar, as at harvest for example, were not bought, they were made by farmers and were expected largesse. Evidence from manufacturing also indicates that drinking customs continued to be linked to beer consumption, quite often expected from employers as a perquisite.[55] Nevertheless, Medick's linking of new forms of recreation to the early period of adjustment to a money wage and to well-noted irregular rhythms of labour offers a more convincing explanation for the commercialisation of working-class leisure than does a simple downward percolation of middle-class forms. From his approach it is possible to link some eighteenth-century forms of recreation to the revised view of nineteenth-century forms recently presented by Dr Cunningham with its greater emphasis on commercial provision for working-class tastes.[56]

From at least the closing years of the eighteenth century the decline of gentry involvement and even tolerance of plebeian sports was evident. Malcolmson has commented that a result of this withdrawal of patronage by the gentry and the better-off farmers as social distance increased was that 'a solid barrier so developed between the culture of gentility and the culture of the people'.[57]

---

54. Fielding, *Inquiry*, p. 9; cited in P. Corfield, *Impact of English Towns*, p. 80; H. Medick, 'Plebeian culture', pp. 84–113.
55. Rule, *Experience of Labour*, pp. 199–201.
56. H. Cunningham, *Leisure in the Industrial Revolution*, Croom Helm, 1980.
57. Malcolmson, *Popular Recreations*, p. 167.

Northamptonshire mumming, Shrovetide football, and 'Plough Mondays' are examples of practices which were no longer encouraged and to an extent positively discouraged by a gentry which increasingly distanced itself from rude diversions and vulgar games. Evangelicalism became an especially potent force in the attack on traditional pastimes. It was distinguished by a belief in the inherent depravity of popular recreational forms. Such activities were not just a waste of time which could be more usefully passed making profits for capitalists. They were not just inconvenient and disruptive, but sinful. The evangelical movement within the Church of England, from the royal proclamation of 1787 issued at the instigation of William Wilberforce, aimed at stirring up the vigilant suppression of 'vice' and attacked pastimes even when they were not breaking the sabbath. Committed evangelicals were a minority, but the movement greatly influenced the attitudes of a wider section of the ruling classes in the way they came to regard plebeian recreations.[58]

Where Methodism took hold, the force of the new puritanism was vastly more effective, largely because it attached sections of the working class itself to the moral crusade and began that polarisation of 'respectable' and 'rough' which was a developing feature in working-class communities in the nineteenth century. John Wesley had confronted popular recreational forms from the early days of his mission. His *Journal* records his disgust with the 'savage ignorance and wickedness' of the Newcastle colliers who assembled on Sundays to 'dance, fight, curse and swear and play at chuck-ball, span-farthing, or whatever came next to hand'. In 1766 he arrived at Otley on feast day and found the town 'gone mad in noise, hurry, drunkenness, rioting, confusion, to the shame of a Christian country'. Charles Wesley congratulated himself in 1744 that as a consequence of his having preached against wrestling on his visit to Cornwall in the preceding year, the village of Gwennap had been unable to find enough men for their next contest, 'all the Gwennap men being struck off the Devil's list, and found wrestling against him not for him'. By the early nineteenth century even an Anglican clergyman was prepared to give credit to the Methodists for the fact that in Cornwall there were no more 'desperate wrestling matches . . . and inhuman cockfights' and fewer 'riotous revellings'. It was not simply a matter of counter action, for the chapel with its meetings, services, love-feasts, etc. became in itself a centre of non-work-

---

58. For a fuller discussion of pressure on recreations, see Rule, *Labouring Classes*, pp. 216–26.

time activities and as the nineteenth century advanced, a deliberate purveyor of counter attraction.[59]

Such attacks were reinforcing the pressures on time and space which in a changing economy were restricting the room allowed to traditional recreational forms. In 1824 a retrospective view regretted as one of the social costs of enclosure that 'the poor have no place on which they can amuse themselves in summer evenings, when the labour of the day is over, or when a holiday occurs'. It was an echo of Goldsmith's *Deserted Village* written more than fifty years earlier.

> Those healthful sports that graced the peaceful scene,
> Lived in each look, and brightened all the green;
> These, far departing, seek a kinder shore,
> And rural mirth and manners are no more.

Town growth, too, as William Hutton's history of Birmingham indicates, threatened space,[60] especially as much of it was a matter of infilling within existing boundaries. However, even by the middle years of the nineteenth century an industrial city like Manchester had not expanded so far as to prevent its mill workers walking in the country on Sundays. The long, regimented day, six of which made up a working week, obviously constrained the recreational possibilities for factory workers. The evidence is clear, too, that in mining districts the first part of the nineteenth century saw a serious erosion of holidays. In most towns, however, the factory system was hardly evident and many urban workers seem to have been still keeping hold of Saint Monday as, almost, an accepted holiday in 1815. At least, that is what the evidence from both Birmingham and Bristol suggests. As for the countryside, the main complaint of the wage labourer was of underemployment and at certain seasons of the agricultural calendar many of them must have wished they did not have time on their hands. In this respect, as in so many others, the eighteenth-century economy was a developing rather than a developed one. The transformation of leisure, like the transformation of work, had for large numbers of the labouring poor hardly begun even by its end.[61]

---

59. John Wesley, *Journal*, entries dated 1 April 1743, 10 July 1743, 15 May 1749, 4 August 1766; Charles Wesley, *Journal*, 4 August 1744; R. Warner, *A Tour Through Cornwall in 1808*, 1809, pp. 300–1.

60. W. Hutton, *A History of Birmingham*, 1781.

61. For Birmingham, see D.A. Reid, 'Decline of Saint Monday', and for Bristol, M. Harrison, *Crowds and History*, Chapter 5.

CHAPTER SEVEN
The Standard of Living

Money-wage data and real-wage series based on full-time adult male earnings have serious limitations in the assessment of living standards but can convey much useful information on the wage economy. They allow comparisons between occupations; within occupations over time; between male and female workers, and between regions. Joseph Massie's well-known survey of 1759 emphasised two main differentials: that craftsmen's wages were higher than those of common labourers, while in both categories wages were higher in London than in the provinces. A third should be added: that men's wages were invariably higher than women's, even if for similar or even identical work.[1]

Discussion of eighteenth-century wages – money or real – is helped by dividing the period at the beginning of the French wars in 1793, for not only did 1792 represent an earnings peak for many workers, but the wage history of 1793 to 1815 is dramatically different from that of the preceding ninety years. Over the latter generally slowly improving money wages brought a degree of improvement in real wages because cereal prices were generally low over the first half of the century. Thereafter the accelerating rate of population growth coincided with the ending of the bounty of generally good harvests to turn the trend in the cost of living sharply upwards, while in most regions the increase in the labour force changed a labour market in which wages had generally held up for more than half a century. As two leading historical demographers have recently stressed: 'The largest and most obvious effect of the sharp rise in population in the eighteenth century was on the national average wage of labour.' The kinds of productivity change which can in-

---

1. P. Mathias, 'The social structure in the eighteenth century: a calculation by Joseph Massie' in *The Transformation of England*, Methuen, 1979, pp. 186–7, Table 9.1.

crease output sufficiently to offset *rapid* population growth were becoming significant only in the early nineteenth century. This does
not mean that the pace of innovation and of capital formation in
the eighteenth-century economy were negligible. Indeed, they were
sufficient to allow an increase in the labour force of about 5 per
cent at constant wages. Any slower rate, as for example in the first
half of the eighteenth century, allowed real wages to rise.[2] The
demographic acceleration of the second half of the century depressed them quite sharply, except in those areas in the North and
Midlands where manufacturing change and expansion were locally
creating a different labour market.[3] This was a significant exception, but although their higher rate of natural increase and migration into the rising manufacturing districts enlarged the population
of earners in the 'better-waged' districts absolutely and proportion-
ately, this was insufficient to prevent a fall in the national average
real wage.

Figure 7.1 Two real-wage indices: Phelps Brown and Hopkins and a
composite 'national' index

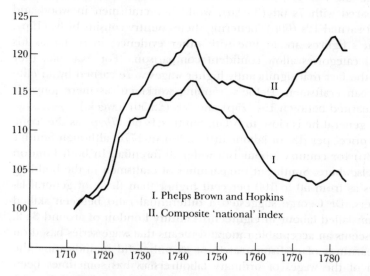

Source: E.A. Wrigley and R.S. Schofield, *The Population History of England
1541–1871.* Cambridge UP, 1989, p. 432.

2. R.D. Lee and R.S. Schofield, 'British population in the eighteenth century' in
Floud and McCloskey, *Economic History of Britain*, p. 28.
3. This key regional variation has recently been re-emphasised in E.H. Hunt and
R.W. Botham, 'Wages in Britain during the industrial revolution'.

REGIONAL DIFFERENCES

Since the long-established, much-criticised index on which Figure 7.1 is based relies on southern wage data for critical years during the crucial third quarter of the eighteenth century, it probably tends to a degree of pessimism, but an insufficient one to affect the trend. This is not surprising if we take account of two factors. Firstly, the dynamism of the newly industrialising areas provided a net rather than an entire gain to manufacturing output, for historians have increasingly come to recognise that it was in part linked to a measure of 'de-industrialisation' in the South and East.[4] Secondly, noticeable as was migration into, for example, west Lancashire, it did not match the continued pouring of people into London, for which city the evidence for a decline in real wages in the second half of the century is ample and conclusive.[5] This is the general picture which needs now to be examined in detail.

According to Massie in 1759, London's labourers earned 9s (45p) a week compared with a country level of 5s (25p). The capital's textile workers, predominantly in silk, earned 10s 6d (52½p) compared with 7s 6d (37½p), while her craftsmen in wood and metal earned 12s (60p), bettering their country cousins by 3s (15p). Massie's figures are in line with other evidence, in so far as his broad categories allow confident comparison. (For example, they hide the fact that significantly higher wages were earned by an elite of urban craftsmen. Defoe's 'topping workmen' as mere journeymen earned between 15s (75p) and 50s (£2.50) a week.)

In general he is close to Adam Smith's 1s 6d (7½p) as the 'common price' per day of labour in London in 1776, although Smith's 8d (3p) for country labour is a wider differential. In both London and elsewhere, Smith put the earnings of craftsmen in the building trades as from 50 to 100 per cent higher than those of general labourers. Dr George suggested a differential ratio between skilled and unskilled labour in eighteenth-century London of around 3 : 2. This seems an acceptable ratio and means that wage series based on the earnings of craftsmen are not as unhelpful in indicating the trend of the wages of ordinary labourers as has sometimes been suggested. While the ability of organised skilled workers to restrict entry to their trade and to develop defensive strategies probably

---

4. See for example M. Berg, *Age of Manufactures*, Chapter 5.

5. This is clear from the migration figures in P. Deane and W.A. Cole, *British Economic Growth*, pp. 108–9. For the standard of living in London, see L.D. Schwarz, 'Standard of living in the long run'.

means their wages rose more sharply when the economy turned up, and fell less quickly on the downturns, this would have the effect of flattening fluctuations rather than of misdirecting trends.[6]

Over the eighteenth century higher London wages had been driving some manufactures into the country. Stocking knitting had been removing to the east Midlands from the last years of the preceding century. Shoe making was progressively employing cheaper labour around and in Northampton, while in the 1780s calico printing moved north to Lancashire. In general the 'topping workmen' were rare enough in London and hardly existed elsewhere, except perhaps in some branches of the metal trades in Sheffield or Birmingham. At the other end of the skilled earning spectrum were those overstocked trades where entry premiums and skill levels were too low to keep wages much above those of common labourers. London's numerous tailors were such a case. For much of the century, their daily rate had been fixed by statute, initially in 1721 at 2s or 2s 6d (10–12½p) per day, but they were hardly ever able to find employment constant enough to earn more than 9s (45p) a week, and in their slack months even less. Required levels of literacy and dexterity kept the supply of compositors, on the other hand, in better balance with the demands of the printing trade. Dr Johnson considered them to be just about worth the guinea a week (£1.05) they generally earned. The saddlers were largely justified in 1777 in stating that their 12 to 15s (60 to 75p) a week was somewhat below the going rate for a skilled trade with a substantial entry premium. Masons seem to have earned around 15s in London over the first three-quarters of the eighteenth century, and if employment was regular, that seems to represent a 'middle line' for metropolitan artisans until the steeply inflationary 1790s.[7]

Wage differentials notwithstanding, the nominal wages of London's skilled men did not much move over the century until the last decade. Bricklayers' money wages, apart from a slight fall from 1736 to 1742, were unchanged from 1717 to 1792, and their labourers' rates shared their constancy at a ratio of 3 : 2. In the face of the low cereal prices of the first part of the century, this meant a rising trend until the mid 1750s then a sharp and sustained deterioration as the cost of living increased. Two periods, 1750–70 and the 1780s, saw especially sharp declines, although the generally high

---

6. Mathias, 'Social structure in the eighteenth century', Table 9.1; Adam Smith, *Wealth of Nations*, I, pp. 84, 116; M.D. George, *London Life*, pp. 160, 168–9. For the effectiveness of eighteenth-century trade unionism, see below pp. 201–13.

7. For these and other examples, see J.G. Rule, *Experience of Labour*, pp. 62–3.

level of economic activity in the latter may have compensated to a degree with fuller employment.

Table 7.1 London bricklayers: decennial averages of real wages

1720–29	140	1760–69	125
1730–39	154	1770–79	109
1740–49	144	1780–89	106
1750–59	140		

Source: L.D. Schwarz, 'The standard of living in the long run: London 1700 to 1850', *Econ. H.R.*, XL, 1987, pp. 40–1.

The figures indicate that the real-wage decline of London's workers was already marked before the impact of the soaring prices of the French war years (1793–1815), for there seems every reason to consider the trend of bricklayers' wages as representative. Both the 1750s and the 1760s contained food-price peaks, 1756–7 and 1766, but there is no escaping the conclusion that the general trend in the standard of living was inexorably downward. Dr Schwarz measures the decline of the 1760s as being as marked as that of the 1790s.[8]

Table 7.2 London bricklayers: changes in real-wage rates

1750–60	–9.5%	1780–90	–11.1%
1760–70	–14.2%	1790–1800	–14.6%
1770–80	–0.5%		

Source: L.D. Schwarz, 'The standard of living in the long run: London 1700 to 1850', *Econ. H.R.*, XL, 1987, p. 31.

Outside of London, too, generally over the South, the West and the South-east, a decline in real wages set in at some point in the two decades centred on 1760, as money wages fell behind rising prices. Dr Gilboy calculated that an annual £15 for the western labourer in 1750 had stretched to only £18.75 by 1775. More recently, Dr Snell has suggested that male real wages rose in the southern part of the country from 1740 to 1770, then stabilised before the whole gain was wiped out in the French war years. But for families standards of

8. Schwarz, 'Standard of living in the long run', p. 25 and appended data.

living were reduced by the fact that women's earnings had been falling from 1760. For these parts of the country the evidence on earnings would seem to justify Adam Smith's observation of 1776: 'the high price of provisions during these ten years past has not *in many parts of the kingdom* been accompanied with any sensible rise in the money price of labour'. The implication is perhaps that there were some parts in which it had; that will be considered below, after we have looked at the pattern of provincial money wages.[9]

Hand-loom weavers in the various textile manufactures were the most ubiquitous of manufacturing workers. For them Massie suggested a mid-century level of 7s 6d (37½p) a week which agrees well enough with a recent estimate of around £20 a year for West-Country woollen weavers in regular employment. Two of these reported earnings of 13s (65p) and 18s (90p) to a parliamentary enquiry in 1757, but calculated this on the basis of a fourteen- to sixteen-hour day by a family working as a unit. Where employed, living-in journeymen got their keep and 6s (30p), which rate was said to have persisted since the 1730s. These figures were produced in support of the employers' position in the course of a bitter wage dispute; the weavers claimed that on some types of cloth they could hardly make 4d (2p) a day. A line between these polemical extremes would come close to Massie's 7s 6d (37½p).[10]

Queen Anne's time had been the 'golden period' for the serge weavers of the Exeter region. Although an Exeter weaver could still make 9s (45p) a week in 1750, a level still persisting in nearby Taunton in 1764, by 1787 he had fallen to 8s (40p) and to 7s (35p) by 1791. Against this wage trend, the rising prices of the latter part of the century were bound to make for severe reductions in living standards. Professor Hoskins, basing his cost-of-living calculation on a range of local price data, not simply cereals, calculated that whereas real wages of labourers and craftsmen fell by around 30 per cent over the second half of the eighteenth century, those of most woollen workers fell by nearer 50 per cent. Earnings of other textile workers in the southern and eastern parts of the country, disclosed by Arthur Young in his *Tours* of the 1770s, suggest a range from the 10 to 12s (50–60p) earned by the specialist blanket weavers of Witney and carpet weavers of Wilton to a low of 5s (25p) scraped by Norwich worsted weavers at a time of serious decline in their trade.

9. E.W. Gilboy, *Wages in Eighteenth-century England*, pp. 220–1, 224; K.D.M. Snell, *Annals of the Labouring Poor*, Chapter 1; Smith, *Wealth of Nations*, I, p. 83.

10. For sources for textile wages, see Rule, *Experience of Labour*, p. 63.

In isolated centres of woollen or worsted weaving, like Romsey, Banbury and Kendal, around 9s a week (45p) seems to have been a 'seventies' norm for urban weavers.[11]

Wool combers, essential preparatory workers in the production of worsted yarn, earned more. Adam Smith presented them as an example of a small group of workers so strategically placed in the chain of production that they could command high wages. These hardly moved in money terms through the eighteenth century. At Tiverton in 1809 they had claimed they had received the same rate for 300 years! For most of the century they earned from 10 to 12s a week (50–60p), and could, it was often argued, have earned more if they had chosen to work more hours. Shearmen, who cut the pile to finish woollen cloth, were similarly paid. Cotton weavers hardly existed before the 1770s, during which decade they do not seem to have been able to command wages above the low norm of weavers in general, for although on some types of cloth as much as 12s (60p) could be earned, the average, like that of bleachers and dyers, seems to have been around 7s (35p). However, their fortunes were soon to enter on that switchback which took them first to a golden age, and then through impoverishment to extinction as they became first the beneficiaries of factory-produced yarn, and then the victims of their own expansion in numbers and, ultimately, of the power loom.[12] Framework knitters received comparable wages for turning yarn into stockings: in the 1770s from 6s (30p) a week down to 4s 6d (22½p) for the coarser varieties. These figures relate to 1778 when the knitters were seeking a parliamentary regulation of their wages to levels about a third higher, restoring earnings to the level of twenty years earlier before a long decline had set in. They did not achieve this, but their future was closely to parallel that of the cotton hand-loom weavers in moving through boom to desperation.[13]

Coal miners usually earned more than farm or common labourers. Estimates of the earnings of pitmen on the Tyne and Wear vary, but they seem to have been around 7s (35p) up to 1740 and then 10s (50p) up to 1790, with, at busy times, earnings reaching from 2 to 4s (10–20p) above this level. For Wigan's colliers a level of 10s 10d (54p) is recorded for 1752, and of 1s 6d (7½p) a day for 1764–5. Lancashire colliers seem to have been able to earn around

---

11. W.G. Hoskins, *Industry, Trade and People in Exeter, 1688–1800*, Exeter UP 1968, p. 56; Rule, *Experience of Labour*, p. 65.

12. Rule, *Experience of Labour*, p. 65.

13. *Ibid.*, p. 69.

1s 9d (8½p) a day by 1786, rather less than the 2s 3d (11p) then being earned on the Yorkshire coalfield, let alone the 3s (15p) for which Staffordshire miners were then striking. The earnings of metal miners are notoriously difficult to estimate because intricate systems of payment by results produced wide fluctuations.[14] Cornish tin and copper miners averaged between 5 and 7s (25–35p) in 1730, 7s 6d (37½p) in 1778 and 10s (50p) by the 1790s. Young estimated the wages of north-country lead miners at 7s 6d (37½p) in 1771.[15] Colliers probably, and metal miners possibly, were among groups who do not seem to have experienced the widespread fall in real earnings after 1760.

Outside London the highest wages were to be found in Birmingham and Sheffield, the great centres of hardware manufacture. Young in 1790 gave 10 to 25s (50p–£1.25) as the range for Birmingham but considered the higher level to predominate, making wages there 'the highest in Europe'. Twenty years earlier he had put the bottom of the range at 7s (35p). Then he had also been astonished to find that some of Sheffield's cutlery grinders earned from 18s (90p) to £1 a week. Daily earnings of 1s 6d (7½p) to 2s (10p) were general, while a small number of razor grinders could make 10s 6d (52½p) a day, 'surprising wages for any manual performance'. In 1792 wages in Sheffield were said to be so high generally as to allow the leisure-preferring cutlers to live comfortably from working only three days a week.[16]

Do the wages of these two great manufacturing centres indicate, along with the evidence from northern and Midland coalfields, that in the dynamic 'industrialising' regions, nominal wages were buoyant enough to maintain or even improve real earnings from mid century through to the 1780s despite the burden of rising prices? The pioneering wage data published by Dr Gilboy in 1934 revealed a very different trend in Lancashire after 1750 from that in London and the South. Her index of money wages for Lancashire (1700 = 100) rose from 133 in 1750, through 200 in 1780 to 267 by 1793. Over the third quarter of the century she estimated a rise in annual earnings of 50 per cent in the North against 7 per cent in the West and no rise at all in London. Reworking of her indices by Deane and Cole suggests that between the quinquennium 1750–4 to 1785–9 money wage rises in the South varied between less than 4 per cent for London labourers and 19.4 per cent for those of Kent, whereas

14. *Ibid.*, p. 65.
15. *Ibid.*, pp. 65–7.
16. *Ibid.*, pp. 67–8.

in Lancashire labourers gained 64 per cent and craftsmen 40.5 per cent over the period. As Dr Von Tunzelmann has pointed out, if the same price data are used, with the Lancashire wage data it would produce an increase in real wages from 1750 to 1780 of around 20 per cent, while with southern wage data a fall of around 15 per cent appears.[17]

The manufacturing and mining district of north Staffordshire has recently been claimed to share the Lancashire trend. An 18 per cent improvement in the real wages of general labourers between 1754–5 and 1788–92 has been estimated. The wages of building craftsmen rose from 1s 4d (6½p) a day in the 1750s to 2s (10p) in the mid 1770s and 2s 6d (12½p) around 1790, with the most distinct upward trend peaking around 1780. Carpenters gained a real-wage improvement of 10 per cent and bricklayers one of 14 per cent between 1750–4 and 1788–92. The major manufacture of the area, pottery, exhibits a wide variety of skills with corresponding wage levels, but skilled male potters seem to have enjoyed an unusually rapid wage increase from the late 1760s to the early 1790s, bringing a real-wage improvement of almost 50 per cent. The daily rate of hewers on the north Staffordshire coalfield advanced from 1s 5d a day to 2s 6d (7p to 12½p) between 1774–5 and 1789–92, a 75 per cent increase in money wages bringing a real improvement of 60 per cent. Wage information from Yorkshire is similarly supportive of the Gilboy position, suggesting a 50 per cent increase in the money wages of craftsmen and labourers in the West Riding between 1750 and 1780 and in the North Riding an increase of 100 per cent for the former and 33 per cent for the latter. Taking the evidence from those areas where industrial employment was expanding, Professor Malcolmson has accepted that they 'unquestionably experienced a general increase in real wages' during the last third of the eighteenth century, and qualify the generally unhappy standard of living experience over the rest of the country.[18]

The evidence for this regional divergence does not rest only on wage levels in manufacturing and mining. An important part of the argument is that the competitive effect of these expanding sectors in the district labour market was to raise the wages of agricultural labour. It began that division of agricultural England into a high-wage North and a low-wage South which is best known from Sir

---

17. Gilboy, *Wages in Eighteenth-century England*, pp. 220–4; Deane and Cole, *British Economic Growth*, pp. 18–19; G.N. Von Tunzelmann, 'Trends in real wages', pp. 39–40.
18. Hunt and Botham, 'Wages in Britain in the industrial revolution', pp. 388–97; R.W. Malcolmson, *Life and Labour*, p. 146.

James Caird's map drawn when the dichotomy was at its peak in 1850. Dr Hunt has pointed out that the geography of farm wages changed far more between 1750 and 1790 than at any time in the period 1790 to 1914.

The changes in fact were sufficient to transform the pre-industrial pattern of regional wages. In the 1760s most of England's high-wage counties were in the south-east and the greatest concentration of low-wage counties was in the north; by the 1790s, eight out of the eleven highest-wage counties were in the north and midlands and only three were in the south-east.[19]

Table 7.3: Regional wages in agriculture (pence per week rounded to nearest)

	South–east	South Midlands	East	South–west	West Midlands	North Midlands	North
1767/70	104	87	95	82	80	87	78
1795	114	95	114	94	92	117	124
1824	121	100	107	92	105	123	139

Source: G.N. Von Tunzelmann, 'Trends in real wages, 1750–1850, revisited'. *Econ. H.R.*, XXXII, 1979, p. 47.

It should be stressed that it is not nearness to industry *per se* which drew agricultural wages upwards, but proximity to the *expanding* newer industrial regions. Old centres of woollen manufacture and of mining in the South-west had no such effect. Comparing levels over twenty- or thirty-year periods does not reveal how even was the wage performance over them. Dr Schwarz has suggested that the evidence points to the regional divergence becoming a clear trend only after 1770, with falls in real wages in the 1760s being avoided only by some groups in Lancashire and Yorkshire.[20] Further, it seems likely that although it may have been the case in the earlier nineteenth century that the proportion of the English population living in the higher-waged North increased both as a result of a higher natural rate of increase and from in-migration, in 1801 53 per cent of the population still lived south of the Severn/Wash line, while north of it counties like Herefordshire and Worcestershire

19. Hunt, 'Industrialization and regional inequality', pp. 935–66.
20. Schwarz, 'Trends in real wage rates', p. 94.

were not high-waged. Deane and Cole have pointed out that the statistics of migration during the early industrial revolution suggest little in the way of a south-to-north population drift: 'What is surprising is the comparatively minor role played by migration in the early development of the main industrial areas.'[21] On the whole, up to 1780 the group seems to have lost population, then to have shown a small net gain before a more general movement becomes clear after 1801.

There seems little point in balancing group against group and region against region. What matters is that economic advances in some regions offset to a degree the general pressure on real wages of the rising population. That this was so, and that its effect was emphasised by the fact that it was largely in these same regions that opportunities for women and children to earn expanded when elsewhere they may even have declined, explains why home demand at least did not collapse despite increasing dependency ratios, very slowly growing income per capita and a deterioration in real wages on the part of, probably, the majority of the working population.

WAGES IN THE FRENCH WAR YEARS

The long stability of nominal wages ended abruptly in the 1790s. It had to, for the cost of living soared. The gentle price rise gave way to a rapid one, especially for food. Between 1783 and 1793 wheat had averaged 47s (£2.35) a quarter; between 1793 and 1801 it averaged 77s (£3.85) and from 1803 to 1813 92s (£4.60). In 1812 it had been an incredible 126s (£6.30). A cost of living index based more widely than on wheat, gives the estimates in Table 7.4.

The average from 1781 to 1790 had been 117.7, with the cheapest year, 1785, at 112.3 and the dearest, 1790, at 125.9. Faced with such an upward price trend it is hardly surprising that historians have tended to present the war years as a time of deteriorating living standards. According to Professor Thomis, it is 'an area of agreement' that wages were generally unable to keep up with steeply rising food prices, while Mathias, pointing to rising money wages as a feature of the period, concludes that inflating prices generally outpaced them.

21. Deane and Cole, *British Economic Growth*, pp. 111–13.

Table 7.4 The cost of living 1791–1815 (1850=100)

1791	121.2	1804	160.9
1792	118.3	1805	186.7
1793	127.3	1806	178.5
1794	130.7	1807	169.1
1795	153.8	1808	180.5
1796	159.5	1809	204.9
1797	138.8	1810	215.4
1798	136.9	1811	204.9
1799	155.7	1812	235.7
1800	207.1	1813	230.6
1801	218.2	1814	203.3
1802	160.9	1815	182.6
1803	156.8		

Source: P.H. Lindert and J.G. Williamson, 'English waters' living standards during the industrial revolution: a new look'. *Econ. H.R.* XXXVI, 1983, p. 11.

All this, supported by literary evidence, suggests deterioration: bleaker diets (but with the poor still demanding wheat), a decline in non-food purchasing, with standards probably lower than at any other time since the wars at the beginning of the eighteenth century.[22]

Von Tunzelmann, remarking that prices had the greater influence on real wage trends over this period, finds that the indices available are much closer to each other than they are for the periods on either side. They point to a real wage drop of 10 to 12 per cent from 1790 to 1795, then a slight recovery to around 5 per cent below the 1790 level over 1797–8, followed by a plunge bottoming in 1800–1 at 30 per cent below the 1790 level. Recovery took 1802–3 wages back to that level, but then a fall took them down 10 per cent by 1808–9, before they recovered this in 1810–11 then fell back somewhat to end the war years perhaps 5 to 8 per cent above the level at which they had begun it.[23]

If the food-crisis peaks of 1795, 1800–1 and 1812–13 are disregarded – for it can be firmly concluded that in those years, as in 1739–40 and 1766–7, the living standards of wage-earners must have been substantially, though temporarily, reduced – then the general real-wage trend of the war years suggests no marked movement

22. M.I. Thomis, *The Town Labourer and the Industrial Revolution*, Batsford, 1974, p. 153; Mathias, *First Industrial Nation*, p. 196.
23. Von Tunzelmann, 'Trends in real wages', p. 40.

either way. Instead it allows for the discovery of both marginal gainers and losers. Professor Flinn found no very wide gulf between wage and price increases and concluded that 'contrary to the very commonly made generalisation that rapidly rising prices tended to erode real wages . . . it seems that for many groups of workers . . . wage rates in general broadly kept pace with rising prices'.[24] The food price trend, as opposed to short-term fluctuations, over the war years was in the region of plus 65–85 per cent. If we take the optimistic view, we could suggest that any group of wage-earners who managed to secure a wage increase of 60 per cent cannot have ended the period to any real degree worse off than they began it. Williamson has suggested that the nominal money earnings of common labourers (non-agricultural) increased by 75 per cent from 1797 to 1815. This group benefited most from the increasing absorption of men into the Army and Navy which peaked at around 10 per cent of the adult male labour force, nullifying the effect of population increase on the labour market.[25] Yet the figures for this group in Bath produced by Professor Neale, calculated on average weekly earnings rather than on nominal annual wages, present a very different picture. Weekly earnings in 1812 were only 16 per cent above their 1793 level, although they had been 25 per cent higher in 1808. On a 1780 base (=100) the real-wage index was 86 in 1793, and even if the 1801 and 1812 price extremes are excluded (55 and 53) the average real-wage index for the remaining war years is still only 77.7 compared with 91.2 for 1780 to 1792. Flinn considered Neale's Bath labourers to have been 'a particularly unfortunate exception', but possibly average weekly earnings are a more realistic basis for assessing living standards than are nominal wage rates, and local labour market conditions occasioned considerable variation not only in wages but in the regularity of employment.[26]

All sectors of the economy do not respond alike in times of war. The Army might take up men, but the effect on the labour market can be offset if women take their place in occupations like weaving. Some manufacturers lose export markets, while others find war increasing the demand for their products. Nor do the years 1793 to 1815 mark an equally suitable period over which to examine wage movements for all trades. The 'good years' of textile out-workers,

24. M.W. Flinn, 'Trends in real wages, p. 408.
25. J.G. Williamson, *Did British Capitalism Breed Inequality?*, p. 8.
26. R.S. Neale, *Bath: A Social History 1680–1850*, Routledge, 1981, pp. 85–6; Flinn, 'Trends in real wages', p. 408.

for example, began before the war but lasted only over the first half of it. In such circumstances, the historian can only present a number of different wage histories.

For farm workers the North–South divide continued, indeed it probably worsened, and countrywide averages are no more helpful than for the 1760 to 1790 period. In Wiltshire, the poorest of counties, winter rates of 6s (30p) rose to 7s (35p) in 1794. They then made hard progress to 8s (40p) over the next decade before enjoying a moment of relative prosperity in the last years of the war, reaching 12s (60p) in 1814. Professor Mathias correctly sees the high demand of the war years for cereals as keeping agricultural wages up with prices, but they started from such a low level that in years of scarcity like 1795 and 1801 they could hardly have sustained life.[27] This is what the budgetary evidence of Eden and Davies revealed, and was the context for the Speenhamland experiment in supplementing wages from the poor rate.

Weekly Earnings of a Berkshire Farm Labourer

A man and his wife, and five children, the eldest eight years of age and the youngest an infant. The man receives the common weekly wages of 7s eight months in the year, and by task work the remaining four months about 1s weekly more. The wife's common work is to bake bread for the family, to wash and mend ragged clothes, and to look after the children; but at beansetting, haymaking, and harvest she earns as comes one week with another about 6d.

From this Davies calculated weekly expenses of 8s 11¼d, leaving a deficit of 5¼d and no allowance for replacing clothing, utensils or bedding.[28]

Dr Horn's assessment is that by the 1790s the southern farm labourer's standard of living had been falling for thirty years, and that an increase of around 85 per cent in money wages over the war years kept it just about level up to 1815. On Arthur Young's calculation higher wages did not restore living standards to the levels of the 1780s, for weekly earnings then would have bought fourteen loaves in Winchester, whereas in 1815 they could buy only nine.[29]

The post-war farming depression meant that by 1817 earnings were once again back at the level of the late eighteenth century.

27. Sources for farm wages are given in Rule, *Labouring Classes*, pp. 38–9; Mathias, *First Industrial Nation*, p. 196.

28. Rev. D. Davies, *Labourers in Husbandry*, 1795, extracts in E. Royston Pyke, *Human Documents of Adam Smith's Time*, Unwin, 1974, pp. 170–5.

29. P. Horn, *Rural World*, pp. 33, 37, 47; Malcolmson, *Life and Labour*, pp. 145–6.

There they stayed for a generation of misery. With rising rural population and the end of the cereal boom, farm wages away from industrial areas simply stagnated. In Herefordshire, for example, they did not change over the forty years ending in 1805.[30]

For some sections of the labour force, prosperous years which had begun in the 1780s continued at least for the first part of the war. Notable among these were textile out-workers. Weavers and knitters flourished in an Indian summer during which power spinning provided abundant yarn, while power weaving lay still in the future. According to Eden, in 1797 Manchester cotton weavers earned around 16s (80p), and that from choosing to work something less than a full six-day week. In fact the war years were a period of mixed fortunes for cotton manufacture. It was in some degree of difficulty in 1793, 1796–7, 1800–1, 1808, and 1811–12. In the good years, such as 1792 and 1802, cotton weavers' wages over most of Lancashire reached the level of skilled artisans. However, by the last years of the war the onset of a falling trend in earnings was unmistakable as the full extent of overstocking, concealed by brisk times like 1802 and most of 1810, became clear. The 225,000 hand-loom weavers in 1811 were three times the number of 1795.[31] In a handbill of 1818 the cotton weavers looked back to earnings of 15s 9d (78p) a week in 1802–3, which had been 'pretty near upon a par with other Mechanicks and we maintained our rank in Society'. The weavers' claim may even have understated their past prosperity for Wood's figures suggest that average weekly earnings of hand-loom weavers exceeded £1.00 each year from 1802–6, peaking at £1.3s (£1.15) in 1805. William Radcliffe, however, in a much-quoted description, placed their 'golden age' between 1788 and 1803.[32] There were to be some more good periods, like the first part of 1810, or 1813–14 when wages again averaged 16s (80p) a week. The ending of the war brought this to an end. Demobilisation intensified the overstocking of the trade, and by 1818 the depressed weavers were claiming earnings had fallen to as little as 5s (25p) a week for a journeyman and were asking 'whether such a paltry sum be sufficient to keep the soul and body together'. Possibly this was an extreme claim, but Wood's figures for average earnings suggest that

30. Horn, *Rural World*, p. 46.
31. On cotton weavers' wages, see J. Foster, *Class Struggle and the Industrial Revolution*, pp. 43–6.
32. For Woods' figures see: Foster, *Class Struggle and the Industrial Revolution*, pp. 43–6. Hammonds, *Skilled Labourer*, p. 88; Thompson, *Making of the English Working Class*, pp. 304–5.

hand-loom weavers earned 8s 3d (41p) in 1818, less than half of their 1814 wages of 18s 6d (92½p).[33]

For framework knitters in the hosiery manufacture of the east Midlands, their historian William Felkin described a golden age lasting from 1755 to 1785, but a more recent authority has suggested that although knitters by the time of Luddism's outbreak in 1811 looked back to pre-war wages of 10 to 12s (50–60p) for plain work and up to 30s (£1.50) for skilled, they were generally prosperous down to 1809. The price list agreed by masters and men in 1787 was generally observed for the next twenty years and with employment brisk, knitters were able to earn, up to 1810, 14 to 15s (70–75p) a week for a twelve- to thirteen-hour day: too much for their own good, according to a local clerical magistrate.

> Abundance thus rapidly acquired by those who were ignorant of its proper application hastened the progress of luxury and licentiousness, and the lower orders were almost universally corrupted by profusion and depravity scarcely to be credited by those who are strangers to our district. Among the men the discussion of politics, the destruction of game, or the dissipation of the ale house was substituted for the duties of their occupation during the former part of the week, and in the remaining three or four days a sufficiency was earned for defraying the current expenses.[34]

Nineteenth-century legs were no longer to be clad in fancy hose, and by 1810 with most of even the skilled stockingers crowded into the plain branch, prices and wages began to tumble. Employers desperately seeking a cheaper product in a crisis of over-production began to introduce 'cut-ups' made on wide frames in the stead of 'fully fashioned' stockings. By the time General Ludd began to destroy the wide frames in 1811, wages for those in employ were only 7s (35p) a week from which deductions for frame rent were made. Even so, those who were fully employed were the fortunate ones, for half the population of Nottingham was on poor relief.[35]

Woollen weavers in the West Country and in the West Riding generally had a good war. In the former district prosperity lasted throughout the war years, which had seen the increasing use of the flying shuttle (spring loom). Clothiers in Gloucestershire did not reduce piece rates, and so weavers were able to profit from their

33. Hammonds, *Skilled Labourer*, p. 88.

34. M.I Thomis, *Politics and Society in Nottingham 1785–1835*, Blackwell, 1969, pp. 15–16; Hammonds, *Skilled Labourer*, p. 23.

35. William Felkin, *History of the Machine-wrought Hosiery and Lace Manufactures*, 1867, rept. David and Charles, 1967, pp. 230–1.

enhanced productivity. Retrospective evidence from 1840 suggests that up to 1796 when it came into use, a master weaver could earn around 12s 6d (62½p) a week, but from this he had, essentially on the old two-man loom, to pay a journeyman 3s 6d (17½p) and his board, and a further 2s (10p) to a child assistant. With the flying shuttle he could earn £1. 2s 6d (£1.12½p) and dispense with the services of a journeyman. In 1803 a weaver claimed that the new loom increased a range of clear earnings from 6 to 7s (30–35p) to 9 to 11s (45–55p). The employers put it even higher: from 10 to 12s (50–60p) to 18 to 21s (90p–£1.05). In this district increased trade absorbed the extra productivity and maintained brisk employment. In the West Riding woollen manufacture the independent working clothiers had long used the spring shuttle, and as a group who produced much of the food needs of their households were well enough protected from the high food prices of the war years. Weavers of worsteds, who worked on a putting-out basis, took to the flying shuttle around 1800 when less breakable yarn became available. Like the West Country weavers they benefited from the introduction, one weaver in 1838 recalling that his wages had increased from around 5s (25p) to between 12s 9d (64p) and 17s (85p) a week.[36]

Coal miners, too, seem to have been among the groups to have kept ahead of the wartime price surge. On the Tyne and Wear the daily rate for pitmen more than doubled from 1793 to 1815, from around 2s (10p) to 4 to 5s (20–25p), bringing a real improvement of 20 to 30 per cent. In an industry expanding in output and where technology increased rather than decreased the demand for adult male labour, it seems probable that this experience was matched on the country's other coalfields. It has been suggested that although some occupations in north Staffordshire experienced real-wage falls over the war years, these were generally of no more than 10 per cent, and it seems that colliers, like potters, were among the groups who could maintain living standards by working harder and longer, even if at times money wages lagged.[37] Metal miners also experienced marked increases in money wages, but it is less clear if they managed to keep fully abreast of price increases. Eden estimated that the Cornish tin and copper miners earned around 10s (50p) a week in 1797, while a select committee of 1799 gave a monthly range of £1 10s to £2 2s (£1.50p–£2.10). This suggests a money increase in the order of 50 per cent from 1790 to 1800. Statistics for

36. Hammonds, *Skilled Labourer*, pp. 128–9, 150–1.
37. R. Colls, *Pitmen of the Northern Coalfield*, pp. 49–50.

the next fifteen years are scarce, but under the tribute system copper miners were paid according to the selling price of the ore they raised. This was low in 1801 and 1802 but high over the next five years; it was on the low side in 1812 and 1813, recovered in 1814, but was falling again as the wars ended. It was, on average, considerably higher between 1805 and 1815 than it was to be from 1815 to 1825. In general the years from 1793 to 1815 do not seem to have been particularly bad in real-wage experience for the Cornish miners, though they suffered like others from the famine price levels of 1795, 1801 and 1812, in each of which crises they rioted.[38] Lead miners in the northern Pennines were earning 10s (50p) a week by 1797 and 11s 6d (57½p) by 1815, whereas before the war they had been earning 7s 6d (37½p); a money-wage increase of around 50 per cent over the war years seems indicated, implying a real-wage fall of about 10 per cent.[39]

An index of real wages for London artisans, constructed by R.S. Tucker in 1936, indicated that an index improvement of 23.7 points in money wages from 1793 to 1814 was insufficient to prevent a real-wage fall of six points. His measurement has underwritten an orthodoxy that the capital's wage-earners suffered declining fortunes which were reversed only by the post-war deflation. If this was so, then it was despite the considerable success of many groups of skilled workers in obtaining a succession of wage increases. Artisans' nominal earnings, which had hardly changed from the 1720s to the 1790s, then experienced a series of sharp increases. By the end of the wars they were 50 per cent above their 1789 level. The upward movement peaked in 1810–11. Saddlers' wages moved from a band of 14 to 16s (70–80p) in 1786 to 25 to 27s (£1.25–£1.35) by 1811, and compositors from 24s (£1.20) in 1777 to 36s (£1.80) by 1800.[40] Yet in a time of 'unprecedented inflation, unprecedented wage demands and an unprecedented number of strikes', most groups can be considered as having *limited* the fall in real earnings rather than as having maintained, let alone increased them.[41] Francis Place produced data on three groups in 1818.

38. Rule, *Experience of Labour*, p. 66.
39. C.J. Hunt, *The Lead Miners of the Northern Pennines in the Eighteenth and Nineteenth Centuries*, Manchester UP, 1970, pp. 73–83.
40. R.S. Tucker, 'Real wages of artisans in London 1729–1939', in Taylor (ed.), *Standard of Living in Britain*, pp. 27–9; George, *London Life*, pp. 166–7.
41. I. Prothero, *Artisans and Politics*, p. 40.

Table 7.5. Money and real wages of London artisans (Francis Place)

	Compositors		Tailors		Typefounders	
	M	V	M	V	M	V
1777	£1 4s	39	£1 1s 9d	36	18s	30
1795	£1 4s	23	£1 5s	24.5	18s	17.75
1796	£1 7s	36	£1 5s	35.3	18s	26.33
1797	£1 7s	34	£1 5s	31.75	18s	22.75
1798	£1 7s	38	£1 5s	35.33	18s	26.33
1799	£1 7s	34	£1 5s	31.75	18s	22.75
1800	£1 10s	22	£1 5s	18.75	18s	13.5
1801	£1 10s	20	£1 7s	18.5	18s	12.5
1802	£1 10s	34	£1 7s	31	18s	20.5
1803	£1 10s	38	£1 7s	34	18s	22.75
1804	£1 10s	38	£1 7s	34	18s	22.75
1805	£1 16s	29	£1 7s	22.3	18s	14.75
1806	£1 16s	3?	£1 7s	26	18s	17.33
1807	£1 16s	36	£1 10s	30	18s	18.00
1808	£1 16s	36	£1 10s	30	18s	18.00
1809	£1 16s	30	£1 10s	24.5	18s	14.75
1810	£1 16s	27	£1 13s	24.75	18s	13.5
1811	£1 16s	29	£1 13s	27	18s	14.75
1812	£1 16s	23	£1 13s	21.5	18s	11.75
1813	£1 19s	24	£1 16s	24.33	18s	12.25
1814	£1 16s	35	£1 16s	35.3	18s	17.33
1815	£1 13s 6d		£1 16s			
1816	£1 13s 6d		£1 16s			
1817	£1 13s 6d		£1 16s			
1818	£1 13s 6d	33			18s	16.75

M Weekly money wage.
V No. of loaves purchasable.
Source: Francis Place, *Gorgon*, 1818–19.

Tailors in 1814 were very much on a level in terms of real wages with 1795, but in the intervening years had been significantly down on that level in eight years, and very seriously below it in 1800 and 1801 when their weekly wage would buy only half the quantity of bread it had purchased from 1777 to 1795. Their increase in money wages had been from 21s 9d to 36s (£1.08–£1.80), an increase of 66 per cent. Compositors with a wage increase of 40 per cent did less well, while typefounders, oppressed by a tightly knit group of employers, were unable to secure a money increase and stayed for seventy years on 18s (90p) a week, experiencing an evident decline in living standards not only in 1795 and 1800–1, but over the last ten years of the wars.

Exceptional groups profited from the war – notably those like shipbuilders and coopers whose specialised services were much in demand for the naval war. The former could earn 5s 3d (26p) a day for much of the war, but the link between these earnings and the war economy was emphasised by a fall to 3s 6d (17½p) during the brief peace of Amiens.[42] By drawing so many men into the services, the war may also have enabled the wages of labourers to keep in touch with prices, assisted by the local increase in demand from the construction of London docks. Spitalfields silk weavers had mixed fortunes, with the war affecting both the extent of foreign competition they faced and the cost and supply of raw silk. Their wages had been regulated by act of parliament since 1773 and they were awarded an increase in 1795. The years from 1800 to the end of the war were generally prosperous, except from late 1807 to mid 1808 when imports of raw silk were almost entirely cut off.[43] For London, as for most of England, the years from 1793 to 1814–15 brought mixed wage experiences, but while the short-term price peaks of 1795 and 1800–1 stand out as years of exceptional distress, there is no clear suggestion of a marked downward trend in real wages. In so far as war recruitment affected the labour market, by emphasising labour shortage in the brisk years it may have helped advance money wages, while in the worst years it may have limited the extent of unemployment.[44]

One group of male workers merits special attention: the cotton spinners, who were the first real group of factory workers. How did they fare in comparison with traditional workers in manufacturing? Well, it would seem. For reasons linked to the physical strength needed to operate them at the beginning, spinning mules were operated by men. These mule spinners, assisted by women and children, were an elite group in the early textile mills. Factory spinning was still in its infancy when the French wars began; by their end mule spinners probably numbered less than 15,000. Their earnings varied according to their skill level, but in 1806 fine spinners could earn 33s 3d (£1.66) a week, those on medium counts around

42. *Ibid.*, pp. 47–8.

43. *Ibid.*, pp. 66–7; Hammonds, *Skilled Labourer*, p. 173; George, *London Life*, pp. 191–4.

44. Schwarz, 'Standard of living in the long run', pp. 28–9; Prothero, *Artisans and Politics*, pp. 66–7.

30s (£1.50), while even coarse spinners could exceed £1. Foster has concluded that by the second decade of the nineteenth century, the well- organised mule spinners had 'fought themselves' to near parity with London's building craftsmen. Frances Collier's detailed studies show a skilled group living at the advancing edge of technology yet who were largely able to offset the falling piece rates thus entailed by greater output. At one mill from 1804 to 1814 the weight of wool spun weekly increased from 12 to 18 lb per man, but wages advanced from 32s 6d to 44s 6d (£1.62½–£2.22½). Little is known of precise wage levels before the beginning of the nineteenth century, but retrospective evidence suggests that Manchester's spinners were earning between 30 and 38s (£1.50–£1.90) in the 1790s, twice as much as the weaver exampled by Eden. The worst time began in the autumn of 1810, which year had up to then been one of peak earnings. Wage reductions were imposed and, until mid 1813, short-time working. In 1811 most mule spinners could earn only half of their peak earnings; even so this was in most cases more than the earnings of fully employed weavers. From late 1813 trade improved, and it was for a time in 1814 brisk again.[45]

FAMILY EARNINGS

It was not, however, only from his good wages and comparatively secure employment that the mule spinner's family enjoyed a standard of living well above that of most of the working class. As Collier put it: 'The greatest number of families were in a better economic position after the introduction of the factory system because of the increased earnings of women and children.' It was not that the wives and children of hand-loom weavers did not work. They did, but for the most part *within* their family economy – that is to say they were not separately waged but included within the household. In cotton manufacture in 1810 children of fourteen earned around 7s 6d (37½p) a week and those of ten 2s 6d (12½p). Women who spun, although there were very few of them, could earn around 15s, while the larger number who were employed as reelers or stretchers earned about the same. Clearly, combined earnings of more than

45. Foster, *Class Struggle and the Industrial Revolution*, p. 82; N.J. Smelser, *Social Change in the Industrial Revolution: An Application of Theory to the Lancashire Cotton Industry*, Routledge, 1959, pp. 213–15; F. Collier, *The Family Economy of the Working Classes in the Cotton Industry 1784–1833*, Manchester UP, 1964.

£2 a week must have quite commonly been brought into the house-holds of mule spinners, while £2.50 would hardly have been exceptional. So far as the households of *weavers* were concerned, putting two or three children to mill work would have doubled the earnings of the father.[46]

How far were such opportunities a new departure? Answering this question requires a fuller investigation of the availability and remuneration of work for women and children in both the agrarian and manufacturing sectors of the eighteenth century, but there are no series comprehensive enough to talk of trends and movements in women's wages. Few women had the opportunity to earn other than low wages; many had small opportunity of regular waged employment at any level of remuneration. In contrast to the chances afforded by the cotton mills, consider Davies' comment of 1795 on the condition of Berkshire farm labourers' families, scarcely able to live on wages of 8 to 9s (40–45p) a week, whose wives earned only from 6d to 1s (2½–5p) weekly when their seasonal and casual earnings were averaged out.

> If any one should think that the women's earnings are stated too low in these accounts, he will be convinced that they are not, on considering that these women commonly begin the world with an infant, and are mere nurses for ten or twelve years after marriage, being always either with child, or having a child at the breast; consequently incapable of doing much other work beside the necessary businesses of their families, such as baking, washing, and the like. In winter they earn next to nothing, few of them having in their youth learnt to knit and spin; and if in summer they are able to go to harvest work, they must pay some person a shilling a week out of their earnings for looking after their children. It is probable therefore that from 6d to 9d a week is as much as labourers' wives in general, hereabout, earn on an average the year through.

Work for children was equally inconstant and low paid. A sixteen-year-old boy is described as earning 2s 6d (12½p) and one of thir-teen 1s 6d (7½p), 'but not constantly'.[47]

In contrasting the earnings during the French wars of a mill-employed Lancastrian family with those of a southern farm labourer's family, we are perhaps dealing with extremes. If living near one of the more expanding manufacturing or mining centres was likely to bring higher adult male wages, it was also likely to offer better prospects of regular waged work for women and children. In the 1770s

---

46. Collier, *The Family Economy*, p. 20 and wage data throughout.
47. Pyke, *Human Documents*, pp. 175–6.

in the Potteries women could earn 7s (35p) a week as gilders, though men at the same trade could earn 12s (60p). In the Birmingham hardware trades the increasing use of stamping and piercing machines from the mid eighteenth century increased the employment of women, who usually earned between 2s 6d (12½p) and 7s (35p) a week, similarly well below the wages of male artisans. At the Sheffield plate works women earned 4s 6d to 5s (22½p to 25p) and in Worcester at glove making their 4 to 5s (20–25p) a week was several shillings below the rate of their male colleagues.[48]

There is a large degree of uncertainty about the extent to which women worked underground in the eighteenth-century coal industry. Accident reports from the first decade indicate that some did on the Great Northern Coalfield, but hardly any did so by 1780. By 1800 the only females were girls of eleven to sixteen years picking coal at the surface for 6d (2½p) a day. At that time women were still employed underground in Cumberland filling the baskets as well as at surface tasks, while the wives of Staffordshire pitmen were said seldom to 'do more than attend to the necessary calls of the Family' except for helping with the harvest. In Lancashire at this time, as in Cumberland, women were still working moving coal in the pits.[49]

In metal mines women practically never worked underground, but work was available at the surface breaking and sorting ores. Defoe met a lead miner's wife in Derbyshire around 1720 who, 'when not preoccupied with the children', earned 3d (1½p) a day washing ores. This was considerably less than the 5s 6d (27½p) a week that Arthur Young considered women similarly engaged at Askrigg in the Yorkshire lead mining district to earn.[50] In the far South-west, Cornish mining took on female labour to a degree unusual in the southern part of the country. Here, there was from the 1740s a considerable expansion in the number of women working at the surface, for from then to the 1850s the mining of copper was of greater importance than tin and, as was pointed out in 1810, 'the copper mines when in full working employ a good number of women and children who are useless about tin'. A parliamentary committee in 1799 considered there to have been between 4,000

48. Wage data all drawn from Arthur Young, *A Six Weeks Tour through the Southern Counties of England and Wales*, 1768; *A Six Months Tour through the North of England*, 4 vols, 1771; and *A Farmer's Tour through the East of England*, 1771.

49. For women's work underground in coal mines, see A.V. John, *By the Sweat of their Brow: Women Workers at Victorian Coal Mines*, Croom Helm, 1980, pp. 19–32.

50. Daniel Defoe, *A Tour Through the Whole Island of Great Britain*, II, Everyman, 1962, p. 162; Arthur Young, *A Six Months Tour Through the North of England*, II, p. 189.

and 5,000 women working at copper mines, but this was an overestimate for an enumeration of 1838, after a considerable expansion, counted 4,526. A count of women and children at copper mines in 1787 suggests that then women workers may have numbered around 1,500. Information on earnings is sparse, but in the 1770s wages were probably around 2s 6d (12½p) a week. It is difficult to estimate their pattern of increase thereafter, but by the 1840s a full-grown young woman could earn 15s (75p) a week, and a twelve-year-old girl 2s (10p).[51]

The recognised craft trades open to women, usually involving needlework, were most often low paid, sometimes exceedingly so. In a survey of London's trades in 1747, the wages of milliners were said to be 'poor and mean': 'Though a young woman can work neatly in all manner of Needle Work, yet she cannot earn more than Five or Six Shillings [25–30p] a week, out of which she is to find herself in board and lodging.' The writer was persuaded that half of the 'common women of the Town' had come from their ranks. Stay makers earned the same, while journeywomen in mantua making made such 'small wages' that, like the milliners, they were in moral danger.[52]

So well organised in support of their pay were the highly skilled journeymen calico printers in the late eighteenth century that even before the advent of machine printing de-skilled them, some employers turned to alternative methods of patterning cloths which used cheaper female and child labour. In the 'picotage' method, printing blocks were studded with tens of thousands of pins or studs which were set by young women who could, after completing their apprenticeship, earn the very high wage for women of 12 to 14s (60–70p) a week. When patterns were pencilled on by hand, good workwomen could earn £2 a week, although most received much less. But these were the pattern-*creating* branches of the trade; once a block had been set, the dye could be splashed on to it by children and the pattern applied to the cloth by lowly paid female labour. This method was considered so cost-effective that some firms continued to employ it even when machine printing offered an alternative way of evading skilled men's wages.[53]

51. Rule, 'The labouring miner in Cornwall, 1740 to 1870', PhD thesis, University of Warwick, 1971, pp. 100–1; F. Michell, *Annals of an Ancient Cornish Town*, Redruth, 1978, p. 45.

52. Richard Campbell, *The London Tradesman*, 1747, rept David & Charles, 1965, pp. 206–9, 225–8.

53. Berg, *Age of Manufactures*, pp. 146–8.

In all these examples the women worked away from home and for the most part received independent wages. Some women worked away from home and yet in 'team' with their menfolk, husbands or fathers, or were included in the 'bargains' made by their husbands. This was not uncommon in some mining districts and even existed in the craft trade of hat making, the artisans who took in their wives to pick the coarse hairs from their material saving the 6 to 9s (30–45p) a week which they would otherwise have had to pay from their wage.[54] Most exploited in this respect were the women farm workers, usually young female relatives rather than wives, who under the 'hind' system of employment in the North were supplied as a condition of the male worker's annual agreement (bond). Described by a recent historian of the North-east as 'one of the most rigorously controlled and poorly paid of all British labour', even in the mid nineteenth century it paid only about 3s (15p) a week. The system which probably developed in the late eighteenth century seems to have been especially increasing from 1790.[55]

In most southern counties wives earned increasingly poorly and casually from day work in agriculture, especially where arable farming was the dominant or developing form. In pastoral areas a high demand for female labour persisted, and in the dairying regions even increased. Here, however, it was above all the labour of unmarried young women as living-in farm servants which was sought. Arthur Young in 1771 on his eastern tour found the dairymaids earned an average of £3 12s (£3.60 per annum). In Devon in 1796 female farm servants earned an annual £3 to £3 5s (£3.25) over their board. This was in a generally low-waged county; in 1794 in Durham their earnings were from £4 to £6.[56] Dr Snell considers there to have been no downward movement in female servants' wages after mid century in the western pastoral counties of Monmouth, Herefordshire, Worcestershire, Shropshire, Gloucestershire, Brecon, Glamorgan, Somerset, Wiltshire, Devon and Dorset. Indeed, with farming especially brisk and with recruitment affecting the labour market, the French war years were associated with 'buoyant and rising' female wages This may also have been the case in Leicestershire, Nottinghamshire and Rutland. By contrast, in areas

---

54. Rule, *Experience of Labour*, p. 42.

55. Rule, *Labouring Classes*, p. 110; Colls, *Pitmen of the Northern Coalfield*, p. 134.

56. Young, *A Farmer's Tour through the East of England*, IV, p. 293; William Marshall, *Rural Economy of the West of England*, 1796, extract in Pyke, *Human Documents*, p. 138; I. Pinchbeck, *Women Workers and the Industrial Revolution*, p. 19.

with a growing specialisation in cereal production there was a lessening of the demand for women workers, which was accentuated by a growing tendency for men to take over harvest work. In the eastern counties Snell examined (Cambridgeshire, Bedfordshire, Huntingdonshire, Northamptonshire, Suffolk, Norfolk, Buckinghamshire, Berkshire, Oxfordshire and Hampshire) female real wages were falling after 1760 for the sharply declining numbers still required. For young countrywomen able and willing to move to London, however, money wages in domestic service seem to have moved in pace with prices and even to have moved quite sharply upward from around 1800.57.

Up to the last years of the eighteenth century, declining levels of employment in agriculture for the wives and daughters of the countryside could have been offset by the taking in of manufacturing work. Paramount among such activity was the spinning of wool for cloth or hose making. It was generally supposed that in the days of wheel spinning six spinners were needed to keep a weaver at work, and the area around the centres of cloth manufacture within which spinning was put out was so much more extensive than that in which the weaving was undertaken that spinning was done 'almost everywhere'. Wages were low; a woman on her own could hardly ever exceed 3d or 4d (1–2p) a day, although with the assistance of one or two children of suitable age, the family income could be more substantially increased.[58] There seems to have been no clear trend in earnings over the period up to the rapid triumph of machine spinning after 1800; in the West of England rates per pound of wool spun were only marginally higher in the 1770s than in the century's first decade. In 1793 a woman with two active children could earn between 4 and 5s (20–25p) a week. There were, of course, short periods of brisk demand when clothiers had to pay higher rates, as in 1760, when one Wiltshire clothier noted in his diary: 'we have this year a very great trade, which has thrown the country into a strange hurry, even into a kind of madness in trade. Our wages are strangely advanced (particularly chain spinning from 11d a score to 15d, and some gave 17d [5p to 6p to 7p].' But the opposite happened in slack periods. In the same county in 1738, the rate fell to 6d (2½p) a score.[59]

Rates reported by Arthur Young on his various *Tours* around

57. Snell, *Annals of the Labouring Poor*, pp. 22, 29–40, 46ff.
58. Malcolmson, *Life and Labour*, p. 47.
59. Mann, *Cloth Industry in the West of England*, pp. 322–6, and *Documents Illustrating the Wiltshire Textile Trades in the Eighteenth Century*, Devizes, 1964, p. 203.

1770 suggest that regional variations were less significant than the type of cloth or the fineness of the yarn (see Table 7.6).

Table 7.6 Rates for domestic spinning *c.* 1770.

Place	Cloth	Weekly rate
Sudbury	worsted	2s 9d
Witney	wool	4s 6d to 5s 6d
Romsey	worsted	2s 9d
Norwich	worsted	2s 6d to 3s 0d
Leeds	worsted	3s 6d to 4s 0d
Kendal	stocking yarn	3s 0d
	linsey-woolsey	4s 6d to 5s 0d
Warrington	sailcloth	1s 0d
	sacking	6s 0d
Manchester	cotton	2s 0d to 5s 0d

Source: Arthur Young, *Tours.*

The higher rates given by Young must be considered unusual, for when he visited a silk mill in Sheffield, which like the more famous example at Derby offered a rare chance of factory employment, he judged the women's earnings of 5 to 6s (25–30p) a week to be 'very good wages, much more than by spinning wool in any part of the kingdom'.[60] The advent of the spinning jenny did not at first destroy home employment in spinning. The early, smaller jennies were used at home, and although the rate paid in the West of England in 1798 was, at 6½d (2½p) a score, only half the rate of the 1770s, the extra output usually more than compensated. In the 1760s those who had jennies in their cottages possibly earned 1s to 1s 3d (5–6p) a day, two to three times as much as hand-wheel spinners. In some districts at least in the 1760s and 1770s, jenny spinners could earn as much as many weavers. However, first larger jennies and then the application of power to them and to the mules took spinning from the cottage through the workshop to the factory where, as we have seen, it became a male employment. Some women took to the loom, further diluting the labour supply in that branch, and others were able to enter the factories, but for many, especially in the de-industrialising South, the loss of home spinning was a real and much commented-on aggravator of female unemployment and depresser of living standards, especially marked

60. Young, *Tour through the Northern Counties*, I, p. 124.

around the turn of the century. William Cobbett was to regret the taking away of such cottage employments, 'so necessary to the well-being of the agricultural labourer', as 'one of the great misfortunes of England'.[61]

There were some cottage industries which came to take up part of the 'space' left by factory spinning, such as straw-hat making and lace making, but they were more localised and tended even by the standards of hand spinning to be low-paid. In the small Dorset town of Corfe Castle in 1795 the earnings of 129 females in poor households were listed. A few still spun, but the great majority were hand knitters. Their average earnings were 1s 5d (7p) a week, and fifty of them earned only 1s (5p).[62]

A distinguishing feature of spinning when put out to the cottage women and children was that it created the possibility of increasing the *money* earnings of the family from an occupation distinct from that of the man. In the households of the small master clothiers of the West Riding woollen manufacture, though not in its differently organised worsted branch, the wives, daughters and female servants may well have spun wool for the household's own cloth – 'Prithie, who mun sit at bobbin weel?' asks the wife in a poem of 1730 when set another task by her husband – but even so yarn had still to be taken in from other spinners. But elsewhere, if wives and children in weaving cottages spun wool or cotton, then along with those in the cottages of farm workers they spun at piece rates for the merchant clothiers. Otherwise women and children did not earn *independently* in the proto-industrial household in its cloth or hosiery branches. No more did they do so in the Black Country's nail-making trade, where the family's output depended upon women as well as men working at the anvil.

> In some of these shops I observed one, or more females, stript of their upper garment, and not overcharged with their lower, wielding the hammer with all the grace of the sex. . . . Struck with the novelty, I enquired, 'whether the ladies of this country shod horses?' but was answered with a smile, 'they are nailers'.

Elsewhere in the Black Country in 1741, William Hutton might also have seen women at the family forges making chains, nuts, bolts and screws, though these were much less populated trades than was nail making.[63]

61. Mann, *Cloth Industry in the West of England*, p. 325; Berg, *Age of Manufactures*, p. 255; Snell, *Annals of the Labouring Poor*, p. 59.
62. For details of the Corfe Castle listing, see above pp. 117–8.
63. Pinchbeck, *Women Workers and the Industrial Revolution*, pp. 271–80.

Dr Berg has suggested that the spread of family-based cottage manufactures played a part in determining the low status and value of women's work even though it, and that of the increasing number of children they produced, was both necessary for the manufacture and significant for family earnings. It was the premium put upon child labour within the domestic family economy of textile manufacture which provides the context for Defoe's observations of around 1720 on Norfolk that 'the very children after four or five years of age, could earn their own bread', while at Taunton 'there was not a child in the town, or in the villages round it, of above five years old, but, if it was not neglected by its parents, and untaught, could earn its own bread'.[64]

Defoe considered it to be manufacturing which conferred this 'blessing' on a vicinity. It is true that William Cobbett, born in 1766, was to write, 'I do not remember the time when I did not earn my living', but he was the son of a moderately successful small farmer in a district where hop growing enabled a decent living from small acreages for a family with three sons to help work it. His father had been the son of a labourer who had earned 2d a day from ploughing, and such low-paid occasional work was typical of what was available for the children of farm labourers until, in such places as it was not in decline, they could be put to live-in farm or domestic service at around the age of fourteen. Before the coming of the cotton mill there were few opportunities for children to make a steady monetary contribution to family earnings. William Hutton, the son of a framework knitter, was sent to work at Derby's silk mill in 1730; he later cursed his luck for having been born in the one city in the world where such could have been his fate. Mining sometimes offered independent employment for children. Two rare 'lives' of working-class Cornish children in the third quarter of the eighteenth century reveal both their subjects, the sons of small farmers, to have worked around tin stamps. Arthur Young suggested that children at the Askrigg lead mines could earn from 1s 10d (9p) to 4s 2d (21p) a week in the 1770s. Pin making was the manufacture most dependent on the labour of children. Young described it at Warrington, Gloucester and Bristol. In these small manufactories adult labour was confined mainly to supervision and it was nimble-fingered children who, for wages of between 1 and 2s (5–10p) a

---

64. Berg, *Age of Manufactures*, p. 132; Defoe, *Tour*, I, pp. 17, 62, 266, II, p. 193.

week, produced the pins.[65] Such examples apart, a consequence of the decline of cottage spinning and knitting was that it removed the earnings of children as well as of grown women. A family might earn from spinning as much as 4s (20p) a week in the days before the mill, but that only at favourable times of the family cycle when two or perhaps three children were working as well as the mother. The changing age structure of the mid eighteenth century significantly increased the number of dependent children in the population and, as Dr Cunningham has pointed out, explains the coexistence of the two views that child employment was desirable and that it was insufficiently available.[66]

---

65. W. Reitzel (ed.), *The Autobiography of William Cobbett*, Faber, 1967, p. 11; William Hutton, *Life*, 1817, p. 82; J.H. Drew, *Samuel Drew M.A.: The Self-taught Cornishman*, Ward & Co., 1861, pp. 17, 22; J.B. Cornish (ed.), *The Autobiography of a Cornish Smuggler*, 1894, p. 2; Young, *Tour through the Northern Counties*, II, p. 189, III, p. 165; Young, *A Six Weeks Tour through the Southern Counties of England and Wales*, p. 109.

66. H. Cunningham, 'The employment and unemployment of children', p. 131. The dependency ratio is discussed in Wrigley and Schofield, *Population History of England*, pp. 443–50. For a discussion of the importance of the family cycle for living standards, see Rule, *Labouring Classes*, pp. 41–3.

CHAPTER EIGHT
Social and Industrial Protest

FOOD RIOTS

Throughout the period living standards were more affected in the short term by price rises than by wage movements. When 80 per cent or more of working-class incomes was spent on food, and most of that on bread, then even in the modernising economy of later eighteenth-century England the state of the corn harvest remained by far the most important determiner of well-being. Poor harvests increased food prices to pressure budgets barely adequate at most times, while seriously deficient harvests brought not just high prices but real scarcity, and for some of the poor absolute want. Furthermore, food prices could sharply distinguish the standard of living in one year from both the preceding one and the next. Small wonder, then, that even among miners and manufacturing workers the most common form of protest was the food riot. To varying extents, food rioting has been recorded in 1727–9, 1737, 1740–1, 1748, 1756–7, 1766, 1771–3, 1782–4, 1789, 1792–3, 1794–6, 1799–1801, and 1812. Thereafter they were more widely spaced in both chronology and geography but have been recorded in 1817–18, 1831 (confined to Cornwall), 1847 (again confined to Cornwall in England, though extensive in Scotland) and final episodes in Devon in 1854 and 1867.[1]

In some of these years, for example 1757, 1766, 1795 and 1801, they were very extensive indeed. The *Annual Register* for 1766 lists more than fifty outbreaks in forty places, and at least as many seem

1. For geography and chronology, see A. Charlesworth (ed.), *An Atlas of Rural Protest*. A general survey is provided in J. Stevenson, *Popular Disturbances*, Chapter 5. The most recent critical survey of writings is Randall and Charlesworth, 'Morals, markets and the English crowd'. The late examples in Devon are described by R. Swift, 'Food riots in mid- Victorian Exeter, 1847–67', *Southern History*, II, 1980, pp. 101–27.

to have escaped its notice.[2] Pioneering scholarship in the 1960s by Rudé and Rose suggested that food rioting first occurred in Oxfordshire in the closing years of the seventeenth century and then spread over the South and West and into the Midlands, but were uncommon in the northern counties.[3] Later research suggests, however, that they were more common in the North-west than had been supposed and probably began in the South-east in the late sixteenth century, and has cast doubt on the validity of seeking to impose too rigid a geographical pattern on food rioting from the *recorded* incidence.[4] Rose and Rudé did, however, establish the essential forms and functions of the food riot, and the next outstanding contribution was to come from E.P. Thompson in 1971 who introduced the hugely influential concept of the *moral economy* into the study of popular protest. He emphasised the extent to which rioters were concerned to fix 'just' prices on seized corn, or, as they sometimes put it, sought to 'regulate' prices. They saw themselves as acting legitimately in the context both of custom and of paternalist legislation of the Tudor and Stuart era which had sought to control the marketing of corn, flour and bread in the interests of the poor consumer. This had included restricting the activities of middlemen (factors or 'badgers') who were suspected of enhancing prices and of allowing the fixing of prices by local justices. In addition to dealers, other objects of anger were farmers who were thought to be withholding grain from the market and thus creating an 'artificial' scarcity; merchants who attempted to buy up corn to move it from the district in which it had been grown at times when local markets were under-supplied; and millers who were considered to be either bulk buying and hoarding corn or else charging the poor too much for grinding grain. Commercial users of grain such as brewers of beer or vinegar or producers of starch were also picked out from time to time. Cereals either as corn, flour or bread were the main concern but other foods, notably cheese and meat, were also seized and re-sold at 'just' prices.[5]

The incidents of 1766 can serve to illustrate the usual and recurrent forms of food rioting, although the geographical pattern

2. *The Annual Register* account is reproduced in G.D.H. Cole and A.W. Filson, *British Working Class Movements*, pp. 20–5.

3. R.B. Rose, 'Eighteenth-century price riots and public policy in England', *Int. Rev. Soc. Hist.*, VI, 1961, pp. 277–92; G. Rudé, *The Crowd in History*, Wiley, 1964, Chapter 2.

4. A. Booth, 'Food riots in north-west England, 1790–1801', *Past and Present*, **77**, 1977, pp. 84–107; R. Wells, 'Counting riots in eighteenth-century England', *Bulletin of the Society for the Study of Labour History*, **37**, 1978, pp. 68–72.

5. E.P. Thompson, 'Moral economy'.

reflects the fact that the North had a better harvest than the South that year. In Gloucestershire and Wiltshire cloth workers destroyed mills and took grain which they distributed among themselves. At Exeter, another clothing centre, cheese was seized and sold at a lowered price, while the Cornish miners forced butchers to lower the price of meat, which also happened in Wolverhampton. At Derby cheese was taken off a boat on the Derwent, while at Lechdale a wagon of cheese intended for London was intercepted. In Devon wheat removed from the granaries of farmers was carried directly to market and 'sold openly from four to five shillings a bushel' after which the crowd returned both the money and the empty sacks to the farmers. This sense of purpose and of confinement to 'legitimate' objectives is briefy conveyed in a single sentence describing events at Malmesbury: 'They seized all the corn; sold it at 5s [25p] a bushel, and gave the money to the right owners.'[6]

Although a fully national market for grain hardly existed in the eighteenth century, a widespread trade was being operated as increasing urbanisation extended the demand for food supplies over greater distances. London, the greatest market of all, was well enough supplied and mostly escaped food rioting, but its reach was vast. Supplied in normal years by the South and the East, it extended to the North and even to Cornwall in years of short supply. Cornwall can serve as an illustration of the problems faced in some areas. Not only did factors draw on it in some years for London, but later in the century the rise of Plymouth as a naval centre provided a counter attraction for corn from its eastern half which might otherwise have gone into the increasingly populous western mining districts. By the mid eighteenth century the rise of tin and copper mining had in any event produced a precarious balance between local grain supplies and a growing population. In years of scarcity, therefore, the miners faced not only enhanced prices but a real deficiency in supply as the activities of agents buying for London increased and as farmers displayed an increasing preference for selling in large quantities rather than piecemeal in local markets.

> We have had the devil and all of a riot at Padstow. Some of the people
> have run to too great lengths in the exporting of corn. . . . Seven or
> eight hundred tinners went thither, who first offered the cornfactors
> seventeen shillings for twenty-four gallons of wheat, but being told they

6. Cole and Filson, *British Working Class Movements*, pp. 20–5.

should have none, they immediately broke open the cellar doors, and took away all in the place without money or price.[7]

From this account of 1773, two things can be noted: the miners first offered a price, and the objects of their anger were merchants intending to remove corn from the locality. There were also many incidents in which the crowd distinguished between dealers and farmers selling their own produce directly: 'At Nottingham fair the mob seized upon all the cheese the factors had purchased, and distributed the same among them, leaving the farmers' cheese unmolested.' Given such selectivity the term 'mob' seems inappropriate, as it does to the Cornish miners who themselves punished some of their number who stole spoons from a farmhouse.[8]

If it seems surprising that the same forms of rioting should recur from one place to another over lapses of time, it should be remembered that food rioting was neither an isolated nor a continuous form of popular action. It was a recurrent one, withdrawn from the popular memory when pressure situations arose. In some places the proclivity to riot was especially marked. Some consuming communities were more vulnerable than others to the effects of high prices and scarcities. John Stevenson has noted the importance of transport networks, with riots occurring not only at sea ports but also along inland waterways where corn might be moved out of a district, such as on the Trent or Avon.[9] Large industrial or mining communities increased the incidence not only because of the ease with which crowds could be formed, but because of their dependence on buying food in local markets. This explains the sense of *invasion* when miners, or weavers, came in force to the market towns: Cornish tinners into Truro, Penryn or Penzance; Kingswood colliers into Bristol or those of Bedworth into Coventry. Rural clothing workers in the West Country or East Anglia were also prominent and textile expansion seems to have brought food rioting to places like Halifax, Huddersfield and Rochdale in the 1780s.[10]

---

7. For the sources for food riots in Cornwall, see my fuller account, 'Some social aspects of the industrial revolution in Cornwall', in R. Burt (ed.), *Industry and Society in the South-West*, Exeter UP, 1970, pp. 87–100.

8. Cole and Filson, *British Working Class Movements*, p. 25; Rule, 'Industrial revolution', p. 88.

9. Stevenson, *Popular Disturbances*, p. 99.

10. R.W. Malcolmson, 'A set of ungovernable people: the Kingswood colliers in the eighteenth century' in J. Brewer and J. Styles (eds), *An Ungovernable People*, pp. 85–27; R.A.E. Wells, 'Revolt of the South-west', p. 742; Stevenson, *Popular Disturbances*, pp. 92, 99.

Women were often the instigators of market riots, but many incidents reveal prior intent and planning. In 1737 a Falmouth merchant buying up corn for shipping to London was warned:

> I am told you have bought up a large quantity of corn lately, which has been the means of raising the price of corn to such a degree, as to incense the tinners so much against you . . . that I am credibly informed no less than a thousand of them will be with you tomorrow early: they are first to assemble at Chacewater and then proceed for Falmouth. This I am told was publicly declared at Redruth market last Friday.[11]

Anonymous threats were frequently sent to those suspected of hoarding or of enhancing prices, or warnings to justices that unless they intervened direct action would be undertaken.

> This is to latt you to know and the rest of you Justes of the Pace that if Bakers and Butchers and market peopel if thay do not fall the Commorits at a reasnabell rate as thay do at other Markets thare will be such Raysen as never was known.

This was received by a Norwich magistrate in 1766, and there was indeed to be a very fierce riot in that town. The farmers of Odiham in Hampshire got an even more pointed warning.

> To the Damd Eternal Fire Brands of Hell belonging to Odiham and its Vicinity. In other Words to the Damd Villans of Farmers that with hold the Corn. . . . This is to inform you all that me and my Companions have Unanamously agreed and likewise made Oath to Each other that if There is not a speedy Altaration made for the Good of the poore that you have corn thinking to make your fortunes of shall have it burnt to the Ground whether it Be in Stacks or Barns for the fire that took place Last Week was but the begining of your Troble, we know every Stack of Corn about this Country, and Every Barn that hath Corn concealed in it for the Purpos of starving the Poore But we are Determind if thare is to Be Starvation it shall be a General thing not a parcial one for both Gentle and Simple shall Starve if any Do.[12]

Posters appeared in some villages advertising what was intended the next market day and calling on 'one and all' to join in. One old miner even recollected seeing one which called upon the fathers of starving children 'in the name of God and the King' to prevent vessels laden with corn from leaving Cornish ports.[13] The size of

---

11. Rule, 'Industrial revolution', p. 88.
12. E.P. Thompson, 'The crime of anonymity: Appendix – A sampler of letters' in D, Hay *et al.*, *Albion's Fatal Tree*, pp. 328, 332–3.
13. Rule, 'Industrial revolution', p. 102.

crowds assembled was considerable; although the evidence is impressionistic they must have commonly numbered several hundreds and perhaps, on occasion, more than a thousand.

In the crowds were to be found most kinds of urban and industrial workers but hardly ever farm labourers; in many cases they were shielded from the market by receiving part of their wages in kind, and in general the authority structure of the countryside was sufficient to deter them from rioting. From time to time strong ceremonial and ritual elements emphasised the importance of legitimacy and tradition. Processions were headed by fife and drum, banners proclaimed 'bread or blood', loaves were carried on pikes. In Cornwall in 1796, 1801 and 1812 a noose and contract was taken around to farmers, who were threatened with the former if they did not agree to sign the latter.[14] Actual violence as opposed to threat and intimidation was not much present in the English food riot. As Dr Stevenson has put it: 'English crowds appear to have killed no one deliberately in the various food disturbances which occurred from the beginning of the eighteenth century to the beginning of the nineteenth.'[15] In this context the often conciliatory responses of the magistracy can be noted. In general they did not seek harsh retributory sentences once order had been restored and in a surprisingly large number of cases actually went some way towards meeting the wishes of the crowd by doing something to encourage a lowering of prices and initiating or participating in relief measures. It was perhaps with the expectation that food rioting sometimes secured short-term remedy that the eighteenth-century crowd resorted to it so frequently.

INDUSTRIAL PROTEST

Although industrial disputes were much less common than food riots, historians have recently come to recognise that they were much more frequent than had been allowed. Professor Malcolmson considers them to have been 'fairly common', and Dr Dobson listed 383 between 1717 and 1800.[16] He divided these into more than thirty occupational groupings, some of which, woollen workers for

14. *Ibid.*, pp. 90–1.
15. Stevenson, *Popular Disturbances*, pp. 105–6.
16. Malcolmson, 'Workers' combinations', pp. 149–61; C.R. Dobson, *Masters and Journeymen*, pp. 22, 24–5.

example, could be further subdivided. Weavers and combers might at most times make common cause against clothiers, but when the import of ready-combed Irish wool was the issue at Tiverton in 1749 they came to blows.[17] That so many disputes were reported in the range of newspapers consulted by Dobson is indicative of a much larger population, either not yet discovered by historians or not reported in their own time. This 'dark figure' is unknowable, but there is a clear enough indication that organisations of a type which would later become familiar as 'trade unions' but were better known to their own time as workers' 'combinations' were well established and widespread among skilled workers in the eighteenth century. Professor Christie has even suggested that they played a sufficiently significant part in the lives of 'multitudes of craftsmen and artisans' to take the edge off the development of revolutionary consciousness.[18] Professor Fox has recently emphasised the importance of an early development for the later history of British trade unionism: 'The artisan-craft tradition by which the British trade union movement more than any other was deeply marked is a pre-industrial and pre-capitalist tradition.'[19]

'Pre-capitalist' is perhaps misleading. The rise of a class of capitalist employers predicated the emergence of defensive labour organisations, but this separation of interests long pre-dated the arrival of the factory and the 'industrial revolution' as normally envisaged. The Webbs in their celebrated history of trade unionism recognised this, but their insistence on a clean break between the guild organisation of the crafts which embraced masters and journeymen and the beginnings of trade unionism was overdrawn. Unions of journeymen commonly sought to retain the restrictive and regulative customs of the 'trade' over such institutions as apprenticeship and expected of the state that it continue to guarantee 'rights' against, in particular, the 'infringements' of innovating masters. They even inherited much of the ceremony and ritual. At Exeter in 1726 the serge weavers were said to have 'Clubs, where none but weavers are admitted; and that they have their ensigns and flags hung out at the door of their meetings'.[20]

17. Rule, *Experience of Labour*, p. 183.

18. I.R. Christie, *Stress and Stability in Late Eighteenth-Century Britain: Reflections on the British Avoidance of Revolution*, Oxford UP, 1984, pp. 124, 141.

19. A. Fox, *History and Heritage: The Social Origins of the British Industrial Relations System*, Allen & Unwin, 1985, p. xiii.

20. See E.P. Thompson, 'English trade unionism and other labour movements before 1790', *Bulletin of the Soc. for the Study of Labour Hist.*, **17**, 1968, pp. 19–24; *Journals of the House of Commons*, XX, 1725, pp. 598–9, 602.

It is at least possible that workers' combinations operated in more propitious circumstances in the eighteenth century than they did in the early nineteenth. In the latter they had to cope with de-skilling innovations in technology and organisation as well as with the effects of rapid population growth on the labour market.[21] Marx recognised as much when he interposed the 'period of manufacture' between that of guild manufacture and that of 'machino-facture': 'Inasmuch as handicraft skill formed the basis of manufacture and inasmuch as the integral mechanism which was at work in manufacture had no objective skeleton existing apart from the workers themselves, capital had continually to wrestle with the subordination of the workers.'[22]

To Adam Smith, disputes between masters and journeymen were endemic in eighteenth-century manufacturing.

> What are the common wages of labour, depends everywhere upon the contract usually made between those two parties, whose interests are by no means the same. The workmen desire to get as much, the masters to give as little as possible. The former are disposed to combine in order to raise, the latter in order to lower the price of labour.[23]

The first recorded use of 'strike' in its modern sense is probably in the evidence of a journeyman tailor at the Old Bailey in 1765, but the thing long pre-dated the word.[24] By the time Smith wrote in 1776, some form of workers' organisation approximating to trade unionism has been found among many groups including hatters, wool combers, tailors, weavers, cabinet makers, wheelwrights, curriers, carpenters, bricklayers, masons and calico printers.

Most of these would have qualified even under the Webbs' strict insistence that only 'continuous associations' qualified as trade unions. This insistence is, however, inappropriate to the actual situation of most eighteenth-century manufacturers. An industrial relations expert, who has written a history of cotton unions, has remarked that whereas general historians of the labour movement report only sporadic trade unionism in that industry in the eighteenth century, historians of the district or of the industry tend to assume a continuous collective labour presence. Following the Webbs too closely means that the surviving documentation of intermittent eruptions is interpreted as indicating ephemerality. But

21. See my Introduction to *British Trade Unionism*, p. 3.
22. For a fuller discussion, see my 'The property of skill in the period of manufacture' in P.K. Joyce (ed.), *Historical Meanings of Work*, pp. 99–102.
23. Adam Smith, *Wealth of Nations*, I, pp. 74–5.
24. See *Old Bailey Sessions Papers*, 1765, p. 173.

continuous association need not imply permanent formal organisation. Members of a trade regularly brought together in workplace or community could acknowledge regular leaders and develop and insist on customary work practices without embedding any of this in formal regulations and procedures. Such a collective presence may have been submerged at times, but did not necessarily disappear. It would not disappear. Thus Turner has written that the sporadic appearance of trade unionism arose not from the absence of collective association but from the 'intermittence' of the actual need for collective action'. When that need arose there is clear enough indication of the availability of collective response from a continuing association which does not always need to have been preserved as a formal organisation.[25]

For rural weavers the habit of association was in itself sufficient to produce at need an organisation to provide deputations or conduct strikes, and this habit was reinforced rather than created by more formal links such as village friendly or burial clubs. The habit of association among hand-loom weavers could last as long as the class of workmen itself, or at least until it became too unstable and diluted to preserve it. Country cotton weavers claimed in 1756 to have been long accustomed to meet weekly at a public house to discuss trade matters and that their friendly society or 'box club' had developed from this and in its turn found itself exercising trade-union functions. Town weavers in places like Manchester worked in small numbers in workshops. That the 'shop' was a natural unit for trade unionism is confirmed even in present-day language. Through delegation to central meetings, a structured union organisation could develop organically. The very simplicity of the structure meant that even formal break-up might be only a temporary interruption since the survival of the essential units made for easy reconstruction. Turner has demonstrated that so far as cotton weavers were concerned, associational persistence can be reconciled with only sporadic incidence, since the true foundation was the durable one of the habit of association within a 'community' of workers, or indeed, in the case of the manufacturing village, within an occupational community.[26]

Cotton weavers can be viewed as representative rather than exceptional. Dr Randall has shown, in studies of the food rioting of 1766 and of the industrial strife of 1765–6 among the Gloucester-

---

25. H.A. Turner, *Trade Union Growth, Structure and Policy: A Comparative Study of the Cotton Unions*, Allen & Unwin, 1962, pp. 45, 77–89.

26. *Ibid.*, pp. 79, 85.

shire woollen workers, 'a community of shared values and expectations' incorporating beliefs and attitudes inexplicable by purely economic considerations underlying both forms of protest. He writes of an 'industrial moral economy'.[27] A Norwich wool comber protested to the employers in a dispute in 1752: 'We are social creatures and cannot live without each other, and why should you destroy community . . .?'[28] Where weavers, knitters and the like existed as communities of producers the defence of customary standards and expectations was more evident than calculative bargaining. Even what appears to be what Adam Smith called an 'offensive' combination – one which 'without any provocation . . . combine of their own accord to raise the price of their labour'[29] – may turn out to have been workers taking advantage of a temporary shift in the labour market to restore previously enjoyed conditions of employment. Employers naturally represented such actions as 'unjustified' rather than admit to their remedial nature. Against the sometimes successful upward negotiation of wages by some groups of urban artisans must be set the long persistence of 'customary' rates in other trades. One West-Country weaver referred to in 1802 stated that his rate per yard had never altered, 'nor yet in my father's memory'. Nor were all urban craftsmen able to lift their earnings. The London masons complained in 1775 that their 50s (£2.50) a week had not changed for seventy years.[30]

Defensive combinations were not, of course, confined to rural workers. Other artisan groups also from time to time found themselves on the receiving end of employer 'impositions'. The shipwrights of Exeter, for example, bound themselves in 1766 not to work for masters who were seeking to employ them at 'less wages than have been from time immemorially paid to journeymen shipwrights', to 'deprive' them of 'several of their ancient rights and privileges' and to impose longer hours than had been 'usual and customary'.[31] In the royal dockyard at Portsmouth the shipwrights struck in 1775 against the imposition of a piece-rate system which, they claimed, 'would occasion progressive suicide in our bodies'.[32]

---

27. A.J. Randall, 'The industrial moral economy of the Gloucestershire weavers in the eighteenth century' in Rule (ed.), *British Trade Unionism*, pp. 29–51.
28. Malcolmson, 'Workers' combinations', p. 149.
29. Smith, *Wealth of Nations*, I, p. 75.
30. *Minutes of the Committee . . . on the Woollen Trade*, VII, BPP, 1802/3, p. 35; M.D. George, *London Life*, p. 166.
31. Devon County Records Office, 146/B add. Z1.
32. A. Geddes, *Portsmouth during the Great French Wars 1770–1800*, Portsmouth City Council, 1970, p. 19.

However, among shipwrights and other skilled workers, especially in London, there is clear enough evidence of a more modern trade-union consciousness, still based on the 'trade', and jealous of its practices and 'rights' but operating in what Dobson has called an 'industrial relations system', that is an arena of interaction within which employers and workers perceived their roles and the moves which were open to them. Here it is possible to refer to 'conflict resolution' and 'bargaining' based on a mutual appreciation of strength.[33]

Among several groups, such as the weavers and combers of the south-western serge manufacture and the tailors, hatters and printers of London, there is clear evidence that organisations recognisable as trade unions were in existence by the first two decades of the eighteenth century. Twenty-three of the disputes listed by Dobson occurred before 1730. A proclamation was issued in 1718 against 'unlawful Clubs, Combinations, etc.' of wool combers and weavers:

> . . . which had illegally presumed to use a Common Seal, and to act as Bodies Corporate, by making and unlawfully conspiring to execute certain Bylaws or Orders, whereby they pretend to determine who had a right to the Trade, what and how many Apprentices and Journeymen each man should keep at once, together with the prices of all their Manufactures, and the manner and materials of which they should be wrought; and that, when many of the said Conspiritors wanted work, because their Masters would not submit to such pretended Orders and unreasonable Demands, they fed them with Money, till they could again get employment, in order to oblige their masters to employ them for want of other hands.[34]

The details of a complaint by the master tailors of London in 1721 show that the organisation revealed in evidence at a trial in 1765 and described again in 1818 by Francis Place as a 'perfect combination' had been by that last year in existence for a century. It was claimed in 1721 that more than 7,000 journeymen had:

> . . .lately entered into a combination to raise their wages, and leave off working an hour sooner than they used to do; and for the better carrying on their design, have subscribed their respective names in books . . . at the several houses of call or resort (being public houses in and about London) where they use; and collect several considerable sums of money to defend any prosecutions against them.[35]

33. Dobson, *Masters and Journeymen*, Chapter 10.
34. Cole and Filson, *British Working Class Movements*, p. 86.
35. J.T. Ward and W. Hamish Frazer (eds), *Workers and Employers: Documents on Trade Unions and Industrial Relations in Britain since the Eighteenth Century*, Macmillan, 1980, pp. 5–6, 18–19.

They warned that the 'ill example' was already spreading to journeymen curriers, smiths, farriers, sail makers, coach makers, carpenters, bricklayers, joiners and 'artificers of divers other arts and misteries'. They might also have mentioned the hatters who seem to have been organised by 1700 and who had by 1777 a 'congress' which made by-laws, extracted fines and sought to limit the number of apprentices masters could take. The masters were forced to give in to wage demands in 1772 and 1775. The congress levied a weekly subscription of 2d (1p). One master complained that when five of his employees refused to join, he was visited and told to discharge them, otherwise his workforce would be called out. Later he put out some work to one of the five, but the journeymen returned, demanded he take it back and levied a charge of 3 guineas (£3.15) for their loss of time in attending to 'this act of justice'. When he refused, all his journeymen quit. Petitions from Manchester, Newcastle under Lyme, Burton on Trent, several towns in Leicestershire, Derby, Bristol, Liverpool, Chester and Hexham in 1777 indicate the geographical range of the hatters' union. Such a reach was enabled by the 'tramping' system. It was widespread among craft unions like the wool combers who were said to have become 'one society throughout the kingdom . . . if any of their club is out of work they give them a ticket and money to seek for work at the next town where a box club is'. If there was no work there, the tramping artisan was fed, given a bed for the night and a few pence to see him on to the next town on the official tramping route. In the craft trades it became the 'very backbone of union' without which information about rates, conditions and disputes could not have been spread and the federation of local clubs into wider organisations could hardly have developed.[36]

When calico printing moved from London to Lancashire in the 1780s, a ready-made journeymen's union went with it, whose members were so assured of their status and craft autonomy that the employers christened them 'gentlemen journeymen'. At the peak of their power, just before machinery threatened their hold, their effectiveness was evident.

> By their combination they prevent the master employing any
> journeymen they do not approve of, who as *they* say is not a fair man;
> and all journeymen must ask the constable of the shop, for the time
> being, (an officer appointed by the combination) for work before they

36. For the hatters, see Rule, *Experience of Labour*, pp. 156–7. For the tramping system see E.J. Hobsbawm, 'The tramping artisan', in *Labouring Men*, pp. 34–63; R.A. Leeson, *Travelling Brothers*, Granada, 1980, pp. 79–122.

ask the master. They can discharge a journeyman from service without his master's content; they can advance their wages, and in many instances, prevent the master taking more apprentices than they approve of, and such a number, as the nature of the work requires. In any case where the master does not show a readiness to comply with their demands, they order both journeymen and apprentice, to *strike, and turn out* (as they term it,) and leave their work.[37]

Among such workers more sophisticated means of conducting disputes had emerged over the century. There was a clear appreciation of the right time to strike. The serge weavers in 1725 were said to have chosen the spring at the seasonal peak of demand. Royal dockyard workers took advantage of the fitting out of the fleet for war, fellmongers of the large number of deteriorating hides on their masters' hands after the pre-winter livestock slaughter, and Coventry's weavers of demand for black ribbons on the death of a popular member of the royal family.[38] It was not simply a matter of timing, for there is evidence of preparing for the moment by building up the organisation and, most important, a strike fund. The journeymen wool sorters of Exeter did this in 1787 before striking at the time when their employers had large wool stocks on hand. They named their fund the 'loaves and fishes'![39] Francis Place described the same process among London's leather-breeches makers in 1793, the book binders built up theirs over four years before striking for a reduction in hours, and the calico printers seem to have been constantly engaged in building and rebuilding strike funds. They, along with compositors, paper makers, wool sorters and colliers, had developed the rolling strike, or strike in detail, whereby shops were turned out one at a time with those in work supporting those who were withdrawn.[40]

In the only passage where he concedes any degree of effectiveness to workers' combinations, Adam Smith said of the wool combers: 'By combining not to take apprentices . . . [they] . . . reduce the whole of the manufacture into a sort of slavery to themselves, and raise the price of labour much above what is due to the nature of their work.'[41] This element of control over entry to the trade was crucial to the prospects of artisan unions. A frontier of

37. 'A history of the combination of journeymen calico printers', 1807, rept in K. Carpenter (ed.), *Trade Unions under the Combination Acts*, Arno Press, New York, 1972.

38. Rule, *Experience of Labour*, p. 179.

39. Devon Records Office, Mss. Law Papers G. 6.

40. Francis Place, *Autobiography*, pp. 113–16.

41. Adam Smith, *The Wealth of Nations*, ed. E. Cannon, 2 vols, rept Methuen, 1961, I, p. 141.

skill had to be defended against dilution by the unskilled, including large numbers of women. 'Unfair' workers, 'knobsticks' as the calico printers called them, were not to be worked with, and in this defence, fundamental to all other purposes such as maintaining or improving wages or hours, the artisans were able to claim a legitimacy not only from the 'customs of the trade' but from the statute of artificers passed in 1564 and popularly known as '5 Elizabeth'. This statutory requirement for an apprenticeship to be served before a trade could be taken up was not repealed until 1814 in the face of organised trade-union opposition. Although throughout the preceding century case law decisions had narrowed its scope and denied its extension to any trade not in being at the time of its passage, it had remained nevertheless of great importance as a legitimating symbol of skilled labour's 'rights'. In the late eighteenth century an 'Ode to the Memory of Queen Elizabeth', composed after the saddlers had been in a dispute, proclaimed:

> Her memory still is dear to journeymen,
> For sheltered by her laws, now they resist
> Infringements, which would else persist:
> Tyrannic masters, innovating fools
> Are check'd, and bounded by her glorious rules.
> Of workmen's rights she's still a guarantee.[42]

The passing of the proscriptive Combination Acts in 1799 and 1800 is a well-known landmark in trade-union history, but they are much misunderstood if they are seen as placing trade unions in a novel position of illegality. Adam Smith had maintained in 1776 that 'those laws which have been enacted with such severity against the combinations of servants, labourers and journeymen' were a major weapon in the hands of employers, as were the powers to deal with riot and disorder when frustrated workers began to attack persons or property.[43] In the preamble to around a dozen eighteenth-century statutes prohibiting trade unionism in specific English trades, combinations are *already* described as unlawful, the purpose of the statute being to offer the employers the chance to secure quick, summary punishment. Not only were there also one or two very old statutes to which resort could be made, but the common law of conspiracy was generally held to preclude collective actions designed to harm employers' interests: 'it is not the denial to work except for more wages than is allowed by statute, but it is for a

---

42. E.P. Thompson, 'English trade unionism', p. 23.
43. Smith, *Wealth of Nations*, I, p. 74; Rule, *Experience of Labour*, p. 175.

conspiracy to raise their wages, for which these defendants are indicted', concluded a famous judgement against some striking tailors
of Cambridge in 1721.[44]

That the law was available does not mean that masters always, or
even often, made use of it. It was not in their financial interest to
provoke or prolong strikes or to create bitterness and resentment
when trade was brisk and labour not in demand. Accordingly workers striking on an economic upswing often found employers more
ready to negotiate than to prosecute, although if masters decided to
combine to take on the union by resisting a wage demand or even
enforcing a cut and bound themselves not to employ each other's
dismissed workmen, the law might be a more ready resort. The
Sheffield cutlery trades, London printing, paper making, coal mining and woollen manufacture all provide well-documented examples. In Exeter the wool staplers moved quickly in 1787 to imprison
some striking wool sorters who were seeking to advance their wages,
but at several other times since the statute they employed had been
enacted in 1726, they had conceded advances sought by their journeymen. Use of the law was capricious, so unions operated in a
context of risk rather than of full and constant constraint.[45]

In 1799 parliament turned a petition for an act specific to journeymen millwrights into a general prohibition of trade unionism
over matters of wages or hours which was slightly amended in 1800.
This action is commonly attributed to the fear of the working class
stirred up by the course of events in France. In the debate Lord
Holland recognised the dread among the upper classes that the
lower orders might be seduced by subversive principles, 'particularly
afloat at this moment', but also considered that some masters were
taking advantage of this moment to 'enforce their views and render
their workmen more dependent than they had hitherto been and
than in all fairness and equity they ought to be'. The Combination
Acts brought the state into a more manifestly repressive role against
trade unions, although the initiation of proceedings still rested on
the employers. The simultaneous withdrawal of the state from regulative intervention in labour matters clearly advantaged employers
and it is hard to deny that all this amounted to class legislation.[46]

44. Cole and Filson, *British Working Class Movements*, pp. 88–9.
45. Rule, *Experience of Labour*, pp. 175–6; Devon Records Office Mss. Law Papers
G. 6.
46. The most recent account of the passing of the Combination Acts is J. Moher,
'From suppression to containment: roots of trade union law before 1825', in Rule
(ed.), *British Trade Unionism*, pp. 74–97. See also my summary 'The Combination
Acts: their making and unmaking', *History Sixth*, 7, 1990, pp. 32–6.

Over fifty years ago Dorothy George contested the views of writers like the Webbs and the Hammonds that 1799 and 1800 amounted to 'the most unqualified surrender of the State to the discretion of a class in the History of England'. She denied they were in any sense a new departure and asserted them to be 'a very negligible instrument of oppression'. The grip of her revision is surprising, for it has long been in need of revision itself. That the acts were not a new departure is argued by those who draw attention to the pre-existing illegality of trade unions under the law of conspiracy and under around forty statutes, a number of which were specific to particular trades. This 'forty' seems to have assumed almost biblical status among historians. It is a seriously distorting figure. Of thirty-four statutes repealed along with the general act in 1824, twenty had been passed since 1714; ten of these had been passed in Dublin and did not apply to England and one was specific to Scots miners. Eight of the nine specific to particular English trades balanced prohibition of combination with wage-regulating clauses binding on employers. The exception was an act relating to paper making which had been passed in 1796. Clearly, even if the acts were not a new departure in terms of the basic question of legality, they were hardly more of the same.[47]

As for the claim that the older acts and the common law had allowed the imposition of harsher penalties, this was not for the simple fact of combination but for activities linked with industrial disputes that could have attracted prosecution for riot, intimidation, assault or destruction of property as much after 1799 as before. Further, employers could not have it both ways; if they sought summary conviction before justices of the peace, they could hardly have had penalties of a harshness imposable only by the courts. This leaves the common law of conspiracy under which prosecutions continued to be brought while the acts were in force. Common-law decisions are not made in a vacuum. In 1799 parliament had pronounced its opinion on the illegality of trade unionism and this was part of an atmosphere in which courts were expected to find against it. Nor should it be forgotten, as Professor Orth has pointed out, that in 1799 penalties were prescribed for the first time for *workmen as a class*, not for hatters or paper makers as a special group; in other words, the language of the act was concerned with a horizontal

47. M.D. George, 'The Combination Laws reconsidered', *Economic Journal. Economic History Supplement*, No. 2, 1927, pp. 214–18. Her reconsideration has recently been shown to be seriously misleading by J.V. Orth, 'English Combination Laws reconsidered'.

social division, not with the reconciliation of difference within the vertical structure of a craft.[48]

The Combination Act of 1800 had a varied effect. The verdict of the clerk to the select committee of 1824 which reviewed it was that it had been a dead letter so far as 'those artisans on whom it was intended to have an effect', namely printers, tailors, shoe makers and shipbuilders in London who continued 'their regular societies and houses of call as though no such act were in existence'. A recent study of London's trades has noted the spread and organisational development of unionism during the period.[49] When a deputation of framework knitters from the east Midlands came down to London in 1812 to lobby in support of a bill to regulate the hosiery trade, they had no difficulty in making contact with trade unionists. They met up and talked with the carpenters' committee, who would have lent £3,000 out of their fund of £20,000 had they not been astonished to learn that the knitters had themselves no permanent fund 'to answer any demand at any time'. Instead they dispensed a condescending homily.

> What would our trade be, if we did not combine together? Perhaps as poor as you are, at this day! Look at other trades! they all combine, (the Spitalfields weavers excepted, and what a miserable condition are they in). See the tailors, shoemakers, bookbinders, gold beaters, printers, bricklayers, coatmakers, hatters, curriers, masons, whitesmiths, none of these trades receive less than 30s a week, and from that to five guineas this is all done by combination, without it their trades would be as bad as yours.[50]

It was among out-working trades like weaving and knitting that the Combination Acts had most effect. For them and for some of the new workers of the industrial revolution in the Midlands and North, the acts brought an era of 'secret unionism'. This effect has been given a special significance in the writings of E.P. Thompson and John Foster who see repression carrying trade unionists into an undercover association with the Jacobin republican movement – the very alliance their passing had been intended to inhibit. According to Foster, in the cotton districts of south-west Lancashire union

48. Orth, 'The legal status of English trade unions 1799–1801', in A. Harding (ed.), *Law-Making and Law-Makers in British History*, Royal Historical Society, 1980, pp. 205–6.

49. Quoted in A.E. Musson, *British Trade Unions 1800–1875*, Macmillan, 1972, p. 24; I. Prothero, *Artisans and Politics in Early Nineteenth-Century London: John Gast and His Times*, Dawson, Folkestone, 1979, pp. 41–3. See also R.A. Leeson, *Travelling Brothers*, Granada, 1980, p. 111.

50. E.P. Thompson, *Making of the English Working Class*, pp. 263–4.

leadership fell into the hands of political radicals who were reported to be drinking the prime minister's health in consequence![51]

In fact the acts symbolised repression as much as they enabled it. It seems to have been the case that attempts to defend their interests by knitters, wool and cotton workers met with a much greater degree of hostility from masters and magistrates than did those made by urban artisans. The first factory unions, formed by the mule spinners, were similarly treated. Incidence of prosecution was not high. Foster noted only seven convictions in Lancashire during five years of trade-union activity between 1818 and 1822, but like Thompson he insists on their general prohibitive influence. Prosecutions might have been made under the law of conspiracy or under 5 Elizabeth for leaving work unfinished, but to trade unionists they were all 'the laws against combination'. Gravenor Henson, the leader of the Framework Knitters' Union, regarded the existence of the acts as 'a tremendous millstone round the neck of the local artisan, which has depressed and debased him to the earth, every act which he has attempted every measure that he has devised to keep up or raise his wages, he has been told was illegal: the whole force of the civil power and influence of the district has been exerted against him because he was acting illegally'. Other witnesses, some of whom had themselves been imprisoned, spoke feelingly of the dread of the Combination Laws in the east Midlands and their use to cower the knitters into defeat, at a time when wages had sunk to 7s (35p) a week. The tendency of historians to play down the general effect of the Combination Laws seems rather insensitive to the feeling of oppression widely found in these manufacturing districts.[52]

MACHINE BREAKING

According to Adam Smith, attacks on machinery were symptoms of desperation on the part of workers nearing the end of their ability to remain on strike. Sometimes they probably were, but more often they formed part of a purposive policy of intimidation which Professor Hobsbawm called 'collective bargaining by riot'. The place of

51. *Ibid.*, pp. 551–62; J. Foster, *Class Struggle and the Industrial Revolution*, pp. 49–50.

52. Select Committee on Artisans and Machinery, Fifth Report, V, BPP, 1824, pp. 265, 269–74.

violence in English labour history has been reconsidered since the earlier historians, notably the Webbs and Hammonds, followed a Fabian predisposition to exclude it from the mainstream of labour action. Intimidation also embraced the sending of threatening letters, sometimes warning of intended attacks on machinery but other times threatening private property or the person. In 1799 the shearmen of Wiltshire threatened those who were introducing dressing machinery: 'if you follow this practice any longer . . . we will keep som people to watch you about with loaded Blunderbuss or Pistols And will certainly blow your Brains out it is no use to destroy the Factorys But put you Damn'd Villions to death'.[53]

Hobsbawm emphasised an important distinction between machine breaking where the machine itself was seen as a threat to employment, and those cases where machinery was destroyed simply as a means of putting pressure on employers in disputes unconnected with its use. Miners, for example, have no quarrel with pithead gear; they cannot work without it. So when the Wigan colliers threatened in 1792 to throw down the engines, they were seeking both to pressure the mine owner and to prevent him from reworking the pit with 'blackleg' labour, also the likely object of Cornish miners who pulled up the ladders in a dispute of 1795.[54]

A sharper awareness among historians of the purpose of actions previously dismissed as desperate or revengeful has helped explain why groups of workers not infrequently combined intimidatory action with more 'legitimate' forms. The weavers and combers of the serge districts in 1725–6 had their 'clubs' with by-laws seeking to 'regulate' apprenticeship, wages, hours and methods of working, but they forced entry into houses, spoiled wool, cut cloth and roughly treated both masters and those journeymen who refused to join the combination. The woollen workers who rioted in Melksham against wage-cutting clothiers in 1738 were from a group of workers sufficiently well organised to petition both parliament and local justices. Pressure on masters and on strike-breakers was part of the structure of many disputes and, as Hobsbawm points out, no less effective than most other options open to protesting workers.[55]

53. Smith, *Wealth of Nations*, I, pp. 75–6; E.J. Hobsbawm, *Labouring Men*, p. 7; E.P. Thompson, 'The crime of anonymity' in D. Hay *et. al.*, *Albion's Fatal Tree*, p. 320.

54. Hobsbawm, *Labouring Men*, p. 7; Rule, 'The labouring miner in Cornwall, 1740–1870', PhD thesis, University of Warwick, 1971, p. 382; A. Aspinall (ed.), *The Early English Trade Unions*, Batchworth, 1949, document 8, p. 7.

55. *Journals of the House of Commons*, XX, 31 March 1726, p. 648; W.E. Minchinton, 'The petitions of the weavers and clothiers of Gloucestershire in 1756', *Trans. Bristol and Gloucs Arch. Soc.*, LXXIII, 1954, pp. 216–26.

Despite the long history of machine breaking, it was the concentrated events of 1811–16 which gave 'Luddism' to the language. In 1811 letters and proclamations signed 'Nedd Ludd' or 'Captain Ludd' or even 'General Ludd' preceded or followed attacks on machinery in the framework-knitting districts of Nottingham. Throughout 1811–12 attacks on machinery took place not only through the stocking-making counties of Nottinghamshire, Leicestershire and Derbyshire but also in the woollen districts of the West Riding and the cotton districts of Lancashire. Objectives differed, but 'Ludd' as leader of the 'army of redressers' was invoked in each case. There were further less extensive outbreaks in 1814 and 1816. At the peak of the agitation more than 12,000 troops were stationed in the disturbed regions of the Midlands and the North – more soldiers than Wellington took with him on his first expedition to Portugal in 1808 in the Peninsular War.[56]

A prelude to 1811–12 had been played out in the woollen districts of Wiltshire between 1799 and 1802. Here the shearmen fought vigorously and, as Dr Randall has demonstrated, with some success against two innovations. These were the gig mills, which raised the nap on the cloth prior to shearing and vastly shortened the time needed compared with the old hand method, and shearing frames, which by mechanically aligning the heavy forty-pound shears reduced the time taken to a quarter. The main target at the height of the riots in 1802 was the gig mill, but that was because very few shearing frames had as yet been introduced. In this respect the shearmen's action was pre-emptive. Attacks on mills took place alongside more 'legalist' methods of protest, including strikes and formal petitioning of parliament. The direct action, by a well-organised union of skilled workers, seems sufficiently to have deterred most clothiers in Wiltshire from introducing machinery for around twenty years.[57] The petitioning of parliament to enforce Tudor statutes proscribing the use of machinery in woollen manufacture, however, had an unintended consequence. After taking much evidence from masters and employers in the woollen manufacture, the statutory outcome was the repeal in 1809 of the old legislation, not only that on machinery but also that requiring apprenticeship. Accordingly when, in 1811, the shearmen of the West Riding, locally known as 'croppers', who had been in regular and supportive contact with the Wiltshire shearmen throughout their struggle, faced

---

56. Stevenson, *Popular Disturbances*, pp. 155–61.
57. A.J. Randall, 'Shearmen and the Wiltshire outrages, p. 304.

the introduction of machinery in their turn, the 'peaceful' option of petitioning parliament had been foreclosed.[58]

The Orders in Council of 1811, imposed as part of the economic war against Napoleon, had hit the hosiers of the east Midlands very hard by closing their American market. It was their wage-reducing attempts to cut costs which led to Luddism. They sought to employ unskilled labour – 'colting' – to make stockings by a cheaper method. These inferior goods were made by producing a woven square on a wider frame which was then 'cut up' and seamed. This, not the introduction of new machinery, was the grievance of the framework knitters. As one of their songs explains, the struggle would continue:

> Till full fashioned work at the old fashioned price
> Is established by Custom and Law.
> Then the Trade when this ardorous contest is o'er
> Shall raise in full spendour its head,
> And colting and cutting and squaring no more
> Shall deprive honest workmen of bread.[59]

At first the knitters concentrated on an unavailing petitioning of parliament, but trouble began during a wage dispute in March 1811 when local justices in Nottinghamshire refused to intervene after hosiers cut the rates they paid to their knitters. Sixty frames belonging to one of the hosiers were smashed, and by November such activity had become widespread, reaching into Leicestershire. General Ludd's anger was discriminating: 'His wrath is entirely confined to wide frames / And those that old prices abate.' During the most active phase, from March 1811 to February 1812, 1,000 frames were destroyed in a hundred separate attacks, and a worried government responded by making machine breaking a capital felony and despatching 2,000 troops to Nottingham. This ended the main phase, and resistance once again concentrated on the attempt, organised by the United Framework Knitters, to secure a parliamentary bill. This failed and with prosecutions under the Combination Acts being set in train, the frustrated knitters turned again to frame breaking which continued spasmodically to 1816.[60]

At the beginning of 1812 the first attacks on shearing frames by the Yorkshire croppers began. 'Ludd' was again invoked, but so too was a new name, 'Enoch', the huge hammer of destruction named,

58. *Ibid.*, pp. 290–1.
59. Hammonds, *Skilled Labourer*, p. 212.
60. *Ibid.*, Chapters 9, 10 and 11, still provides the fullest account.

ironically, after the firm of Enoch and James Taylor who made both
the shearing frames and the sledges which broke them!

> Great Enoch still shall lead the van.
> Stop him who dare! Stop him who can!
> Press forward every gallant man
> With hatchet, pike and gun!
> Oh, the cropper lads for me,
> The gallant lads for me,
> Who with lusty stroke
> The shear frames broke,
> The cropper lads for me.[61]

Threats intensified and an organisation capable of attacking larger
mills was built up. The most serious incident came in April 1812
when two men were killed in attacking the well-guarded mill of William Cartwright. In an aftermath when the relentless and remorse-
less inhumanity of the mill owner and his magisterial friends passed
into local lore, an attempt was made to assassinate Cartwright and
one was successfully carried out on another mill owner, William
Horsfall, who had boasted his intent to ride up to his saddle girths
in the blood of Luddites. After this, West Riding Luddism entered a
phase when machine breaking became a focus for wider grievances
and tensions as disturbances spread out beyond the clothing districts into Rotherham and Sheffield, with raids in search of arms,
bullets and money marking its final stages.[62]

In Lancashire and Cheshire events were less 'pure'. There was a
machinery issue in the introduction of power looms. Several rioters
were killed during an attack on a mill using them at Salford in
1812, but few manufacturers had as yet introduced them, or were
intending to in the near future, and disturbances were intermingled
with food riots and political agitation. Once again the name of
Ludd was invoked and there were rumours of links with Nottingham. An attempt to burn down a warehouse at Stockport was followed by rumours of secret gatherings, armings and oath taking
and there was certainly talk of a general rising.[63]

Until the major reinterpretation by E.P. Thompson in 1963, a
consensus view of Luddism prevailed among historians. The
Hammonds had placed Luddism as the resort to violence by traditional workers who had failed in the face of a growing *laissez-faire*

61. *Ibid.*, p. 247.
62. This attack is the one on which Charlotte Brontë based her novel *Shirley*, but
see E.P. Thompson, *Making of the English Working Class*, pp. 613–16.
63. *Ibid.*, pp. 644–56.

ideology to persuade parliament to protect them by invoking old paternalist statutes. Machine breaking was a final act in the struggle of artisans to maintain or revive customs and laws which the new breed of capitalist employers was determined to evade. However, they were unable to place a violent movement like Luddism into the mainstream history of a developing labour movement. Those knitters who broke the machines had to be separated from the 'constitutionalists' who organised the petitioning of parliament. Anxious to deny any significant revolutionary input, they were at pains to resist any suggestion that machine breaking could have had any links with a revolutionary political movement. They did, however, note that the disturbances of 1811–12 were distinguished by a new level of planning and organisation, but still insisted that the involvement of 'proper' trade unionists was limited to sympathy. Gravenor Henson, the leader of the Framework Knitters' Union, they argue, did not even approve of Luddite actions. They have been more willing than other historians to accept at face value his retrospective remark of 1824: 'The branch who broke the frames never contemplated any such thing as the combining.'[64]

The parallel existence in Nottingham and Leicester of a movement for parliamentary redress alongside machine breaking has allowed historians other than the Hammonds to claim that each was the method of a distinct group. Such a 'compartmentalisation' is less easy in the cases of Yorkshire and Lancashire. Here, too, the Hammonds were concerned to dismiss suggestions that Luddism was anything more than a despairing form of industrial protest without any real degree of political revolutionary intent. Faced with evidence to the contrary, which the government of the day either believed or at least affected to believe, they resort to describing the reports of arms, oaths and plans for insurrection sent in by government spies as exaggerations or fabrications, especially those of Bent, from Lancashire: 'The Home Office Papers contain numbers of illiterate communications from him, full of lurid hints of the approaching outbursts of the lower orders, encouraged by mysterious beings in higher places.'[65] They further discounted reports of oath taking in Lancashire or in the West Riding. Their interpretation remained unchallenged until E.P. Thompson questioned their reading of this evidence in 1963.

64. Hammonds, *Skilled Labourer*, pp. 190, 194–5, 213–17. For the historiography of Luddism, see my Introduction to the 1979 edition.
65. *Ibid.*, pp. 225, 273–5.

. . . a special pleading which exaggerates the stupidity, rancour, and
provocative role of the authorities to the point of absurdity; or by an
academic failure of imagination, which compartmentalises and
disregards the whole weight of popular tradition . . . . We end in a
ridiculous position. We must suppose that the authorities through their
agents actually created conspiratorial organisations and then instituted
new capital offences (such as that for oath-taking) which existed only in
the imagination or as a result of the provocations of their own spies.[66]

Most recent historians would agree that the Hammonds were much
too reluctant to accept that there was even serious talk of revolution, although the majority do not go so far as Thompson in their
assessment of the seriousness of the threat. It is reasonable, however, for Thompson to ask why such a degree of compartmentalisation of objectives should be presumed to have been the case in
1812, when war had been largely continuous over twenty years,
when trade unions were under the interdict of the Combination
Acts, when the hand- loom weavers and knitters were suffering a
catastrophic drop in earnings and when high food prices were producing widespread and severe hunger.

Thompson's view of Luddism is connected to the argument of
The Making of the English Working Class, that a revolutionary underground movement linked the Jacobinian agitation of the 1790s to
the re-emergence of more open radicalism after 1816. It is not a
view shared by historians like Thomis who consider Luddism to
have been 'industrial in its origins and industrial too in its aims'.[67]
Recently Craig Calhoun has also criticised the 'revolutionary' view of
Luddism. To him it was essentially a community-based populist movement which, while it was capable of employing a revolutionary rhetoric,
was not so of organising a revolution.[68] Professor Dinwiddy was
more willing to accept the existence of a revolutionary movement in
Lancashire and the West Riding which had begun to mobilise in a
rudimentary way and which did administer oaths and invoke the
name of Ludd. However, he did not think it was of formidable
enough dimensions even to link the industrial towns of the North,
let alone spearhead a wider rising.[69] It is in the nature of the evidence that the debate will remain inconclusive. At very least, however, the Luddites presented the government with a problem of
order of a magnitude hardly reached since. Well-planned and ex-

66. E.P. Thompson, *Making of the English Working Class*, pp. 629, 631, 636–7.
67. M.I. Thomis, *Luddites*, p. 137.
68. C. Calhoun, *The Question of Class Struggle: Social Foundations of Popular Radicalism during the Industrial Revolution*, Blackwell, 1982, p. 61.
69. J. Dinwiddy, 'Luddism and politics', pp. 33–63.

ecuted night attacks on machinery and factories took place over wide districts and a long time span by men who, having set governmental authority at defiance, disappeared back into the community by day. In the face of an unprecedented presence of troops, Luddism was the nearest thing to a guerrilla campaign waged on English soil. Even if only for that reason, to regard it as simply an expression of industrial grievances is ludicrously inadequate.

LONDON DISORDERS

In London, as Professor Rudé has noted, the incidence of civil disturbance was not so closely tied to peaks in food prices.[70] This does not mean that the capital experienced less frequent disorder; far from it. It was reputed to be one of Europe's most disordered cities, and there was scarcely a year in which some rioting did not take place. Industrial disputes were endemic and, when they involved large and close-knit groups like the Spitalfields silk weavers, the coal heavers of the Thames or, most unruly of all, the sailors of Wapping, presented serious problems for the authorities. All three of these groups were active in the period of widespread industrial disputes from 1766 to 1769.[71] Sailors were then protesting about their wages, but they were capable of rallying to other causes. They were the most frequent of the Tyburn rioters who contested with the surgeons' agents for the bodies of the hanged. They formed the great bulk of the riotous crowd in 1749 who, after three sailors had been robbed in a brothel, rioted and burned down bawdy houses in the Strand in a three-day riot, although the only unfortunate Tyburn example made on this occasion was the improbably named Bosavern Penlez, a wig maker.[72] There were occasions when a London crowd was activated by wider considerations. Professor Rudé has shown that its members were not generally from the delinquent, vagrant or criminal poor and were often unfairly described as 'a mob'. They came notably from the petty tradesmen, craftsmen, journeymen and apprentices of the capital's myriad manufactures. Time and again

70. G. Rudé, 'The London "mob" of the eighteenth century', 1959, reprinted in *Paris and London*, pp. 310–11.

71. For a survey of these years, see W.J. Shelton, *English Hunger and Industrial Disorders: A Study of Social Conflict during the First Decade of George III's Reign*, Macmillan, 1973, pp. 165–202.

72. For the Strand riots and their aftermath, see P. Linebaugh, 'The Tyburn riots against the surgeons' in D. Hay *et al.*, *Albion's Fatal Tree*, pp. 89–102.

those brought to trial reveal proper trades and had completed apprenticeships.[73]

Government attempts to restrict the sale of gin in 1736 are usually considered to have been behind disturbances in that year, but these also involved the resentment of building workers and weavers at being displaced from employment by the cheaper Irish. As Robert Walpole explained to his brother: 'Their cry and complaint was of being underworked and starved by the Irish.' At one point the grievance brought out an East End mob 4,000 strong which destroyed some Irish public houses. Among nine taken into custody were a weaver, sawyer, carpenter, brewer, blacksmith and several servants.[74] The riots were in a sense a foretaste of the Gordon Riots of the summer of 1780. These provided the most frightening episode, perhaps, in any Western European city before the French Revolution. Apart from the destruction of Catholic chapels and the houses of some Catholics, the riots included the freeing of prisoners from Newgate and other gaols, an attack on the house of Lord Chief Justice Mansfield and even one on the Bank of England. Statistics reveal the seriousness of the riots. At their height, and they lasted four days, 10,000 troops were called out. Of 162 persons who later stood trial, sixty-two were sentenced to death, of whom twenty-five were hanged. A total of 210 people were killed outright by the soldiers, another seventy-one died later and 173 were less seriously wounded. The extent of the firing of buildings was such that observers thought the whole city was ablaze.

The riots had begun when a crowd of around 60,000, mostly of the 'better sort of tradespeople', were brought together by the Protestant Association on St George's Fields to pressure parliament into rescinding the very limited measures of Catholic relief which had been enacted in 1788. A section of the crowd turned events when it attacked the private Catholic chapels of several embassies. The next evening a mob re-formed. This time it had a more obviously proletarian presence, with working artisans and labourers in evidence. Catholic chapels and private houses were pulled down, and the riots spread to the East End with riots against Catholic inhabitants in Spitalfields. The riots continued for three days, climaxing on 7 June when it was finally quelled and the half-mad leader of the Protestant Association Lord George Gordon taken to the Tower. The biographies of those arrested tell a similar tale to

---

73. Rudé, 'London Mob', pp. 298–302.
74. Rudé, '"Mother Gin" and the London riots of 1736', *Paris and London*, pp. 205–21.

those of other eighteenth-century riots. They were not a common riff-raff. Almost all of them were supplied with sound testimonials and professed a proper trade. Only fifteen were charged with theft. There had been little looting. Property had been thrown out into the streets and burned. The same thing had happened during the riots against the Strand bawdy houses in 1749.[75]

What were their motives, if they were not rapine and robbery? There was strong anti-Catholic feeling but it was mostly against substantial rather than poor Catholics. Rudé has pointed out that hostility against the working-class Irish was much less evident than in 1736 and 1763. In a sense, a very basic one, the riots were political: 'a groping desire to settle accounts with the rich, if only for a day and to achieve some rough kind of social justice'. One rioter, on the point of attacking a non-Catholic property, asserted: 'Protestant or not, no Gentleman need be possessed of more than £1,000 a year.' The attack on the Bank of England may have been 'blind and desperate' but it was unmistakably a gesture against the very symbol of plutocracy.[76] The riots of 1736, too, had crystallized general resentments of the lower orders. Rumours that the increased duties to be levied on gin were but the beginning of a general excise, an indirect tax that would hurt the poor much more than the better-off, fuelled the crowd's antipathy towards the government: 'If we are Englishmen . . . let them see that wooden shoes are not so easy to be worn as they imagine.[77]

'No wooden shoes'; 'No potatoes, No Popery'; no imprisonment without trial; liberty, freedom, and, especially, a sympathy with anyone who seemed to be making a stand against government's inherent tendency towards arbitrary action. These were the factors that moved London's crowds of working artisans, journeymen and apprentices. Those of them which were not about the Englishman's standard of living (no peasant wooden shoes and no Irish potatoes) were shared by many of the 'middling people'; these were the issues and they were more important than any lingering popular Jacobitism, although that sentiment certainly existed.[78]

The disturbances of 1736 and 1780 have organisational similarities. In both episodes, groups of rioters were led by 'Captains'. 'Tom the Barber' was one in 1736, while among those revealed by

75. Account based on Rudé, 'The Gordon riots: a study of the rioters and their victims', *Paris and London*, pp. 268–76.

76. *Ibid.*, pp. 283–9.

77. Rudé, 'London Mob', pp. 311–12.

78. Rudé, 'Mother Gin', pp. 219–21.

the trials in 1780 were a journeyman wheelwright and a coach maker. In both disturbances attacks on property were not indiscriminate. There was talk of a 'list', and in both years the arrested rioters were operating close to their own streets and parishes. In both cases the artisans who made up a high proportion of the arrested do not appear in the rate-books, suggesting that they were not among those tradesmen who could be considered part of the 'middling sort'. But neither were they from the very poor and vagrant population. Rudé's researches established that few of those tried after the Gordon Riots were unemployed, hardly any had previous convictions and all were of settled abode.[79]

There were occasions when riots were connected with more overtly political incidents. Professor Rogers has shown the role of the wider populace when elections were contested in the widely enfranchised Westminster constituency in 1741 and 1749 and has suggested they foreshadowed the riots associated with John Wilkes.[80] The cry of 'Wilkes and Liberty' had first been heard in 1763 when the publisher of the anti-Government *North Briton* had been imprisoned after the issue of a general warrant. The populace generally played little part in that agitation, but when Wilkes returned from the exile in 1768 to which he had fled from fear of imprisonment, debt and the fighting of a duel, to fight the Middlesex election, he became the symbol of a much wider agitation. The winter just ending had been exceptionally severe, causing great hardship to the poorer people. Bread prices were beginning to rise and industrial disputes were entering very bitter phases in several large occupations, including coal heavers, silk weavers and sailors. Wilkes, as a symbol of defiant resistance to government, was taken up by all these groups. The rioters, who held the streets of London for three days after Wilkes' election, although they did not come exclusively from the working classes, were still overwhelmingly so composed. Wilkes had many levels of supporters, from the Middlesex freeholders who voted for him, through City interests 'independent' of those linked through finance and contracting to the government, to the 'middling sort' of householder.[81] Politically it was the awakening of these groups which was most important, for as Professor Christie has concluded:

---

79. Rudé, 'London Mob', pp. 295–6, 300–1; 'Gordon Riots', pp. 283.
80. N. Rogers, 'Aristocratic clientage, trade and independency: popular politics in pre-radical Westminster', *Past and Present*, **61**, 1973, pp. 70–106.
81. For the Wilkes riots, see G. Rudé, *Wilkes and Liberty*, Oxford UP, 1962.

Contrary to their claims that they were fighting off the onset of a Tory authoritarian reaction, Wilkes and his friends in various minor ways were extending the range of civil liberties, liberalising the constitution, and opening the way for developments that would only mature in the years after Waterloo.[82]

Those coal heavers, weavers, sailors, labourers and others of the lower orders who took to the streets in 1768 were to a large extent caught up in a political moment which coincided with longer-running economic grievances. That does not mean that they parroted slogans without appreciating their significance. Reaction to presumed threats to liberty and freedom, as well as a long-standing tendency to support the 'victims' of government, made up the political dimension of London crowd action. That is, they did until the watershed of the 1790s when, inspired by events in France and soon to be given a 'red book' in Tom Paine's *Rights of Man*, the first popular movement for radical reform appeared. It was marked by the formation of the London Corresponding Society at the beginning of 1792 with its low subscription and search for 'numbers unlimited'. But, as the name of the Society implies, its object was to form links with a raised artisan political consciousness in the provinces, with towns like Norwich and, especially, Sheffield in the forefront.[83]

The geographical reach of popular radicalism was long. 'In this neighbourhood Citizens abound,' was the optimistic message the LCS received from west Cornwall in 1796.[84] That was a huge overstatement, but it at least demonstrates how widespread the discourse of political radicalism had become. Membership of the corresponding societies is hard to measure, and wider influence even more so. At its peak in 1792 the LCS had around 800 active members with a further 5,000 attending its divisional meetings from time to time. When in 1795 it began holding a series of open-air demonstrations in London, surprising numbers seem to have attended – possibly more than 100,000, given the tendency for such occasions to become 'fairs' with women and children attending as well as men. Sheffield had the largest membership, certainly in relation to its population and probably in absolute terms as well. Estimates from various sources, some hostile, range between 1,500 and 2,500. Norwich was in the same league, but most large urban centres had much smaller memberships. In a wider context, sales of

82. I.R. Christie, *Wars and Revolutions: Britain 1760–1815*, Arnold, 1982, p. 79.
83. Rudé, 'London Mob', pp. 311–12; Stevenson, *Popular Disturbances*, p. 19.
84. Place Collection, British Museum, MS. 27815, ff 39–40.

Tom Paine's *Rights of Man* were huge especially during 1792 when perhaps as many as 200,000 of the cheap edition were sold.

Edward Thompson has argued that there was a change in popular sentiment in that after 1791 it was no longer possible for the 'establishment' to pressure radicals by raising 'Church and King' mobs against them and their property. Birmingham radicalism had been subdued in this way in the famous riots of 1791 against the radical dissenter Joseph Priestley. The real problem with assessing popular sentiment over the 1790s is the interplay of contradictory forces shifting it between radicalism and loyalism. The outbreak of war with France in 1793, with a developing fear of invasion, brought xenophobia to aid loyalism. The hunger crisis of 1795–6 and the later one of 1800–1 gave radicals the misery of the lower orders to play upon. A decisive victory in a battle brought patriotic celebration, while at other times when things were going less well the failure to seek a peace could swing sentiment the other way.[85]

Even before it proscribed the corresponding societies by law in 1799, thus turning a decade of more open popular radicalism into a following one of underground conspiracy and plans for insurrection, the state had begun to take things very seriously indeed. It redefined treason and sedition and severely constrained the freedoms of meeting, speech and writing, and it funded a massive output of loyalist pamphleteering to counteract the *Rights of Man*. Historians of the conservative tendency, in rejecting the claims of the leading historians of the popular reform movement, seem to be suggesting that it must have been over-reacting. However, that there is no simple way of quantifying the strength of popular radicalism does not deny that the 1790s were a watershed in British political history. At their beginning the members of the LCS debated for five nights in succession: 'Have we, who are Tradesmen, Shopkeepers and Mechanics, any right to obtain a Parliamentary Reform?' They decided that they had. In so doing they served notice that, although enthusiasm would ebb and flow through the following decades, a new and fundamental fact had entered the politics of the nation.[86]

85. Thompson, *Making of the English working class*, pp. 114, 126–7.
86. Thompson, *Making of the English working class*, p. 16.

CHAPTER NINE
Crime and Punishment

THE INCIDENCE OF CRIME

Lord North's anonymous informant, who thought the Gordon rioters were made up mostly of house-breakers, pickpockets and the like, clearly considered London to have a substantial criminal population.[1] That was a widely held view. Although at times, for example in the early 1720s, around 1750 and in the last decade of the century, crime levels became a matter of special concern, throughout the eighteenth century perceptions of a problem of crime and anxiety over its presumed increasing incidence were widely held, especially in the capital. This is hardly surprising, for crime is usually the most obvious and widespread threat posed by the unpropertied to the propertied. Oliver Goldsmith anticipated modern sociology in his interactive view of the relationships of crime, property and the criminal law.

> . . . penal laws which are in the hands of the rich are laid upon the poor . . . and as if our possessions were become dearer in proportion as they increased, as if the more enormous our wealth, the more extensive our fears, our possessions are paled up with more edicts every day, and hung around with gibbets to scare every invader.[2]

From Sir Leon Radzinowicz's magisterial study, the increasing use of capital punishment to cover an increasing range of crimes against property emerges as the main reason for the astonishing increase in the number of hanging offences between 1688 and 1820 from around fifty to 200. Their rapid diminution in the next

---

1. G. Rudé, 'The Gordon Riots' in *Paris and London*, p. 280.
2. Oliver Goldsmith, *The Vicar of Wakefield*, 1766.

decade amounted to one of the most rapidly enacted U-turns in the history of social reform.[3]

Henry Fielding, the novelist, who was appointed magistrate at Bow Street in 1749 and who founded the famous Bow Street Runners, was perhaps the best-known criminologist – although contemporaries would not have recognised the term – of the eighteenth century. His major treatise was published in 1751 as *An Inquiry into the Causes of the Late Increase of Robbers.* It came in a year in which George II's speech at the opening of parliament had expressed the royal alarm at 'outrages and violences, which are inconsistent with all good government, and endanger the lives and properties of my subjects' and it probably influenced the report of a parliamentary committee in that year.[4] In his better-known novels Fielding often seems to have an empathy with some criminal actions and a perception of the pressures which could lead to an individual's turning to crime. He also seems well enough aware of the power of the predominant land-owning class which both made and enforced the laws. An exchange from *Joseph Andrews* begins with a sympathetic squire asking a country justice for what crimes a young couple had been committed.

> 'No great crime,' answered the Justice, 'I have only ordered them to Bridewell for a month.' 'But what is their crime?' repeated the Squire. 'Larceny, an't please your Honour,' said Scout [the lawyer lackey]. 'Aye,' says the Justice, 'a kind of felonious larcenous thing. I believe I must order them a little correction too, a little stripping and whipping'. . . . 'Still,' said the Squire, 'I am ignorant of the crime, the fact I mean.'

The justice then consulted a deposition in which it was stated that in walking through a field, the young man had cut a twig to the value of 7½d (3p), which the young woman had received.

> 'Jesu!' said the Squire, 'would you commit two persons to Bridewell for a twig?' 'Yes,' said the Lawyer, 'and with great lenity too; for if we had called it a young tree, they would have been both hanged.'[5]

In a second major social pamphlet, Fielding also seems to posit a link between the pressures of poverty and the incidence of crime against property: 'They starve and freeze, and rot among themselves; but they beg, and steal, and rob among their betters.'[6] While

3. L. Radzinowicz, *A History of the English Criminal Law and its Administration since 1750,* Vol. I, Stevens, 1948.

4. *Journals of the House of Commons,* XXVI, 1751, p. 3; *ibid.,* 23 April, p. 190.

5. Henry Fielding, *Joseph Andrews,* 1742.

6. Henry Fielding, *A Proposal for Making an Effectual Provision for the Poor,* 1753, collected works, XII, p. 77.

it is true that Fielding considered the Poor Laws of the eighteenth century to have been both misconceived and poorly administered to the extent that they contributed to the 'increase in robbers', he emphasised the *bad management* of the poor, not the bald fact of poverty in itself. Crime to Henry Fielding was certainly not generally explicable in terms of the struggle of the needy to survive. In fact, his keyword is not 'poverty' but 'luxury'. To Fielding that word symbolises the dangerous aspirations of those who sought material possessions and 'diversions' above their station.

> I think that the vast torrent of luxury which of late years hath poured itself into this nation hath greatly contributed to produce . . . the mischief . . . In free countries at least, it is a branch of liberty claimed by the people to be as wicked and profligate as their superiors . . . it reaches the very dregs of the people, who, aspiring still to a degree beyond that which belongs to them, and not being able by the fruits of honest labour to support the state which they affect, they disdain the wages to which their industry would entitle them; and, abandoning themselves to idleness, the more simple and poor-spirited betake themselves to a state of starving and beggary, while those of more art and courage become thieves, sharpers and robbers.[7]

The poor tradesman brought by ill-fortune and failure to highway robbery plays no part in the *Inquiry*. Therein gambling, 'the last great evil which arises from the luxury of the vulgar', is presented as 'a school in which most highwaymen of great eminence have been bred'. Similarly the great gin-drinking epidemic is seen as the cause of poverty rather than as its manifestation, leading to robbery and even murder. Fielding in words makes a statement which is a close parallel of Hogarth's famous engraving of the same year, 'Gin Lane'.[8]

In fact the growth of crime is presented as the obverse of the coin of the consumer revolution. For not only does it reflect the great downward drift of increasing expectations, it also becomes possible on a large scale only because of the vast increase in volume and range of the goods in circulation. A glance at the pages of the Old Bailey proceedings, or for that matter over a page or two of the *Beggar's Opera*, indicates this well enough. Purse cutting could be guarded against by the bill of exchange, indeed the intercepting highwayman had as much to do with that financial development as did the increasing volume of sophisticated commercial transactions.

7. Henry Fielding, *An Inquiry into the Causes of the Late Increase in Robbers etc.*, 1751, in T. Roscoe (ed.), *The Works of Henry Fielding*, 1849, p. 763.
8. *Ibid.*, pp. 766–7.

But watches and silk handkerchiefs, or even periwigs, could be taken from the person, and rolls of cloth and a whole range of other goods from the swelling number of shops.

Unlike currency, stolen goods had to be 'converted' to profit the thief, who hardly ever intended their use. Fielding was especially concerned with the 'receiving' network which flourished in eighteenth-century London. At the top were the great 'fences' like the infamous Mendoza, who like his even greater predecessor of the 1720s, Jonathan Wild, arranged a regular traffic across the sea to Holland.[9] Below them were a range of others of varying underworld stature including, according to Fielding, most pawnbrokers, whom he considered a 'set of miscreants which, like other vermin, harbour only about the poor, and grow fat by sucking their blood'. At the bottom the women of house-breakers and robbers frequently seem to have received the goods along with the problem of shifting them. Edgworth Bess certainly seems to have acted in this way for the celebrated escaper Jack Sheppard. Fielding's proposal to make receiving an original offence, not dependent upon the conviction of the thief, was eventually acted upon.[10]

The greatest operator on the eighteenth-century criminal scene had been hanged in 1725, more than twenty years before the great novelist, who was to use his life as the basis of an allegorical novel, was appointed to Bow Street. Jonathan Wild, by origin a buckle maker from Wolverhampton, followed a crooked path through pimp and brothel keeper to become the most powerful man in the London underworld. His deviant career is indicative of the 'modernisation' of crime in Hanoverian urban England. As his modern biographer points out, he is rather a foreshadower of Al Capone than a parallel of the great bandits of the peasant countryside, who were the archetypal 'robber kings' of eighteenth-century Europe.[11]

It was probably his experience with the willingness to pay of married 'gentlemen' de-propertied in brothels which gave Wild the idea that the safest way to make profit from stolen goods was to 'recover' them for reward from their owners. The intricate details of his unequalled chicanery are fully revealed in the admirable study by Gerald Howson. They can be summarised briefly. Wild first arranged a robbery, then advertised a return through his 'Office for the

9. *Ibid.*, pp. 778–80.

10. *Ibid.*, pp. 779–80; for the criminal careers of Wild and Sheppard, see G. Howson, *It Takes a Thief: The Life and Times of Jonathan Wild*, Hutchinson, 1987.

11. *Ibid.*, p. 7.

Recovery of Lost and Stolen Property'. Audaciously he posed as a 'thief-taker', apprehending wanted felons with a posse of assistants for the reward. He became a celebrity, the 'Thief-Taker General', operating over the South of England, breaking gangs as well as apprehending individuals. It was only when he made himself finally unpopular with his capture of the folk-hero escapee Jack Sheppard that the truth began to come out. Wild was truly a taker of 'blood money'. The felons he passed on to trial and the gallows were often his victims. 'Set up' in the modern phrase, they were delivered because they were underworld rivals, or simply because the bounty on their heads had accumulated to the £40 ceiling. In 1725, after one of his own gang, Blueskin Blake, whom he had betrayed, attempted to cut his throat, Wild was convicted of taking a £10 reward for the return of some lace whose theft he had arranged.

Such a career suggests the existence of a criminal world, apart from that of the labouring poor in general – one with its own customs, language and hierarchy, peopled by a 'criminal class' with a hereditary delinquency and irredeemable proclivity to depredation. Born and raised to thieving, it was neither able nor inclined to practise any other trade. But that is a rather nineteenth-century notion of which there is little sign in Fielding or his contemporaries. Of course, many lived through stealing, receiving or forging and many more at least partly did so, but there was no rigid line of separation between the world of the labouring poor and that of a presumed 'criminal class'. The famous 'canting tongue' which so fascinated contemporaries was understood and used widely among London's lower orders. Laws relating to the materials used by out-working journeymen were, as we have seen, increasingly criminalising what had been considered 'customary' rights to materials used in manufacturing processes. A large proportion of the capital's lower orders lived at least in part from their wits and by taking advantage of opportunities. Most of the hanged came from the same background as the crowds who assembled to bear witness to their last moments at 'Tyburn Fair'; had it been otherwise, public executions might actually have worked as the deterrent that authority intended.

Dr Linebaugh has shown that the proportion of those executed at Tyburn between 1703 and 1772 who had begun or even completed apprenticeships was as high as that of those tried for involvement in the Gordon Riots, used by Professor Rudé to indicate 'respectability' and a social status removed from the 'bottom of the pile'.[12] Nor were most of them the children of London 'rookeries'

12. P. Linebaugh, *The London Hanged*, pp. 91–2, 108–9.

like St Giles, for only 41 per cent of 1,176 jerked out of the world at Tyburn were London-born. A culture of deprivation and poverty, of violence, crime, casual employment and prostitution, was an evident feature of Hanoverian London, but how far was it distanced from the city's working classes in general? As we have seen, even Francis Place, the very model of the aspiring artisan held a rougher world at barely arm's length.

That so many of those executed came from outside London helps explain Fielding's perception of the link between the treatment of the poor and the high incidence of metropolitan crime. The growth of a mobile proletariat freed by the dissolving of what he called 'feudal' bonds was at the root of the problem. It was aggravated by the bad management of the nation's poor, which was deficient in allowing them to wander from their home parishes, where they were known, and to lose themselves instead in the anonymity of the notorious lodging houses of districts like St Giles or Shoreditch, from which narrow alleys they could emerge to rob and return to safety. Even if detected, they could rely on the physical force of their neighbours to help resist arrest. If, nevertheless, they found themselves on trial, then false alibis were often available. It was to improve this situation that Fielding brought into being the professional detective force, later to be known as the Bow Street Runners, and argued for a shift in the prevailing rules of evidence to make for easier conviction.[13]

To Henry Fielding the underlying causes of crime were deep. Increasing depredations on property reflected the related problems of an increase in consumer goods and services and the emergence of a new kind of society – one, as Clive Emsley has pointed out, with a value system rooted in self-interest and individualism. The next major writer on crime to emerge in London saw the 'commercial revolution' in a very different light. Patrick Colquhoun, one of London's first stipendiary magistrates under the Act of 1792, published his *Treatise on the Police of the Metropolis* anonymously in 1795. He expressed much admiration for the *Inquiry*, and certainly shared several of Fielding's prejudices.

> Were we to examine the history of any given number of these our
> miserable fellow-mortals, it would be discovered that their distresses,
> almost in every instance, have been occasioned by extravagance,
> idleness, profligacy, and crimes: and that their chief support is by
> gambling, cheating and thieving in a little way.

13. Fielding, *Inquiry*, pp. 784–5.

Unlike Fielding, however, he did not view the growth of commerce with a jaundiced eye as the solvent of social bonds. Rather he gloried in the wealth and prosperity of London. It is appropriate that his second important book was on the setting up of a police force to protect the cargoes being handled on the docks. The Riverside was the centre of the greatest trading empire the world had yet seen, where the products from the New World were unloaded and, in part, reloaded for re-export. Sugar and above all tobacco were among the imports subject to heavy depredation from those who handled them. It was a campaign both intensive and symbolic, for the Thames was the great artery of empire. The 'population' of seamen, porters, coal heavers, etc. which lived and worked along it was the most international section of the proletariat:[14] seamen who signed on on both sides of the Atlantic; the Irish who monopolised the unloading of coal. Here too lived most of London's black population which probably numbered between 10,000 and 20,000 by 1780. According to Sir John Fielding, when a man ventured into Rotherhithe or Wapping, 'but that somewhat of the same language is spoken, a man would expect himself to be in another country'.[15]

By 1780 concern with crime reached far beyond London. Indeed, statistical evidence derived from indictments suggests that criminal trends exhibit a remarkably similar rhythm in the counties which have so far been examined, with a marked increase in the closing decades of the century which gathered pace into the early nineteenth. How can the pattern be explained? Broadly, as Professor Beattie demonstrated with his study of indictment levels for Surrey and Sussex, there is a correlation with economic pressure. Indictment levels matched to wheat prices and the trade cycle, the former matching best in the rural districts while the latter, considered as a surrogate for employment levels, worked best in urban. This, Professor Beattie suggests, argues 'that a large number of people were close enough to the subsistence line for changes in prices to register immediately in their fortunes and for them to turn to theft to fill the gap'.[16]

Even more marked, however, was the tendency of indictments to increase at the end of wars. This was clearly linked to demobilisation on to a glutted labour market, but even more importantly it

14. C. Emsley, *Crime and Society*, pp. 51–3; Linebaugh, *The London Hanged*, pp. 409–34.

15. M. Rediker, *Between the Devil and the Deep Blue Sea: Merchant Seamen, Pirates and the Anglo-American Maritime World, 1700–1750*, Cambridge UP, 1987, p. 11.

16. J.M. Beattie, 'The pattern of crime in England 1660–1800', *Past and Present* **62**, 1974, p. 88.

reflects the age structure of those committed for trial. Adolescent and young unmarried males were the main group of those enlisted and also the dominant group among those indicted for property offences. Circumstances which affected this group therefore helped determine the overall pattern of indictments. War swept them up and away, peace returned them to inflate the most crime-prone section of the population. In the peacetime years of the middle 1780s around half of all those indicted on the home assize circuit were between eighteen and twenty-six. In Gloucestershire after 1815 there was a massive surge in indictments of this age group. Peter King has argued that this helps to explain why the crime rate was more sensitive to price levels in wartime than it was in peacetime; for in the former, married men feeling subsistence pressure formed a larger proportionate fraction of the population. He has also noted that crimes which were associated with younger men such as highway robbery and horse stealing increased more rapidly in peacetime.[17]

Douglas Hay has noted the effect on Staffordshire indictment levels of the ending of major wars in 1748, 1763 and 1783: 'an immediate increase in committals for theft followed and was usually sustained until the year in which warfare resumed'. Like King he noted that in years of peace high indictment levels correlated poorly with price peaks, but in the twenty-three years of war, fluctuations in the consumer price index could explain around three-quarters of the variation in indictment levels. Hay estimates that in hard years, around a fifth of the population could not have bought sufficient bread for the support of their families even had they spent their whole incomes on it. At such times more men dared to steal: 'as those for whom poverty became a desperate affliction rather than a customary privation increased in numbers, we might expect not only more appropriation, but a change in the kind of offence committed and the kind of person prosecuted'. In fact he showed that it was indictments for less serious offences which were most affected by price levels. Staffordshire wheat prices after 1772 can explain 54 per cent of changes in the level of capital crimes, against 70 per cent of the non-capital. There were also changes within capital indictments. Felonies most associated with violence or professional organisation such as highway robbery, horse theft or pocket picking changed only slightly with the price level, much less than did general thieving or sheep-stealing. Hay found, too, that serious

17. P. King, 'War, judicial discretion and the problem of young adulthood 1740–1815', *Social History Soc. Newsletter*, IX, 1, 1984, p. 9.

crimes increased markedly with the ending of wars, capital offences against property being 47 per cent higher in peace than in war, while non-capital increased by only 17 per cent. His conclusion is that: 'The level of capital crime diminished little if at all during the course of peacetime: it only fell, and then dramatically, when the propertied again sent the unpropertied to fight England's great commercial wars.'

Removal of the younger males also meant that women made up a larger proportion of those indicted in wartime than they did in peace. In Staffordshire the proportions were from 16 to 10 per cent in the case of capital crimes, and from 23 to 12 per cent in the case of lesser thefts. Finally, the test for the kind of explanation of fluctuations these historians are now offering would be a year in which food prices were high, bringing up the indictment level for lesser crimes, and which was also a year of demobilisation, bringing increasing serious crime. Such a year was 1783, which saw the ending of the American war. In both Staffordshire and the home circuit this year saw the largest percentage increase in total indictments over the preceding year.[18]

Contemporaries did not make the sophisticated statistical breakdown which has enabled modern historians to discern patterns. They responded to aggregate increases in committals, brought home to them through long assize and sessions calendars and teeming gaols. One distinction, however, which they might have been aware of and annoyed by, was the legitimacy attached to certain actions outside the law by the labouring poor. It is hardly surprising, when laws were made and enforced by the propertied classes, that not all of them were acceptable to the moral opinion of the lower orders. A notion of 'social crime' helps the understanding of a substantial range of lower-class 'crimes'. Poachers, smugglers or wreckers did not normally think of themselves as criminals, nor were they normally so regarded by the communities in which they lived.[19] 'The common people of this country have no notion that smuggling is a crime,' complained the Sussex smugglers' sworn enemy the Duke of Richmond in 1749.[20] John Styles has shown that in the West Riding in the 1760s and 1770s, forging gold coins had wide acceptance in a bustling commercial district faced with a coin

---

18. D. Hay, 'War, dearth and theft', pp. 117–60. Quotation cited p. 144.

19. For an attempt to define 'social crime', see Rule, 'Social crime in the rural south'.

20. Cited in C. Winslow, 'Sussex smugglers' in Hay *et al.*, *Albion's Fatal Tree*, pp. 148–9.

shortage, but only if recast from gold 'clipped' from official coins, not if made from base metals.[21]

Property redefinitions could bring about such divergences between official and popular views of criminality. After enclosure of a village, for example, trespass would acquire new meanings. Fuel gathering would become hedge breaking or wood theft (easily the most common rural crime), while the new type of cost-conscious farmer might even deny to the village poor the age-old custom of gleaning after the harvest. In manufacturing the change from the independent craftsman to the out-worker making up materials put out by a merchant capitalist was reflected in a number of new laws punishing the 'embezzlement' of spare materials and thus clashing head on with the customary perquisites of the workers.[22]

'Social crime' is a concept which must be used with care. It does not distinguish between professional and casual crime. Although plundering shipwrecks may from its nature have been an *ad hoc* activity, smuggling could be very big business indeed. In its heyday on the south coast it involved raising large sums for the purchase of contraband, the building or adaptation of suitable vessels, and the mobilisation of large numbers of men and horses to carry the goods once landed. Poaching, too, embraced those who took for their own pot as well as organised gangs who procured for profitable sale to inns. Nor is the distinction between 'nice' and 'nasty' crime. Both smuggling and poaching often involved considerable violence – against informers and customs officers in the former case, and against gamekeepers in the latter. The murder of a customs officer and an unwilling informer by the Hawkhurst Gang in 1749 was among the most brutal crimes of the age. What makes them social crimes is the popular sense that they broke laws which only foolish and unreasonable legislatures would impose on actions which could hardly be considered improper. As the poet George Crabbe put it:

> . . . The smuggler cries
> What guilt is his who pays for what he buys?
> The poacher questions with perverted mind,
> Were not the gifts of heaven for all design'd?

21. J. Styles, 'Our traitorous money makers: the Yorkshire coiners and the law' in Styles and Brewer (eds), *An Ungovernable People*, pp. 209–11.

22. For wood stealing, see R.W. Bushaway, *By Rite*, pp. 208–33; For gleaning, see P. King, 'Gleaners, farmers, and the failure of legal sanctions in England 1750–1850', *Past and Present*, **125**, 1989, pp. 116–50. For industrial crime, see Rule, *Experience of Labour*, pp. 125–35; Styles, 'Embezzlement, industry and the law' in Berg, Hudson and Sonenscher (eds), *Manufacture in Town and Country*, pp. 183–204.

There is perhaps a second category of social crime: that in which an action in breach of the criminal law wins popular acceptance, not because of the inherent nature of the crime itself, but because of the protest context in which it is committed. Arson, especially rick burning against unpopular farmers, is sometimes in this category, as also are some cases of assault.[23]

Ascribing motives for crime is an exercise needing caution, however. Sheep-stealing, in contrast to horse-stealing, is often seen as the poor man's crime of desperation. Commonly it was. In a case from 1757, a year of very high cereal prices, a prosecutor admitted that a case of sheep-stealing was 'the effect of necessity only, occasioned by the hardness of the times, and to support a wife and three small children who were starving, the Parish officers having refused him relief'. Such extenuating circumstances were often claimed and largely explain why capital sentences for sheep-stealing were so often mitigated into transportation. But a closer analysis of the evidence reveals that not all sheep-stealers were in the same category. Some stole in consort with butchers. Some took sheep alive in such numbers for sale at fairs, or to add to the stock of their own farms, that they could be considered 'rustlers'. Some specialised in slaughtering sheep for the high-value tallow fat around their kidneys, leaving the main carcass behind. A few even stole or killed sheep as an act of protest or vengeance against their owners.[24]

PUNISHMENT

Concern with crime inevitably led on to consideration of the efficacy of punishment. In London this consideration had been long continuing. As Professor Beattie has pointed out, it is only when the problems of the capital are kept in mind that the need for such measures as the Transportation Acts of 1718 and 1719 can be accepted. In the small towns and villages in which most English people lived, the control of the face-to-face community with the

23. For an extended development of this argument, see Rule, 'Social crime in the rural south'.
24. Hay, 'War, dearth and theft', p. 129. For sheep-stealing generally, see Rule, 'The manifold causes of rural crime: sheep stealing in England c. 1740–1840' in Rule (ed.), *Outside the Law: Studies in Crime and Order 1650–1850*, Exeter UP, 1982, pp. 102–29; R.A.E. Wells, 'Sheep rustling in Yorkshire in the age of the agricultural and industrial revolutions', *Northern History*, XX, 1984, pp. 127–45.

back-up of the exemplary public hanging from time to time seemed sufficient. This is at the heart of the paradox of capital punishment in eighteenth-century England: why with so many capital convictions did so significant a proportion escape hanging? In London and Middlesex between 1749 and 1799, in twenty-four of the fifty-one years, at least half of the capitally convicted were reprieved. This was true of twenty-three of the thirty years 1770 to 1799. Of course, the pattern is very erratic: 90 per cent of those convicted in 1752 – the year following Fielding's influential tract – were hanged, and 81 per cent in 1787 – the year the first convict ships sailed to Botany Bay. In contrast, only one in ten of those capitally convicted in 1794 and one in eight in 1797 were executed. To view this as simply the tempering with mercy of a brutal penal code, an illustration of 'humanity', is to view only the surface appearance. The word to keep in mind is not 'mercy' but 'discretion'. The landed rulers of England did not *need* to hang all those indicted for felony; the assumption was of exemplary rather than retributive punishment.[25]

The assize judges decided at the end of the session which of those they had sentenced should be reprieved. For those they did not spare, there was still the prospect of securing the royal pardon. But, as Fielding was so concerned to point out, this was only the end of a punishment system in which most of those who *committed* capital felonies would not hang. In the first case many would escape detection or arrest. At a time when prosecutions had to be initiated by the victims, many would be reluctant to bring to trial those who had stolen from them. Juries increasingly tended to find those who were committed guilty of petty rather than grand larceny, by consciously undervaluing the goods in question. At times they were even directed in this by the judge. Local persons of influence would use it to incline judges towards reprieves, or the minister towards pardon. All of these Fielding considered misguided and dangerous to the state.

> No man indeed of common humanity or common sense can think the life of a man and a few shillings to be of an equal consideration, or that the law in punishing theft with death proceeds . . . with a view to vengeance. The terror of the example is the only thing proposed, and one man is sacrificed to the preservation of thousands.
>
> If therefore the terror of this example is removed (as it certainly is by frequent pardons) the design of the law is rendered totally ineffectual; the lives of the persons executed are thrown away and sacrificed rather to the vengeance than to the good of the public,

25. J.M. Beattie, *Crime and the Courts*, pp. 620–4.

which receives no other advantage than be getting rid of a thief, whose place will immediately be supplied by another . . . pardons have brought more men to the gallows than they have saved from it. So true is that sentiment of Machiavel, that examples of justice are more merciful than the unbounded exercise of pity.[26]

It is possible that the sharp decline in reprieves in 1752 over 1751 suggests that his view had some short-term influence, but Fielding was arguing against a trend in sentiment. If the death-based punishment regime of Hanoverian England had appeared effective, less concern over it would have been expressed, but the flaw in his argument was that the slaughter at the Fatal Tree seemed to be neither bringing peace of mind nor stemming the 'invasion of property'. None challenged the rightness of the rope for murder, or indeed for other crimes of violence, but then few swung for those crimes. Of the ninety-seven hanged in London and Middlesex in 1785, only one was a murderer and none a rapist, but forty-three had been convicted of burglary and house-breaking and thirty-one of highway robbery. It was, however, a long time before the opposition of powerful interests to the reform of the criminal law was overcome. As the leader of the reform movement, Sir Samuel Romilly, told the House of Commons in 1810: 'The indiscriminate application of the sentence of death to offences exhibiting very different degrees of turpitude has long been a subject of complaint in in this country, but it has still been progressive and increasing.'[27]

Before we turn to examine the trend away from the gallows, there is a need to consider another of the criticisms that Fielding made of the practice of executions in England – that is, their public nature.

> If every hope . . . fails the thief . . . if he should be discovered, apprehended, prosecuted, convicted, and refused a pardon . . . what is his situation then? Surely most gloomy and dreadful, without any hope and without any comfort. This is perhaps, the case with the less practised, less spirited, and less dangerous rogues; but with those of a different constitution it is far otherwise. No hero sees death as the alternative which may attend his undertaking with less terror, nor meets it in field with more imaginary glory. Pride, which is commonly the uppermost passion in both, is in both treated with equal satisfaction. The day appointed by law for the thief's shame is the day of glory in his own opinion. His procession to Tyburn and his last moments there, all are triumphant; attended with the compassion of

26. Fielding, *Inquiry*, p. 791.
27. Speech reported in *Cobbett's Parliamentary Debates*, XV, 1810, p. 366.

the meek and tender-hearted, and with the applause, admiration, and
envy of all the bold and hardened. His behaviour in his present
condition, not the crimes, how atrocious soever, which brought him to
it, are the subject of contemplation. And if he hath sense enough to
temper his boldness with any degree of decency, his death is spoken of
by many with honour, by most with pity, and by all with approbation.[28]

Not all doomed felons had the style of 'Tom Clinch', and Jonathan
Swift's poetic licence must be allowed for, but his verses of 1727
convey vividly the message of a thousand lesser ballads and broadsheets, many of which in a combination of picaresque adventure,
gruesome details and dying confessions were near instant inputs
into the cult of Tyburn.

> As clever Tom Clinch, while the rabble was bawling,
> Rode stately through Holburn to die in his calling,
> He stopt at the George for a bottle of sack,
> And promised to pay for it when he came back.
> His waistcoat, and stockings, and breeches, were white;
> His cap had a new cherry ribbon to tie't.
> The maids to the doors and the balconies ran,
> And said, 'Lack-a-day, he's a proper young man!'
> But, as from the windows the ladies he spied,
> Like a beau in the box, he bow'd low on each side!
> And when his last speech the loud hawkers did cry
> He swore from his cart 'It was all a damn'd lie!'
> The hangman for pardon fell down on his knee;
> Tom gave him a kick in the guts for his fee:
> But I'll see you all damn'd before I will whittle!
> My honest friend Wild (may he long hold his place)
> He lengthen'd my life with a whole year of grace.
> Take courage, dear comrades, and be not afraid,
> Nor slip this occasion to follow your trade;
> My conscience is clear, and my spirits are calm,
> And this I go off without prayer-book or psalm;
> Then follow the practice of clever Tom Clinch,
> Who hung like a hero, and never would flinch.

From the moment the assize judge put on the black cap, to the fatal
drop via the long procession from Newgate to Tyburn Hill, the state
intended to enact an awful theatre before the lower orders. The
problem was that the people turned it into counter theatre and
made a celebration of an intended humiliation. Commenting on
the lapse of time between sentence and execution, Fielding wrote:

28. Fielding, *Inquiry*, pp. 791–2.

'no good mind can avoid compassionating a set of wretches who are put to death we know not why, unless, as it almost appears to make a holiday for, and to entertain, the mob'. In his etching 'The Idle 'Prentice Executed at Tyburn' of 1747, William Hogarth vividly conveys this aspect of public hangings, while Thomas Rowlandson in his 'An Execution' of 1803 makes a related point. The foreground is dominated by two young pickpockets, perhaps ten years of age, cheerfully plying their trade in the very shadow of the gallows. The frequency of executions in London, as Fielding recognised, denied them any potency as lessons. Public hangings had been intended to link shame with death. Fielding argued that private executions would be 'much more shocking and terrible to the crowd without doors than at present, as well as much more dreadful to the criminals themselves'. It was not advice government took. The Murder Act of 1752 required death sentences on murderers to be carried out within two days, and for them to be kept in solitary confinement in the brief interlude, and in 1783 the decision to carry out executions in Newgate ended the procession to Tyburn, but public executions did not end until 1868, by which time only those convicted of the most serious of crimes were hanged.[29]

Secondary punishment

To the modern student, perhaps the most surprising thing about punishment during the period was the scant use of imprisonment for criminal offences before 1770. John Howard's pioneering survey of the prisons in 1776 discovered a total population of only 653 persons in the gaols of England and Wales. Of these, 59.6 per cent were not felons but debtors. Only 15.9 per cent were petty offenders on whom sentence of imprisonment had been passed. The remainder were persons in waiting: waiting for trial, for execution or for transportation. Although they were considerably more common in the counties, prison sentences formed only a very small proportion of those handed out at the Old Bailey: a little over 1 per cent in 1760–4 and a little less in 1765–9, and still only 2.3 per cent between 1770 and 1774. Most of these were short sentences of never more than three years and usually for one year or less for offences like manslaughter, commercial frauds, combining against employers, embezzlement of materials or rioting.[30] Around 1775,

29. For public executions in London, see Linebaugh, 'The Tyburn riots against the surgeons' in Hay *et al.*, *Albion's Fatal Tree*, pp. 65–117.
30. M. Ignatieff, *A Just Measure of Pain*, pp. 15, 28.

however, a new age of punishment began, during which not only would prison provision and the growth of the imprisoned population accelerate, but alongside would develop the notion of reformative incarceration. Between 1775 and 1784 around a third of Old Bailey sentences were for imprisonment. In the second half of the 1780s there was a sharp fallback, but in the 1790s the level returned again to about a third. Two things seem clear: that from the last quarter of the eighteenth century there began an increasing use of imprisonment that amounted to a revolution in the English punishment system, and that up until then transportation had been the enabling instrument of the penal system.[31]

Professor Beattie has described the introduction of transportation to the American colonies in 1718 as a 'fundamental break'. It provided the crucial form of punishment which not only reduced the numbers of those who needed to be hanged, but even further reduced those who had, for want of an alternative, to be freed back into the community. By the time of the approach of the American war in 1775 around 50,000 convicts had been carried over the Atlantic; four-fifths of them were male, and they were typically between fifteen and twenty-nine years old. Most of them had been convicted of theft, the vast majority being neither habitual nor serious criminals. The scope of the first Transportation Act, which was considerable, was extended at several points in the period by adding fresh offences for which it could be inflicted. As a means of filling the sanction gap between whippings and hangings and by offering life or fourteen-year banishment as alternative sentences for serious crime, transportation gave the courts that flexibility necessary to sustain an exemplary approach.[32]

When the revolt of the American colonies changed the situation from 1776, the government resorted to holding would-be transportees in the 'hulks', old moored ships. This could not be a long-term solution. The hulks could have held only around 60 per cent of those under sentence of transportation, which left several thousand to be kept in gaols, in effect, as Michael Ignatieff has noted, transforming imprisonment overnight from an occasional to the most frequent sentence for all minor property crime. The return of peace in 1783 worsened the situation by bringing the customary demobilisation 'crime wave' to a situation in which there was no

31. *Ibid.*, p. 81.
32. Beattie, *Crime and the Courts*, p. 620; K. Morgan, 'English and American attitudes towards convict transportation, 1718–1775', *History*, LXXII, 236, 1987, p. 416. See also Ekirch, *Bound for America.*

receiving shore. The interlude before transportation to Australia began in 1787 was one in which, although there was some decrease in the reprieve rate of convicted felons, a much wider range of opinion began to swing behind the prison reform impetus set in motion by John Howard. Overcrowding between 1776 and 1786 resulted both from the detention of those sentenced to transportation and from the greatest crime wave since 1720 which greeted the end of the war and threw the problems of prison conditions into the public view. Corruption and brutality on the part of gaolers, failure to carry out statutory inspection on the part of the county bench and the ravages of the 'gaol fever' (typhus) all combined to carry forward the reform of the prisons.[33] Although it is true that transportation to Australia restored the old situation from 1787, banishment never again dominated sentencing in the way it had done in the third quarter of the eighteenth century.[34]

At the same time, at the lower end of the scale of offences, whippings and brandings, although they certainly did not disappear, became more often than not attached to prison sentences. Behind this lay the Howard-inspired rebuilding and redesigning of the country's gaols. Prisons were not only made larger to cope with the dimensions of the explosion in committals after the American war, they were re-conceptualised in design to permit the possibility of reforming their inmates. The old open-area prisons with their promiscuously mixed, chained offenders, gave way to cell systems enabling the new offenders to be separated from the corruption of old lags. Brutal regimes were to be replaced by purposeful ones, hygiene practices controlled the ravages of fever, and the high, secure walls which replaced the chains also separated the world of the prison from intercourse with the world outside. In these new conditions a different kind of discipline was instilled: systematic, not haphazard, purposeful, not corrupt. As Ignatieff has concluded:

> In the short space of a decade, the whole strategy of eighteenth-century punishment had been called into question – by a crime wave that refused to respond to the old remedies, by the suspension of transportation, and by the arguments of reformers who contended that there was a more just and rational way for the state to inflict pain on its subjects.[35]

With some regions taking the lead from the zeal of their local reformers, like Sir George Onesiphorus Paul in Gloucestershire, the

33. Ignatieff, *Just Measure of Pain*, pp. 81–2.
34. For transportation to Australia, see Shaw, *Convicts and the Colonies*.
35. Ignatieff, *Just Measure of Pain*, p. 93.

Duke of Richmond in Sussex and T.B. Bailey in Lancashire, a great period of gaol-building began quickly to provide places which were almost as rapidly filled. For it was not so much with the hardened but the reprieved felon that the new imprisonment most concerned itself; the re-availability of transportation could take care of the former, and it continued to do so down to the middle years of the nineteenth century, covering the crucial years which lapsed between the removal of so many capital crimes in the 1830s and the emergence of long-term prison sentences. The punishment reformers were especially concerned to get hold of the first-time offenders. As Paul put it: 'Few men have been hanged for a felony, who might not have been saved to the community for the correction of a former misdemeanour.'[36] It is for this reason that, as Professor Beattie had pointed out, the consequences of crime for many offenders became more serious. This was especially the case with the punishment of summary offences which had previously been dealt with corporally.[37] Now, incarceration into the remoulding, work-educating regime of the new prisons was increasingly likely to happen. The blueprint Fielding had projected in his precocious *Plan* of 1753, for 'County Houses' which could receive and reform both the indigent poor and the petty criminal,[38] was by the end of the eighteenth century becoming reality. Embezzlers of materials, breakers of husbandry or other employment contracts, bearers of bastards, lesser poachers, disturbers of the peace, vagrants, turnip stealers and combining workers – these were the kinds of people mostly affected. The reforming vision was genuine enough, and its perception of the need for a new and more intense and general discipline of the lower orders may well justify the placing of the new prisons alongside the workhouse and, in some respects, the factory. However, the more evident short-term effect was to increase the authority of landlords, employers and parish officials. In the gradual shift in punishment emphasis away from publicly inflicted exemplary assaults on the body, the state intended to suffer no loss of control. In many ways Jeremy Bentham's *Panoptican*, that fantasy

36. *Ibid.*, pp. 94–102. For a view more sympathetic to the humanism of prison reformers, see M. de Lacy, *Prison Reform in Lancashire, 1700–1850: A Study in Local Administration*, Chetham Society, Manchester, 1986.

37. Beattie, *Crime and the Courts*, p. 616. For the punishment of petty crime, see also J. Innes, 'Prisons for the poor, English Bridewells, 1555–1800' in F.G. Snyder and D. Hay (eds), *Labour, Law and Crime in Historical Perspective*, Tavistock, 1987, pp. 42–122.

38. See Fielding, *A Proposal for Making an Effectual Provision for the Poor*, 1752, and the discussion in Ignatieff, *Just Measure of Pain*, pp. 45–6.

gaol run by private enterprise and so designed that ceaselessly watched convicts were forced to manufacture a prodigious output, was the logical end of the new discipline. The great utilitarian had been extolling its virtues since 1791.

> What hold can another manufacturer have upon his workmen equal to what my manufacturer would have upon his? What other master is there that can reduce his workmen, if idle, to a situation next to starving, without suffering them to go elsewhere? What other master is there whose men can never get drunk unless he chooses they should do so? And, who, so far from being able to raise their wages by combination, are obliged to take whatever pittance he thinks it in his interest to allow?[39]

The idea was firmly rejected in 1810. The predominantly evangelical reformers would not support a scheme so blatantly commercial that it seemed to leave scant room for the reformative role of religion. The state was not, then, ready to hand the management of punishment to private enterprise.

LAW AS IDEOLOGY

Because of the increasing role of pardons, the numbers hanged remained surprisingly stable over much of the eighteenth century, despite the great expansion in the number of capital offences and the increase in population. Partly because of this and because of the belief that rising indictments reflected an increase in 'real' crime, contemporary opinion that the penal code was inefficacious became increasingly widespread, especially among the ranks of the propertied beyond the very small ruling elite. The landed gentry took hold readily enough of the use of imprisonment for petty offences, especially, as we have seen, for those sentenced under the growing body of summary jurisdiction with which the landed interest as MPs was conveniencing itself through JPs. Yet despite the persuasive arguments of the criminal law reformers, parliament resisted all proposals. No capital statute was repealed before 1808 and substantial progress had to wait until the second and third decades of the nineteenth century. As Douglas Hay has pointed out, the determination to retain all capital statutes, even when obsolete, and in fact to introduce new ones indicates how deep into the mental

39. Ignatieff, *Just Measure of Pain*, p. 110.

world of the eighteenth-century class the 'bloody code' and the concept of deterrence through terror was rooted.[40]

In a brilliant, if controversial essay, Hay drew attention to the role of the criminal law as ideology and its legitimating function for the rule of the few over the many. For the most part, the small ruling class did not fear or experience much depredation on their property. To this degree they did not, as did the merchants, shopocracy and farmers, perceive that the death-based code was failing to protect property. Little troubled in this regard, they were more concerned with authority. As Hay has put it: 'The criminal law was critically important in maintaining bonds of obedience and deference, in legitimising the status quo, in constantly recreating the structure of authority which arose from property and in turn protected its interests.'[41] The gallows was indispensable to maintaining authority, but the criminal law of which it was both symbol and ultimate sanction became a complex and subtle instrument of class rule. It, not religion, became the chief ideological weapon which in the name of equality could facilitate and justify the hegemony of an elite. Hay picks out three aspects of the law as ideology: majesty, justice and mercy.

Majesty describes the ceremonial and theatrical dimensions, from assize processions of red-robed judges to the rituals of public execution. We have already discussed this aspect. It remains only to remark how much would have been lost without the awful power over life. There were not many 'maiden' assizes, after which the judge could pull on the symbolic white gloves. I doubt there were ever two in a row. But only exceptionally did more than two, three or four prisoners at any one of the twice-yearly county assizes tremble while a full-wigged judge reached for the black cap. London needed such a lesson six times a year, but it was well enough understood that selective terror, not an orgy of executions, was the most effective demonstration of power and preserver of the authority structure.[42]

Justice was a concept which elevated the criminal code into THE LAW, allowing it to appear as something more than the instrument of a ruling class. Equality before the law may have been a fiction in practice, but it was not necessarily perceived as one in legal philosophy. It needs no great sociological insight to see, as Goldsmith did,

40. Hay, 'Property, authority and the criminal law' in Hay *et al.*, *Albion's Fatal Tree*, pp. 23–4.
41. *Ibid.*, p. 25.
42. *Ibid.*, pp. 26–7.

that 'Laws grind the poor, and rich men rule the law',[43] but the broad acceptance of the rule of law in eighteenth-century England depended on the belief that no man was exempt from it. It was one of those shibboleths which, even in the political ferment following the outbreak of the French Revolution, English Jacobinians could insist was a right of the 'Free-born Englishman'. It was equally available to the anti-Jacobinian writer Hanna More, in her tireless crusade to attach the lower orders to the side of government, to put into the mouth of a ploughman:

> British laws for my guard,
> My cottage is barr'd,
> 'Tis safe in the light or the dark, Sir;
> If the Squire should oppress,
> I get instant redress:
> My orchard's as safe as his park, Sir.[44]

From time to time the law despatched the well-born or the well-to-do. When it did so it extracted maximum propaganda advantage from so unusual an occurrence. When the rope took Lord Ferrars in 1760 for the murder of his steward, and when not even his noble body was spared from the dissecting knives of the surgeons, an example was created which was to surface in a thousand justifications. Lower down the social scale convictions of farmers or prosperous tradesmen afforded rare opportunities for exegesis. When a Devonshire farmer, rich enough to have offered a £500 bribe, was executed in 1801 for stealing a sheep, the broadsheet sold at his hanging concluded with a plaudit to English law.

> The excellency of the English constitution in its impartial awards of punishment must excite the admiration of all who see the rich culprit, whose crime was aggravated by the circumstances of his wealth, bend to an equally ignominious death with the meanest criminal.[45]

It is true, as Hay acknowledges, that the parlour justice summarily administered by the squires paid much less regard to the rules of evidence, and did not always impress with its impartiality, especially when offences against the game laws were concerned, or for that matter wood thefts, the commonest trespass against property by the fuel-starved poor. Only a handful of diaries recording the out-of-sessions dealings of justices survive, but one from Wiltshire which does records fifty occasions in the five years 1744–8 on which the

43. Oliver Goldsmith, *The Traveller*, 1764.
44. Cited in Hay, 'Property, authority and the criminal law', p. 37.
45. Broadsheet on execution of Henry Penson, Devon County Records Office.

justice was presented with cases of wood stealing.[46] However, even here the poor could obtain justice for themselves or inform against petty oppressers – so long as the interests of the squire and his neighbours were not threatened.

There is evidence enough that recourse to law was within the *mentalité* of the poor. In 1770 a labourer went into the Anchor public house in Egham. Another labourer, James Turner, who was already there, 'offered to toss up for a pennyworth of gin, which he agreed to, and upon informant's winning, Turner struck him several times and beat him very much and told him that he supposed informant would take the law of him . . .'. He supposed correctly.[47] Reading these 'case books' indicates that justices dealt very often with such complaints, and as often with desperate working-class wives seeking protection from brutal husbands. Sending farm servants and others for short stays in the House of Correction for quitting their masters' employ without notice was another regular event, but so too was the other side. When, in 1744, Wiltshire labourer William Turner was not paid his due wages by his employer, Mrs Tucker, he went directly to the justice, who summoned the lady and settled the matter. Below the level of labourer, even paupers could take to the law, as for example in 1745 when the justice summoned before him the overseers of the poor from a Wiltshire parish to explain why they had refused relief to two female paupers; 'they obeyed the summons and relieved them'. A labourer's wife, who was sold a loaf 5 ounces underweight by an Egham baker in 1774, was soon laying an information on the matter before Justice Wyatt.[48]

Cheating dealers, wage-witholding farmers, over-zealous excisemen, assault-committing neighbours, maladministrators of poor relief, all these were dealt with often enough for many of the poor to feel there was a level of the law which could afford them a degree of redress. Some of Hay's critics have made a good deal of this. Peter King in particular has demonstrated that in Essex even at quarter sessions, many more prosecutions were brought by the labouring poor than Hay's reading of the law as a class instrument seems to allow. It is a point which should not be overlooked. King found that at the Essex quarter sessions between 1760 and 1800

46. E. Crittall (ed.), *The Notebook of William Hunt 1744– 1749*, Wiltshire Record Society, Devizes, 1982.

47. E. Silverthorne (ed.), *Deposition Book of Richard Wyatt, JP*, Surrey Record Society, Guildford, 1978, entry no. 78.

48. Hunt, *Notebook*, no. 102; Wyatt, *Deposition Book*, no. 247.

around a sixth of prosecutors were labourers. Twice as many were farmers, despite their very much smaller numbers in the population. Tradesmen and artisans, like the farmers, accounted for a third of prosecutions, but this was not the only difference. Overwhelmingly labourers brought actions against their own class. Both farmers and tradesmen also prosecuted labourers or servants. That the poor from time to time used the law against the poor seems hardly to affect the different use made of it by the ruling class. Of course, 'patricians' were hardly likely to bring the kinds of action usually tried at sessions, but King points out that assize records for Essex suggest that the gentry were responsible for only 8 to 10 per cent of prosecutions.[49] If anything I find this surprisingly high, for Hay's thesis does not require that the landed ruling class use the law in the same way as farmers or tradesmen, that is in the direct initiation of prosecutions. King's figure further suggests that the 'patrician elite' (his term) was, in contrast to labourers, active well beyond its representation in the population.

Hay's third aspect of the law as ideology was *mercy*. Discrimination was possible at many stages of the path from commission through committal and conviction to punishment. We have already noted Henry Fielding's misgivings over its extent and, in his view, misuse. The de-propertied could decide not to act; the jury not to convict, or to deliberately lessen the offence; the judge to recommend reprieve; and the king to pardon. Hay has been criticised for too marked a concentration on the last acts of discrimination, those taking place after the terrible moment of sentencing. Yet in terms of the analysis of power, that is the place that matters. One measure of the extent of authority are the possibilities for selectivity inherent in its structure. The power to prevent a hanging is as awesome as that to inflict one. At this point, 'equality before the law' is dispensable. Judges recommended before they departed the assize towns, but they were influenced, not only by the extenuating circumstances of particular crimes and the local prevalence of the crime in question, but by character representations made by persons of standing in the court itself, and subsequently through whatever connections with the powerful and influential the convict or his relatives could exploit. In inclining greater men to take up the case, much was made of contacts such as links through service, tenancy or parental acquaintanceship. Noting that as much was made in written pleas of 'respectable parentage' as of previous good charac-

49. King, 'Decision makers and decision making in the English criminal law', pp. 25–34.

ter, Hay has cynically remarked, 'claims of class saved far more men who had been left to hang, than did the claims of humanity'. Sentencing may have been carried out in public, but, as Hay points out, pardoning was essentially an act of private patronage, going on out of sight of the larger population, which allowed the rulers of England the opportunity of making, in part, 'the rule of law' a matter of selective class justice while preserving a public face of impartiality and absolute determinacy: 'It allowed the class that passed one of the bloodiest penal codes in Europe to congratulate itself on its humanity.' To note that only a proportion of the condemned were hanged is to see half the picture; we need to note wherein lay the power to determine *which* convicts made up that proportion. Like other kinds of patronage their power of mercy helped the landed elite to maintain the fabric of obedience, gratitude and deference.[50]

Edward Thompson has pointed out that, 'If the law is evidently partial and unjust, then it will mask nothing, contribute nothing to any class's hegemony. The essential precondition for the effectiveness of law in its function as ideology, is that it shall display an independence from gross manipulation and shall seem to be just.'[51] This does not mean that the public face of the rule of law is a *simple* mask for the rule of a class. It is more complex than that. The law must not only appear impartial, it must also be of some *use* to the wider society. We have seen that despite the overwhelming preponderance of the labouring poor as the victims of the law, they did make some use of it, howbeit at the basement level. Perhaps, however, there is an even more serious point to take. The 'rule of law' as a justifying ideology for an extremely unequal distribution of property and even more unequal one of power enabled the elite to govern without police or standing army, but it established 'rules' which could not then be broken, as at a famous moment in 1794 when the jury at a treason trial refused to convict the leaders of popular radicalism. The leaders of the London Corresponding Society, the first truly 'popular' radical organisation, walked free.[52]

---

50. Hay, 'Property, authority and the criminal law', pp. 41–8.
51. E.P. Thompson, *Whigs and Hunters*, p. 263.
52. For the London Corresponding Society, see above, pp. 224–5. For the arrest, trial and acquittal of its leaders Thomas Hardy, Horne Tooke and John Thelwall, see E.P. Thompson, *Making of the English Working Class*, pp. 144–9.

Change and Continuity

'Times are altered' was Oliver Goldsmith's verdict on England in 1769. It was a view echoed by many other contemporary writers. They perceived an agency which they did not recognise as 'capitalism' but variously labelled 'trade', 'commerce' or simply 'wealth'. This force had corrupted the simple and good manners of a populace which had once contained its expectations and, knowing its place, had relatively prospered in it. 'Ill fares the land,' declared Goldsmith, 'where wealth accumulates and men decay.' He continued:

A time there was, ere England's griefs began,
When every rood of ground maintain'd its man;
For him light labour spread her wholesome store,
Just gave what life required, but gave no more:
His best companions, innocence and health;
And his best riches, ignorance of wealth.[1]

For Henry Fielding in 1751 the main agency of social degeneration was the rise of commerce.

Nothing hath wrought such an alteration in [the] people as the introduction of trade. This hath indeed given a new face to the whole nation, hath in a great measure subverted the former state of affairs, and hath almost totally changed the manners, customs, and habits of the people.[2]

It was not that such writers could not see the material benefits that economic development brought. Fielding wrote of 'many emoluments' which compensated: 'the grandeur and power of the nation is carried to a pitch that it could never otherwise have reached', while 'human life' was 'embellished with every comfort

1. Oliver Goldsmith, *The Deserted Village*, 1769.
2. Henry Fielding, *An Inquiry into the Late Increase of Robbers, 1751, Collected Works*, ed. T.Roscoe, 1849, p. 761.

which it is capable of tasting'. What they lamented was the social change which accompanied it. Half a century after Fielding, when manufacturing might was becoming as visible as expanding commerce, William Wordsworth viewed a textile mill and expressed the same dilemma. He could only 'rejoice' when 'Measuring the force of those gigantic powers / That by the thinking mind, have been compelled / To serve the will of feeble-bodied Man', yet could only hope that men would learn that 'all true glory rests / All praise, all safety, and all happiness / Upon the moral law'.[3]

Their lost world was ill defined. They did not call it 'feudal society' in any complex sense of a peculiar social system, but their vocabulary invoked 'a peasantry' and, especially, 'natural bonds' between rulers and people, lords and vassals and masters and servants. 'Bonds' short-handed social relations and it was a sense of change in these that really concerned the writers. To cite Goldsmith again:

> As nature's ties decay
> As duty, love and honour fail to sway,
> Fictitious bonds, the bonds of wealth and law,
> Still gather strength, and force unwilling awe.[4]

The decline was hardly precisely dated and these writers usually seriously foreshortened the period over which the changes they lamented had been developing. It can, however, be suggested that they represent a sense of change which becomes increasingly discernible in the middle decades of the eighteenth century. Most, if not all historical periods could be presented in a textbook entitled *Continuity and Change*. However, coming as it does between two such contrasting centuries as the seventeenth and the nineteenth, the eighteenth century presents the dichotomy in a particularly sharp manner.[5]

No simple concept such as 'modernisation' can overrule its paradoxes. It was an age in which people could still be drowned by a witch-hunting mob, as at Tring in 1751; in which, until 1790, women were still burned for murdering their husbands, although compassion now decreed they should first be strangled; and in

---

3. William Wordsworth, *The Excursion*, 1814.
4. Oliver Goldsmith, *The Traveller*, 1764.
5. See the discussion of this point by Joanna Innes, 'Not so strange? New views of eighteenth-century England', *History Workshop Journal*, **29**, 1990, pp. 179–83. The latest volume of the *Oxford History of England* – Langford, *Polite and Commercial People* – however, declares an intent 'to emphasise the changes which occurred in an age not invariably associated with change'. In particular it stresses the growing importance of 'a broad middle class'.

which soldiers or sailors could be flogged, sometimes to death, for minor offences. These were hardly manifestations of modernity.[6] But it was also an age which, after first expanding the number of crimes for which people were hanged, was by its close beginning the process of reducing them. It took another generation before executions for the capital crimes which remained ceased to be carried out in public. The availability first of the American and then of the Australian colonies saved the ruling classes from having to hang too many of the poorer sort, but by the beginning of the nineteenth century, humanitarianism was combining with the altering punishment needs of the changing economic system to make a decisive move towards a modern regime based on imprisonment, although the new direction indicated by the Penitentiary Act of 1779 remained an untrodden way for some time to come.

The criminal law was only one aspect of the way in which the eighteenth-century legislature recognised and attempted to deal with social change. In a significant article, Joanna Innes has revealed a House of Commons which also quite thoroughly informed itself on other social issues and enacted a sizeable volume of legislation on matters like poor relief, vagrancy and moral reform. She presents a legislature where the initiative came more often from back-benchers than ministers and which was increasingly responsive to opinions thrust upon it from widespread petitioning. Her picture of this developing feature of Hanoverian England does not fit well with the determination of some historians to insist that it was an *ancien régime* society.[7]

Historians of the conservative tendency, of whom Dr Jonathan Clark has become the best known, tend to stress two factors in arguing that significant social change did not take place in the eighteenth century. These are the continued political domination of the aristocracy and, rejecting the label 'industrial revolution', the undramatic nature of economic change. The first of these is hardly now disputed, but the continuation of aristocratic power is not incompatible with social change. As Dr Porter has pointed out, Dr Clark's argument has an element of inversion: because the eighteenth-century political structure so successfully endured, social developments cannot have been very marked. This would seem to accept that profound social change does threaten the political order, so that the endurance of the latter suggests the absence of

6. The last public execution was carried out at Newgate in 1868.
7. Joanna Innes, 'Parliament and the shaping of eighteenth-century English social policy', *Trans. Royal Hist. Soc.*, XXXX, 1990, pp. 63–92.

the former. In fact social and economic change can continue for some time before it threatens the hegemony of the existing elite. In some respects it might even reinforce it. The increased power of the state, both nationally and internationally, rested on its ability to raise revenues from a growing wealth distributed in a particular way. More generally, the 'old regime' functioned effectively and avoided serious challenge because it was able to adapt to a changing society and move with new economic directions.[8]

Those who reject the validity of even a qualified notion of an 'industrial revolution' in eighteenth-century Britain rest their case substantially on the reworking in recent years of the macro-economic indicators of trends in the national economy.[9] These do indeed suggest that growth was slower, especially in per capita terms, than those assumed in traditional accounts of the industrial revolution, and further that no marked discontinuity in the pace of growth took place in the eighteenth century. Like all dramatic concepts, that of industrial revolution exaggerates the suddenness and completeness of actual happenings, but to what extent and in what ways? National income accounting figures, for that is what the 'new' statistics are, provide only one way of reading economic change. Low figures for annual percentage increases can in themselves be deceptive, unless the student keeps in mind that even so modest a figure as, say, 1.4 per cent, compounds to a doubling in only fifty years. Further, national accounting is perhaps not generally appropriate in that industrialisation was a regional phenomenon. In England it was more widespread than in later industrialisations, much more so, for example, than in Germany. True, some areas in the South and East suffered a measure of de-industrialisation, but if mining and manufacturing are both considered, it is not unreasonable to write of an industrial revolution in the North, west and east Midlands, Cornwall, Shropshire and beyond England in South Wales and lowland Scotland.[10]

Borrowing what is convenient for its purposes from Professor Crafts, conservative historiography has largely ignored his stress on the unusual level of structural change in England. The move out of agriculture was very marked. It came much sooner and proceeded

8. J.C.D. Clark, *English Society and Revolution and Rebellion*; R. Porter, 'English society in the eighteenth century revisited', in J. -Black (ed.), *British Politics and Society from Walpole to Pitt*, pp. 29–52.

9. Especially on the work of Professor Crafts now brought together in *British Economic Growth during the Industrial Revolution*.

10. See the pertinent criticisms of the method in J. Hoppit, 'Counting the industrial revolution', *Econ. Hist. Rev.*, XLIII, 2, 1990, pp. 173–93.

to a markedly greater extent than was the case in later industrialisations. If the proportionate growth of the non-agricultural labour force is considered alongside the wider geographical spread, it could be argued that the peculiarities of Britain's industrial revolution were such that the lives of a larger proportion of the population were directly touched than was the case with later industrialisations, despite their higher initial rates of growth and more evident technological transformation. In the last analysis the crucial fact is that the population of England was able to double between the Hanoverian succession and Waterloo. Only significant social and economic change can explain that, whatever continuities can be found in the political superstructure.[11]

11. See Crafts, *British Economic Growth*, Chapter 6.

Bibliography

This is a select listing of recent secondary works. The footnotes contain full details of all works used and cited in the text. Titles are listed only once, so the assignment between categories is somewhat arbitrary.

GENERAL

Ashton, T.S. *An Economic History of England: The Eighteenth Century.* Methuen, 1955.

Berg, M. *The Age of Manufactures 1700–1820.* Fontana, 1985.

Berg, M., Hudson, P. and Sonenscher, M. *Manufacture in Town and Country before the Industrial Revolution.* Cambridge UP, 1983.

Black, J. (ed.) *British Politics and Society from Walpole to Pitt 1742–1789.* Macmillan, 1990.

Bowden, W. *Industrial Society in England towards the End of the Eighteenth Century.* 1925 rept, Cass, 1965.

Brewer, J. *The Sinews of Power.* Unwin, 1989.

Clark, J.C.D. *English Society, 1688–1832: Ideology, Social Structure and Political Practice during the Ancien Régime.* Cambridge UP, 1985.

Clark, J.C.D. *Revolution and Rebellion. State and Society in England in the Seventeenth and Eighteenth Centuries.* Cambridge UP, 1986.

Clarkson, L.A. *Proto-industrialization: The First Phase of Industrialization?* Macmillan, 1985.

Crafts, N.F.R. *British Economic Growth during the Industrial Revolution.* Oxford UP, 1985.

Deane, P. and Cole, W.A. *British Economic Growth 1688–1959.* Cambridge UP, 1969.

Digby, A. and Feinstein, P. *New Directions in Economic and Social History.* Macmillan, 1989.

Floud, R. and McCloskey, D. *The Economic History of Britain since 1700: I, 1700–1860.* Cambridge UP, 1981.

George, M.D. *England in Transition.* Penguin, 1953.

Gilbert, A.D. *Religion and Society in Industrial England.* Longman, 1976.

Hartwell, R.H. *The Industrial Revolution and Economic Growth.* Methuen, 1971.

Langford, P. *A Polite and Commercial People: England 1727–1783.* Clarendon Press, Oxford, 1989.

Levine, D. *Family Formation in an Age of Nascent Capitalism.* Academic Press, 1979.

McKendrick, N., Brewer, J. and Plumb, J.H. *The Birth of a Consumer Society: The Commercialization of Eighteenth-Century England.* Hutchinson, 1983.

Malcolmson, R.W. *Life and Labour in England 1700–1780.* Hutchinson, 1981.

Mantoux, P. *The Industrial Revolution in the Eighteenth Century.* 1928, rept Methuen, 1961.

Mathias, P. *The Transformation of England.* Methuen, 1979.

Mathias, P. *The First Industrial Nation: An Economic History of Britain 1700–1914.* 2nd edn, Methuen, 1983.

Pawson, E. *The Early Industrial Revolution: Britain in the Eighteenth Century.* Barnes & Noble, New York, 1979.

Perkin, H.J. *The Origins of Modern English Society, 1780–1880.* Routledge, 1969.

Pinchbeck, I. *Women Workers and the Industrial Revolution, 1750–1850.* 1930 rept, Cass, 1969.

Porter, R. *English Society in the Eighteenth Century.* Penguin, 1982, revised 1990.

Roscoe, T. (ed.) *Collected Works of Henry Fielding.* Henry Bohn, 1849.

Rule, J.G. *The Experience of Labour in Eighteenth-Century Industry.* Croom Helm, 1981.

Rule, J.G. *The Labouring Classes in Early Industrial England, 1750–1850.* Longman, 1986.

Rule, J.G. *The Vital Century: England's Developing Economy, 1714–1815,* Longman, 1992.

Thale, M. (ed.) *The Autobiography of Francis Place.* Cambridge UP, 1972.

Wilson, C. *England's Apprenticeship 1603–1763.* Longman, revised 1984.

Wrigley, E.A. 'The growth of population in eighteenth-century England: a conundrum resolved'. *Past and Present* **98**, 1983.

Wrigley, E.A. and Schofield, R.S. *The Population History of England 1541–1871*. 2nd edn, Cambridge UP, 1989.

THE UPPER CLASS

Ayres, J. *Paupers and Pig Killers: The Diary of William Holland, a Somerset Parson 1799–1818*. Alan Sutton, 1985.

Beckett, J.V. *The Aristocracy in England 1660–1914*, Blackwell, 1986.

Cannon, J. *Aristocratic Century: The Peerage of Eighteenth-Century England*. Cambridge UP, 1984.

Corfield, P. 'Class by name and number in eighteenth-century Britain'. *History*, LXXII, No. 234, 1978.

Rogers, N. 'Money, land and lineage: the Big Bourgeoisie of Hanoverian London'. *Social History*, IV, 3, 1979.

Stone, L. and Fawtier Stone, J. *An Open Elite? England 1540–1880*. Penguin, 1986.

Thompson, E.P. 'Eighteenth-century English society: class struggle without class'. *Social History*, III, 2, 1978.

THE MIDDLE CLASSES

Briggs, A. 'The language of class in early-nineteenth-century England' in Briggs, A. and Saville, J. (eds), *Essays in Labour History*. Macmillan, 1967.

Crouzet, F. *The First Industrialists*. Cambridge UP, 1985.

Davidoff, L. and Hall, C. *Family Fortunes: Men and Women of the English Middle Class, 1780–1850*. Hutchinson, 1987.

Earle, P. *The Making of the English Middle Class: Business, Society and Family Life in London, 1660–1730*. Methuen, 1989.

Miles, M. 'A haven for the privileged: recruitment into the profession of attorney in England, 1709–92'. *Social History*, XI, 2, 1986.

Minchinton, W.E. 'The merchants in England in the eighteenth century'. *Explorations in Entrepreneurial History*, X, 1957.

Money, J. 'Birmingham and the West Midlands 1760–1793: politics and regional identity in the English provinces in the later eighteenth century' in Borsay, P. (ed.) *The Eighteenth-Century Town*. Longman, 1990.

Mui, H. and Mui, L.H. *Shops and Shopkeeping in Eighteenth-century England*. Routledge, 1988.

O'Day, R. *Education and Society 1500–1800.* Longman, 1982.

Schwarz, L.D. 'Social class and social geography: the middle classes in London at the end of the eighteenth century'. *Social History,* VII, 2, 1982.

Vaisey, D. (ed.), *The Diary of Thomas Turner, 1754–1765.* Oxford UP, 1984.

THE LOWER ORDERS

Baugh, D.A. 'The cost of poor relief in south-east England, 1790–1834'. *Econ. H.R.,* XXVIII, 1975.

Blaug, M. 'The myth of the old Poor Law and the making of the new', *Jn. Econ. Hist.,* XXIII, 2, 1963.

Blaug, M. 'The Poor Law report re-examined'. *Jn. Econ. Hist.,* XXIV, 1964.

Bushaway, R.W. *By Rite: Custom, Ceremony and Community in England, 1700–1880.* Junction Books, 1982.

Clark, P. and Souden, D. *Migration and Society in Early Modern England.* Hutchinson, 1987.

Digby, A. *Pauper Palaces.* Routledge, 1978.

Hempton, D. *Methodism and Politics in British Society 1750–1850.* Heinemann, 1974.

Henriques, U.R.Q. *Before the Welfare State. Social Administration in Early Industrial Britain.* Longman, 1979.

Hill, B. *Women, Work and Sexual Politics in Eighteenth-Century England.* Blackwell, 1989.

Hobsbawm, E.J. *Labouring Men.* Weidenfeld & Nicolson, 1964.

Horn, P. *The Rural World 1780–1850: Social Change in the English Countryside.* Hutchinson, 1980.

Laquer, T. *Religion and Respectability: Sunday Schools and Working-class Culture 1780–1850.* Yale UP, 1976.

Malcolmson, R.W. *Popular Recreations in English Society 1700–1850* Hutchinson, 1981.

Marshall, J.D. *The Old Poor Law 1795 to 1850.* Macmillan, 1985.

Medick, H. 'Plebeian culture in the transition to capitalism' in Samuel, R. and Stedman Jones, G. (eds), *Culture, Ideology and Politics.* Routledge, 1982.

Sanderson, M. 'Literacy and the industrial revolution'. *Past and Present* **56,** 1972.

Sanderson, M. *Education, Economic Change and Society in England 1780–1870.* Macmillan, 1983.

Snell, K.D.M. *Annals of the Labouring Poor: Social Change and Agrarian England 1660–1900.* Cambridge UP, 1985.

Stone, L. 'Literacy and education in England, 1640–1900'. *Past and Present,* **42**, 1969.

Storch, R.W. *Popular Culture and Custom in Nineteenth-century England.* Croom Helm, 1982.

Taylor, J.S. 'The impact of pauper settlement, 1691–1834'. *Past and Present,* **73**, 1976.

Thompson, E.P. *The Making of the English Working Class.* Penguin, 1968.

Thompson, E.P. 'Patrician society, plebeian culture'. *Jn. Soc. Hist.,* VII, No.4, 1974.

Vincent, D. *Literacy and Popular Culture: England 1750–1914.* Cambridge UP, 1989.

Wadsworth, A.P. 'The first Manchester Sunday schools' in Flinn, M.W. and Smout, T.C. (eds), *Essays in Social History.* Clarendon Press, 1974.

STANDARD OF LIVING

Collis, R. *The Pitmen of the Northern Coalfield: Work, Culture and Protest, 1790–1850.* Manchester UP, 1987.

Cunningham, H. 'The employment and unemployment of children in England *c.* 1680–1851'. *Past and Present,* **126**, 1990.

Defoe, D. *A Tour through the Whole Island of Great Britain.* 2 vols, Everyman, 1962.

Flinn, M.W. 'Trends in real wages, 1750–1850'. *Econ. H.R.,* XXVII, 1974.

Gilboy, E.W. *Wages in Eighteenth-Century England.* Harvard UP, 1924.

Hunt, E.H. 'Industrialization and regional inequality: wages in Britain, 1760–1914'. *Jn. Econ. Hist.,* XLVI, 4, 1986.

Hunt, E.H. and Botham, R.W. 'Wages in Britain during the industrial revolution'. *Econ. H.R.,* XL, 1987.

Mann, J. de L. *The Cloth Industry in the West of England 1640–1880.* 1971, rept Alan Sutton, 1987.

Schwarz, L.D. 'The standard of living in the long run: London 1700 to 1850'. *Econ. H.R.,* XXXVIII, 1985.

Schwarz, L.D. 'Trends in real wage rates, 1750–1790: a reply to Hunt and Botham'. *Econ. H.R.,* XLIII, 1990.

Taylor, A.J. *The Standard of Living in Britain in the Industrial Revolution.* Methuen, 1975.

Von Tunzelmann, G.N. 'Trends in real wages, 1750–1850, revisited'. *Econ. H.R.*, XXXII, 1979.

Williamson, J.G. *Did British Capitalism Breed Inequality?* Allen & Unwin, 1985.

SOCIAL AND INDUSTRIAL PROTEST

Aspinall A. *The Early English Trade Unions*. Blatchworth, 1949.

Charlesworth, A. (ed.) *An Atlas of Rural Protest in Britain 1548–1900*. Croom Helm, 1983.

Cole, G.D.H. and Filson, A.W. *British Working Class Movements: Select Documents 1789–1875*. Macmillan, 1951.

Dinwiddy, J. 'Luddism and politics in the northern counties'. *Social History*, IV, 1979.

Dobson, C.R. *Masters and Journeymen: A Pre-history of Industrial Relations*. Croom Helm, 1980.

Foster, J. *Class Struggle and the Industrial Revolution: Early Industrial Capitalism in Three English Towns*. Methuen, 1977.

Hammond, J.L. and Hammond, B. *The Town Labourer*. 1917, new edition, Longman, 1978.

Hammond, J.L. and Hammond, B. *The Skilled Labourer*. 1919, new edition, Longman, 1979.

Harrison, M. *Crowds and History: Mass Phenomenon in English Towns 1790–1835*. Cambridge UP, 1988.

Joyce, P.K. (ed.) *Historical Meanings of Work*. Cambridge UP, 1987.

Malcolmson, R.W. 'Workers' combinations in eighteenth-century England' in Jacobs, M and J. (eds), *The Origins of Anglo-American Radicalism*. Allen & Unwin, 1984.

Orth, J.V. 'The English Combination Laws reconsidered' in Snyder, F. and Hay, D. (eds), *Labour, Law and Crime: An Historical Perspective*. Tavistock, 1987.

Prothero, I. *Artisans and Politics in Early Nineteenth-century London: John Gast and his Times*. Dawson, 1979.

Randall, A.J. 'The shearmen and the Wiltshire outrages of 1802: trade unionism and industrial violence'. *Social History*, VII, 3, 1982.

Randall, A.J. and Charlesworth, A. 'Morals, markets and the English crowd in 1766'. *Past and Present*, **114**, 1987.

Reid, D.A. 'The decline of Saint Monday 1776–1876'. *Past and Present* **71**, 1976.

Rudé, G. *Paris and London in the Eighteenth Century: Studies in Popular Protest.* Fontana, 1970.

Rule, J.G. (ed.) *British Trade Unionism 1700–1850: The Formative Years.* Longman, 1988.

Stevenson, J. *Popular Disturbances in England 1700–1870.* Longman, 1979.

Thomis, M.I. *The Luddites: Machine Breaking in Regency England.* David & Charles, 1970.

Thompson, E.P. 'Time, work-discipline and industrial capitalism'. *Past and Present,* **38**, 1968.

Thompson, E.P. *The Making of the English Working Class.* Penguin, 1968.

Thompson, E.P. 'The moral economy of the English crowd in the eighteenth century'. *Past and Present,* **50**, 1971.

Wells, R.A.E. 'The revolt of the south-west, 1800–01'. *Social History,* VI, 1977.

Wells, R.A.E. *Wretched Faces: Famine in Wartime England 1793–1803.* Alan Sutton, 1988.

CRIME AND PUNISHMENT

Beattie, J.M. *Crime and the Courts in England, 1660–1800.* Oxford UP, 1986.

Ekirch, A.R. *Bound for America: The Transportation of British Convicts to the Colonies, 1718–1775.* Oxford UP, 1987.

Emsley, C. *Crime and Society in England 1750–1900.* Longman, 1987.

Hay, D. 'War, dearth and theft in the eighteenth century'. *Past and Present,* **95**, 1982.

Hay, D., Linebaugh, P., Rule, J.G., Thompson, E.P. and Winslow, C., *Albion's Fatal Tree: Crime and Society in Eighteenth-Century England.* Penguin, 1977.

Ignatieff, M. *A Just Measure of Pain: The Penitentiary in the Industrial Revolution 1750–1850.* Macmillan, 1978.

King, P. 'Decision-makers and decision making in the English criminal law 1750–1800'. *Historical Journal,* XXVII, 1984.

Linebaugh, P. *The London Hanged: Crime and Civil Society in the Eighteenth Century.* Allen Lane, 1992.

Radzinowicz, L. *A History of the English Criminal Law and its Administration since 1750.* Vol. I, Stevens, 1948.

Rule, J.G. 'Social crime in the rural south in the eighteenth and early nineteenth centuries'. *Southern History,* I, 1979.

Shaw, A.G.L. *Convicts and the Colonies: A Study of Penal Transportation from Great Britain and Ireland to Australia and Other Parts of the British Empire.* Faber, 1966.

Styles, J. and Brewer J. *An Ungovernable People: The English and their Law in the Seventeenth and Eighteenth Centuries.* Hutchinson, 1980.

Thompson, E.P. *Whigs and Hunters: The Origins of the Black Act.* Penguin, 1977.

URBANISATION

Abrams, P. and Wrigley, E.A. (eds) *Towns in Societies. Essays in Economic History and Historical Sociology.* Cambridge UP, 1968.

Borsay, P. *The English Urban Renaissance: Culture and Society in the Provincial Town, 1660–1700.* Oxford UP, 1989.

Borsay, P. (ed.) *The Eighteenth-century Town.* Longman, 1990.

Clark, P. (ed.) *The Transformation of English Provincial Towns.* Hutchinson, 1984.

Corfield, P. *The Impact of English Towns 1700–1800.* Oxford UP, 1982.

George, M.D. *London Life in the Eighteenth Century.* Penguin, 1966.

McInnes, A. 'The emergence of a leisure town: Shrewsbury 1660–1760'. *Past and Present,* **120**, 1988.

Index